China–India Relations

This book examines the dynamics of the modern relationship between China and India. As key emerging powers in the international system, India and especially China have received much attention. However, most analysts who have studied Sino-Indian relations have done so through a neorealist lens which emphasizes the conflictual and competitive elements within the overall relationship. This has had the effect of obscuring how the China–India relationship is currently in the process of transformation. Drawing on detailed and systematic analysis of the interlinked and increasingly important issues of maritime security in the Indian Ocean region, energy demands and concerns, and economic growth and interchange, the author shows that not only is there an absence of mutual threat perception, but Sino-Indian bilateral trade is increasingly being framed institutionally and China and India are also beginning to coordinate policy in important areas such as energy policy. He concludes that neorealist accounts of Sino-Indian relations have difficulty in explaining these recent developments. However, rather than rejecting neorealist explanations in their entirety, he points towards a theoretical pluralism with an appeal to 'soft' realism and theories of neoliberalism and peaceful change. Overall, this book provides a comprehensive account of contemporary relations between China and India, and is important for all scholars of international relations, not only China and India specialists.

Amardeep Athwal received his PhD in political science from the University of Toronto, Canada.

Routledge Contemporary South Asia Series

Pakistan
Social and cultural transformations in a
Muslim nation
Mohammad A. Qadeer

**Labor, Democratization and Development
in India and Pakistan**
Workers and unions
Christopher Candland

China–India Relations
Contemporary dynamics
Amardeep Athwal

China–India Relations
Contemporary dynamics

Amardeep Athwal

Routledge
Taylor & Francis Group

LONDON AND NEW YORK

First published 2008 by Routledge
2 Park Square, Milton Park, Abingdon, Oxon, OX14 4RN

Simultaneously published in the USA and Canada
by Routledge
605 Third Avenue, New York, NY 10017

Routledge is an imprint of the Taylor & Francis Group, an Informa business

Typeset in Times New Roman by
RefineCatch Limited, Bungay, Suffolk

British Library Cataloguing in Publication Data
A catalogue record for this book is available from the British Library

Library of Congress Cataloging in Publication Data
   Athwal, Amardeep, 1980–
   China–India relations : contemporary dynamics / Amardeep Athwal.
     p. cm. – (Routledge Contemporary South Asia series; 3)
   Includes bibliographical references and index.
   1. India–Relations–China. 2. China–Relations–India. I. title.
   DS450.C5A85 2007
   303.48′251054—dc22
   2007013246

ISBN 13: 978–0–415–43735–6 (hbk)
ISBN 13: 978–0–415–54473–3 (pbk)
ISBN 13: 978–0–203–93444–9 (ebk)

To my Mom, Dad and the late Daljit Athwal, a wonderful person who passed away far too soon

Contents

Preface

This study examines the modern-day dynamics of the Sino-Indian relationship—with particular focus on issues relating to maritime security, economics, energy and elite bilateral dialogue. Since the 1962 Sino-Indian War, most neorealist analysts have continued to emphasize the conflictual and competitive elements within the Sino-Indian relationship.

The book first explores the crucial post-independence history of Sino-Indian relations to provide the appropriate contextual background. Thereafter, it explores the geopolitical significance of the Indian Ocean in the light of soaring global energy demands. While acknowledging the credibility of neorealist insights in the realm of maritime rivalry by detailing China's and India's naval build-up and naval strategy, it finds that the security dilemma argument is overstated. Therefore, it seeks alternative explanations for both Chinese and Indian activities in Southern Asia.

Hence it explores positive elements within the Sino-Indian relationship, such as growing economic interdependence, energy convergence and elite consensus. In the economic realm, Sino-Indian bilateral trade is rapidly expanding every year. The study highlights how China and India are beginning to coordinate energy policy to transform the Sino-Indian relationship from a framework of conflict and competition to cooperation. The study concludes that there are serious mitigating factors in the Sino-Indian relationship, but argues that an exclusively neorealist outlook is impoverished. Theoretical insights from neoliberal institutionalism and constructivism point to how emerging economic interdependence creates dependable expectations of peaceful change and point towards stability in the Sino-Indian relationship.

Acknowledgements

I am grateful to many people for helping me with my book. First, I would like to thank my supervisor Arthur Rubinoff as well as Louis Pauly, John Kirton, Steven Bernstein, Jeremy Paltiel and three anonymous reviewers. Second, I would like to thank the Institute for Defence Studies and Analyses in New Delhi for providing me with research facilities during my 2005 summer trip to India and the Sahota family for their hospitality. I would especially like to thank the Director of IDSA, CMDE C. Uday Bhaskar, WG CDR A.V. Lele, CDR Gurpreet Khurana and Srikanth Kondapalli for their particular assistance while at IDSA. I also benefited from many helpful discussions and interviews with Sujit Dutta, R.R. Subramanian, CDR Alok Bansal, G.V.C. Naidu, Udai Bhanu Singh, Raviprasad Nairayan and Nanda Kumar.

I would also like to thank Swaran Singh, Madhu Bhalla and C. Raja Mohan from Jawaharlal Nehru University. CDR Vijay Sakhuja from the Observatory Research Foundation, Bharat Karnad and Brahma Chellaney from the Centre for Policy Research and Brig-Gen. Arun Saghul from the United Services Institute of India. I am also grateful to the Indian Ministry of External Affairs and the Ministry of Defence and several anonymous sources.

I also benefited from many useful comments and suggestions from my colleagues. In this regard I would like to thank Chris Alcantara, Erick Lachapelle, Patrick Lennox and Vincent Pouliot. I am grateful to Jeffrey Kopstein who suggested that I should study India in the first place.

Finally, I would like to acknowledge financial support provided by the Government of Ontario in the form of an Ontario Government Scholarship. In this regard I would also like to thank the Trudeau Centre for Peace and Conflict Studies at the University of Toronto, which awarded me a Beattie Fellowship.

List of abbreviations

ARF	ASEAN Regional Forum
ASEAN	Association of South East Asian Nations
ASW	anti-submarine warfare
ATV	advanced technology vessel
AWACs	Airborne Warning and Control Systems
BARC	Bhabha Atomic Research Centre
BCIM	Bangladesh, China, India and Myanmar
b/d	barrels per day
BHEL	Bharat Heavy Electricals Limited
BIMST-EC	Bangladesh-India-Myanmar-Sri Lanka-Thailand-Economic Cooperation
BJP	Bharatiya Janata Party
BLA	Baluchistan Liberation Army
BLF	Baluchistan Liberation Front
BMD	Ballistic Missile Defense
CBMs	confidence-building measures
CCP	Chinese Communist Party
CMC	Central Military Commission
CNOOC	China National Offshore Oil Corporation
CNPC	China National Petroleum Corporation
CNS	Chief of the Naval Staff
COM	Chief of Material
COP	Chief of Personnel
CTBT	Comprehensive Test Ban Treaty
DCNS	Deputy Chief of Naval Staff
DRDO	Defence Research and Development Organization
EEZ	exclusive economic zone
ETIM	East Turkestan Islamic Movement
FDI	foreign direct investment
FENC	Far Eastern Naval Command
FOC-in-C	Flag Officer Commanding-in-Chief
FTA	free trade agreement
GAIL	Gas Authority of India

GDP	gross domestic product
GOI	Government of India
HQ	headquarters
IAF	Indian Air Force
ICSID	International Centre for Settlement of Investment Disputes
IITF	India International Trade Fair
IMF	International Monetary Fund
INDFEX	India-Far East Express
IOC	India Oil Corporation
IOR	Indian Ocean region
IR	international relations
ITBP	Indo-Tibetan Border Police
JSG	Joint Study Group
JWG	Joint Working Group
KMT	Kuomintang
LAC	line of actual control
MFN	most-favored nation
MIGA	Multilateral Investment Guarantee Agency
NATO	North Atlantic Treaty Organization
NEFA	North East Frontier Agency
NELP	New Exploration Licensing Policy
NHQ	Naval Headquarters
NPT	non-proliferation treaty
NSSP	Next Steps to Strategic Partnership
ODI	overseas direct investment
OECD	Organization for Economic Cooperation and Development
ONGC	Oil and Natural Gas Corporation
OPEC	Organization of Petroleum Exporting Countries
PLA	People's Liberation Army
PLAN	People's Liberation Army Navy
PNE	peaceful nuclear explosion
PSLV	Polar Satellite Launch Vehicle
PSO	Principal Staff Officer
PWR	pressurized water reactor
R&D	Research and Development
RCAs	Revealed Comparative Indices
SAARC	South Asia Association for Regional Cooperation
SAMs	surface-to-air missiles
SARS	Severe Acute Respiratory Syndrome
SATCOM	satellite communications
SCO	Shanghai Cooperation Organization
SDPC	State Development Planning Commission
SEZ	Special Economic Zone
SFF	Special Frontier Force
SLBM	submarine-launched ballistic missile

SLOCs	sea-lines of communication
SNEP	subterranean nuclear explosion
SOE	state-owned enterprise
SS	submarines
SSBN	ballistic missile class submarine
SSMs	surface-to-surface missiles
SSN	nuclear-powered submarine
TMD	Theatre Missile Defense
UN	United Nations
UNCITRAL	UN Commission on International Trade Law
USSR	Union of Soviet States of Russia
VCNS	Vice Chief of Naval Staff
WTO	World Trade Organization

Introduction

The neorealist account of Sino-Indian relations: competition and rivalry

Both China and India are rapidly industrializing states and ascending powers in international politics. The Indian Ocean itself and its sea-lines of communication (SLOCs) have become increasingly important for China over the decades and have always been important to India. Both countries now rely heavily on petroleum and natural resources to safely transit the Indian Ocean.

However, India and China have a history of conflict. They fought a border war in 1962 and still have an undemarcated border between them. Relations between the two states remained detached and hostile during the Cold War, warmed briefly following the collapse of the Soviet Union and became cold again following India's nuclear weapons tests in 1998. To add to the tension in South Asia, India and China have also been rapidly modernizing their navies and increasing their presence in the Indian Ocean region (IOR).

China continues to cooperate with Pakistan and has been a key backer of the controversial Gwadar maritime access project. Following the 1999 Kargil Crisis, when the vulnerability of Karachi was revealed by an Indian naval blockade, Pakistan, with the cooperation and funding of China, decided to develop a deep-water port at Gwadar in Baluchistan province. Upon completion, the port will rival Karachi.

China also continues to strengthen its ties with Myanmar. Most indicative of this is Chinese support for the Irrawaddy Corridor project at Kyaukpyu. There now exists an integrated transportation system linking China's Yunnan province with Kyaukpyu port on the northern end of Ramree Island. At Kyaukpyu, a new modern port has also been constructed to accommodate ocean-going ships picking up and delivering cargo transiting the road–river line to Yunnan.

As China has enhanced its naval and military ties with Pakistan and Myanmar in recent years, India has developed its "look east" policy. This has involved deepening economic and strategic ties with states such as Vietnam, Laos, the Philippines, Thailand, Cambodia, Japan, Indonesia and South Korea. India's bilateral engagement with these Asian states has resulted in the signing of numerous defense accords and has produced reciprocal expressions of goodwill and calls for further strategic coordination.

Based on such developments, many analysts of Sino-Indian relations have concluded that China and India are currently engaged in a regional struggle for power (Garver 2001b, 2002; Malik 2001; Lee 2002; Mohan, 2003). Many of these scholars either implicitly or explicitly characterize the Sino-Indian relationship in terms of a security dilemma (Jervis, 1978) and in broader neorealist terms. For instance, as John Garver has noted:

> The concept of a security dilemma casts considerable light on a central dynamic of the complex relationship between China and India—the constant pulling and tugging between those two countries over China's security ties with countries in the South Asian-Indian Ocean region. The existence of a security dilemma, focused on Chinese ties to the South Asian and Indian Ocean states other than India, throws much light on the deep-rooted suspicion between those two Asian powers.
>
> (2002: 1)

Drawing on neorealist theories of international relations (Waltz, 1979; Mearsheimer, 2001) that characterize the international arena as the realm of great power politics, those within the Sino-Indian neorealist school have applied the neorealist model to the South Asian regional subsystem. As Dabhade and Pant (2004: 158) note, "If we take South Asia as a regional subsystem, then the two major powers whose behavior substantially impacts the foreign policies of smaller states in the area are China and India." In their analysis of Sino-Indian activity in Nepal, Dabhade and Pant conclude:

> Chinese and Indian strategies reflect their respective desires to expand their relative influence over Nepal at each other's expense. Both powers display a lack of satisfaction with the current status quo and have pursued strategies that are aimed at maximizing their share of regional power.
>
> (ibid.: 167)

The "Sino-Indian neorealist school" (as it is labeled here) continues to emphasize how conflict and competition between both China and India are inevitable, as, "one mountain cannot accommodate two tigers." As Malik notes:

> In the international status stakes, it is China with which India wants to achieve parity. India and China share similar aspirations towards status and influence, with China further advanced towards their achievement than India. And this inevitably introduces a more competitive aspect into the Sino-Indian relationship ... The Chinese know India is the only Asian country determined to resist China's preeminence in Asia by developing the full spectrum of economic and military capabilities. It is

safe to conclude that China's foreign and defense policy initiatives will continue to be designed to reduce India to the status of a subregional power by increasing Chinese influence and leverage in the South Asian region.

(2001: 90)

The certainty of rivalry between India and China is indeed a central theme taken up by the Sino-Indian neorealist school. Many analysts have concluded that with the "dual rise of Beijing and New Delhi in international society, their respective interests and influence will inevitably encounter each other in the Asian subregions" (Guihong Zhang, 2005: 61). As China's interest in the IOR expands, then competition and rivalry with India are likely to follow as India tries to assert its influence in its own backyard. As Jae-hyung Lee notes:

China has been expanding its sphere of influence into the Indian Ocean region as an initial stage of a broader scheme of involvement throughout the Asian region. China's fast-growing economy has increased significantly its patterns of oil consumption, thus making it a net oil importer since 1993 . . . by 2000 China had become the third biggest oil consumer in the world.

(2002: 552)

It is no surprise then that the Straits of Malacca and Hormuz have become crucial waterways for China. Close cooperation with Myanmar and Pakistan, therefore, becomes essential to guarantee the security of SLOCs in the IOR. For neorealist scholars though, this has come at the cost of India's security (Garver, 2001b, 2002). Referring to the emergence of new bases in the Indian Ocean such as Gwadar and Karwar (one of India's newest naval bases), Donald Berlin (2004: 239) has concluded that "this new 'great base race' will make war, at least among the [Indian] ocean's littoral states, a more practicable option than previously."

China and India's naval modernization programs have drawn much attention in recent years (Goldstein and Murray, 2004; Margolis, 2005). Both states have spent billions of dollars acquiring modern naval equipment and weapons systems from abroad (and especially from Russia). India and China are also involved in overhauling their indigenous naval production capabilities. Both India and China have long-term plans in place to acquire blue-water naval capabilities and the end result has been a marked increase in the number of frigates, destroyers and submarines on both sides. India and China's navies now rank only behind the world's elite naval powers: the United States, Britain, France, Russia and Japan.

The current pattern of Sino-Indian relations, as characterized by the Sino-Indian neorealist school, closely follows central neorealist assumptions about international relations (this can be considered the "hard core" of neorealism). Neorealists have long held that the international system is best characterized as anarchic (Waltz, 1979; Mearsheimer, 1995; Frankel, 1996; Schweller, 1997). Furthermore, neorealists argue that states are the main actors in the international system and moreover that these states are "rational" utility maximizers (Keohane, 1986: 164–165; Legro and Moravscik, 1999). In this calculus, states seek power and calculate interest in terms of power—material capabilities therefore play a key role in determining outcomes in international relations. Furthermore, as Waltz (1986: 102) notes, because the future is always uncertain, states are more concerned about relative gains than absolute gains and how gains will be divided. For this reason, cooperation is hard to achieve in international relations. The basic nature of international relations is therefore essentially conflictual (Gilpin 1996: 7–8; Schweller, 1997: 927). States will inevitably find themselves at odds with one another as their interests and goals overlap and this will lead to conflict.[1] In analyzing South Asia as a regional area of great power competition, the Sino-Indian neorealist school concludes that conflict between China and India is inevitable. As "rational" utility-maximizers pursuing their respective interests in terms of power, both India and China will have to reckon with one another in the IOR. The uncertainty of the future and the constant concern of relative power capabilities will make Sino-Indian cooperation extremely difficult.

From neorealism to the research puzzle: explaining emerging empirical discrepancies in the neorealist account

At first sight it appears that the neorealists capture important elements of the Sino-Indian relationship. The case of China and India, in some ways, characterizes a security dilemma. There are two rising states with a history of conflict, an undemarcated border, potentially explosive irritants (Sino-Pakistani nuclear cooperation and Tibet) and a strong sense of nationalism that are undergoing a massive military restructuring and modernization.[2] Moreover, the long-term fortunes of both states are increasingly tied to the same geostrategic region, the IOR, as China and India have emerged as major importers of hydrocarbon resources. These very hydrocarbons are needed domestically in China and India to satisfy energy demands and to continue rapid economic growth. Nonetheless, one of the questions asked in this book is whether it is possible despite the billions being spent on naval modernization, China's push into the IOR and India's expansion of its "look east" policy for there to be other important factors in play that the neorealists have overlooked.

This leads to the central research questions of this book as well as the puzzle. One question is how accurate are neorealist accounts of the current state of Sino-Indian relations? Another is, "What is the nature of the Sino-Indian relationship and is it in the process of transformation?" Overall it appears that the neorealists may be onto something and that there are signs of a Sino-Indian power struggle and rivalry. The puzzling thing though is that serious cooperative trends or mitigating factors are also beginning to emerge in the Sino-Indian relationship. Although neorealist theory does not preclude cooperation between states, particularly in the form of strategic alliances, on the whole, self-help systems "make the cooperation of parties difficult" (Waltz, 1986: 336). As two analysts note, "realism presents a fundamentally pessimistic analysis of the prospects for international cooperation" (Grieco, 1990: 27) and under conditions of anarchy, any cooperation will be "tenuous, unstable and limited to issues of peripheral importance" (Weber: 1990: 58–59). As Adler and Barnett (1998: 10) note, "neorealist theories ... stress the notion that while war does not take place all the time, like rain, it is always expected."

Thus, recent agreements reached by China and India such as the 10 April 2005 accord aimed at resolving the border dispute and plans to enhance annual bilateral trade from $13.6 billion in 2004 to $30 billion by 2010 appear to indicate that there is more going on in the Sino-Indian relationship than what the neorealists have portrayed. In recent years there has been a substantial increase in economic interaction between China and India. Moreover, high-level diplomatic exchanges have become more frequent and both China and India are beginning to express mutual goodwill. This represents a marked change in the Sino-Indian diplomatic environment from even five to seven years ago, as tensions increased following India's nuclear tests.

One of the central tasks of this book will be to deal with this emerging empirical discrepancy and to reconcile it with existing neorealist accounts of Sino-Indian rivalry. Instead of entirely dismissing neorealist insights into the Sino-Indian relationship in favor of alternative theoretical approaches, this book will instead moderate the neorealist position and complement it with theoretical illuminations from both neoliberal and sociological perspectives. The neoliberal additions will draw from theorists such as Robert O. Keohane and Joseph Nye (1977) and Richard Rosecrance (1986) and their studies of interdependence and international trade. The sociological additions will draw primarily from Emmanuel Adler and Michael Barnett's (1998) study of peaceful change. An examination of these two theoretical approaches will help demonstrate that the Sino-Indian relationship is best perceived through a multifarious theoretical lens.

In short, it will be held that while Sino-Indian relations can still be characterized in neorealist terms, important economic and diplomatic changes are taking place that require theoretical attention. This book will argue that both China and India are beginning to realize that there is much more to be gained from cooperation than from conflict. Three emerging factors will be analyzed that best exemplify this argument: (1) Sino-Indian economic integration; (2) soaring Chinese and Indian energy demands pushing towards convergence; and (3) a growing Sino-Indian elite consensus. All three of these factors are closely interlinked and the energy sphere serves as a bridge to security issues.

The economic forces of globalization and the mutual benefits of trade are the driving forces behind the transformation of the Sino-Indian relationship.

Moreover, in the field of energy, where both India and China have become major importers of oil and gas, there are pressures to coordinate policy. This is because both India and China's economic growth and ability to continue modernizing depend upon energy supplies and both have major interests in ensuring the safety of shipping in the IOR. This shared vulnerability creates a structural pressure to coordinate energy policy. China needs India's help in combating piracy and terrorism against its merchant marine in the Indian Ocean and India in turn needs China's help to ensure that its ships transporting gas from the Russian far east and trading in South-East Asia are secure. As the energy demand in China and India continues to soar in the future, this shared vulnerability or common aversion should also grow and should push both states towards convergence. Furthermore, as both states continue the process of economic liberalization, total trade and total Sino-Indian bilateral trade should also continue to grow. The economic pressure to integrate with the global economy and with one another can also be expected to intensify in the future. Thus, there are serious factors pushing China and India towards convergence and pulling them away from the conflictual security dilemma. Finally, these pressures for convergence are also reflected by a growing elite consensus between India and China. Top military and political leaders in both states are starting to change their hostile tune from the days of the Cold War and Pokharan II nuclear tests and are commenting on the benefits of Sino-Indian integration.

These changes cannot easily be incorporated into a neorealist framework but can be explained by neoliberal and sociological theories of international relations. Although realists may say that they are not concerned with "emerging discrepancies," empirical data that fail to corroborate existing theory require explanation and cannot be taken for granted. Critics of neorealism have long argued that neorealist scholars have a tendency to be so focused in their own theoretical bubble that they obscure the "reality" they are observing (Ashley, 1986). With their narrow focus, neorealists often miss or completely ignore other phenomena that help provide a more complete understanding of events (Ashley, 1986; Cox, 1986; Buzan *et al.*, 1993; Lebow, 1996).

The problem with the neorealist account of Sino-Indian relations is that it is beginning to lose its heuristic power and is not anticipating novel facts such as the economic and diplomatic shifts in Sino-Indian relations. It no longer makes sense to view the Sino-Indian relationship in theoretically monist terms. However, instead of offering a competing theory, the argument here is that theoretical insights from neoliberalism and constructivism can complement a neorealist framework for a more complete explanation of Sino-Indian relations. Both neoliberal and constructivist explanations would help explain recent developments in Sino-Indian relations.

There are few general works on Sino-Indian relations emanating from North America let alone neoliberal or constructivist accounts (Frankel and Harding, 2004: xi). Indeed, as discussed at the outset, most analysts, given the conflictual history of Sino-Indian relations, have continued to examine the relationship in neorealist terms (Kondapalli, 2005b). Since it is extremely difficult to eliminate research programs (as even Lakatos admits), theoretical synthesis is one way to achieve theoretical pluralism and to make progressive theory shifts. This synthetic technique has been employed and advocated by many key international relations theorists. Following Dougherty and Pfaltzgraff (1981), Alker and Biersteker (1984: 123) note that international relations should be perceived as an "interdiscipline, constituted at least as much by its principled differences in research approaches, teaching and practice as by its communalities." As Wendt notes of his own *Social Theory of International Politics*:

> Its substantive argument cuts across the traditional cleavages in IR between Realists, Liberal, and Marxists . . . Readers will find much . . . that is associated usually with Realism: state-centrism, the concern with national interests and the consequences of anarchy. There is also much associated with Liberalism: the possibility of progress, the importance of ideas, institutions, and domestic politics. There is a Marxian sensibility in the discussion of the state.
>
> (1999: 33)

As Adler and Barnett have put it:

> By examining the dynamic relationship between state power, international organizations and institutions, and changes in security practices, the study of security communities offers a blend of *idealism*—which recognized state interests but also envisioned the possibility of progress and a promise for institutions in helping states overcome their worst tendencies—and *realism*, whose main proponents saw the worst but continued to write about the conditions under which there might be peaceful change and new forms of political organization. *Theories of international politics, therefore, can and should occupy a pragmatic middle ground between the view that identities and international practices cannot change, and the view that everything is possible. They should be able to blend power, interests, and pessimism with norms, a dynamic view of international politics, and moderate optimism about the possibility of structural change that enhances human interests across borders.*
>
> (1998: 14–15; emphasis added)

If the range of international relations theories are conceptualized between holism and individualism, on the one hand, and materialism and idealism, on the other, the horizontal and upward pressure on neorealism by introducing neoliberal (economic interdependence) and constructivist ideas can be visualized (see Figure 0.1).

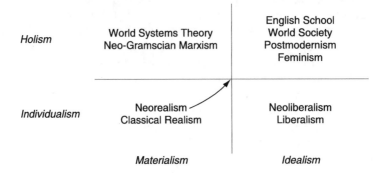

Figure 0.1 Matrix of international relations theories.

Source: Loosely reproduced from Wendt (1999: 32, figure 2).

The rigidity of neorealism: economic interdependence and sociological transformation

From a broader theoretical perspective such a move can be justified by examining the criticisms that have been made about the neorealist paradigm's "hard core." The problem with the neorealist "hard core" is that it is often too rigid to provide empirically accurate or rich analyses. As Ashley notes:

> [Neorealism reduces] political practice to an economic logic, and it neuters the critical faculties of the latter by swallowing methodological rules that render science a purely technical enterprise . . . What emerges is a positivist structuralism that treats the given order as the natural order, limits rather than expands political discourse, negates or trivializes the significance of variety across time and place, subordinates all practice to an interest in control, bows to the ideal of a social power beyond responsibility, and thereby deprives political interaction of those practical capacities which make social learning and creative change possible . . . What emerges is an ideology that anticipates, legitimizes, and orients a totalitarian project of global proportions: the rationalization of global politics.
>
> (1986: 258)

In a similar vein, Robert Cox (1986) has criticized the ahistorical nature of neorealism. As Cox (ibid.: 214) notes, "The error . . . consists in taking a form of thought derived from a particular phase of history (and thus from a particular structure of social relations) and assuming it to be universally valid . . . is an error of neorealism." This has been a particular problem for analysts of Sino-Indian relations. Many theorists continue to see the relationship from an increasingly less relevant historical lens of conflict. Although China and India may have been enemies in the past and although neorealist accounts of that relationship may have been accurate at that time, it does not necessarily mean that this will continue to be the case. For Cox, theories such as neorealism cannot account for the succession of different historical structures. These are the problems inherent in neorealism's positivism. According to Cox, the dynamics between social forces, institutions and ideas need to be analyzed together with material capabilities for an accurate analysis of international change.

John Ruggie (1986) has also criticized neorealists (specifically Waltz) for their inability to adequately explain structural change.[3] Ruggie draws attention to the shift from the medieval to the modern international system and notes that the neorealist reluctance to problematize the second image or the unit-level is a major problem. This is because unit-level change can lead to systemic change. The modern international system, according to Ruggie, consists of property exclusiveness and the totalization of authority (division of public and private realms). In the medieval system this was not the case, and hence there has been major systemic change that can only be explained at the unit-level. This is the level most neglected by Waltz and other neorealists.

For Ruggie (1998: 7), Waltz's structural neorealism is "strictly physicalist in character." Similarly, Ruggie (1998) is critical of neoliberals such as Keohane (1984) who provide an only slightly less undersocialized ontology. Ruggie refers to these commonalities as the "convergence of the neos."[4] Indeed, both of these theories share the same "neo-utilitarian" analytical foundations, assuming that states are rational actors maximizing their utilities defined in relative material power (under conditions of anarchy). According to Ruggie (1998: 11), the neo-utilitarian research program has an "increasingly narrow analytical frame" that invites challenges from sociologically oriented approaches.

Notwithstanding Ruggie's criticism of neoliberalism, neoliberal scholars have made key contributions to international relations that are applicable here (and improve upon the neorealist position). Of particular relevance is how neoliberals highlight the importance of trade and integration in addition to power and interest. As Richard Rosecrance illustrates:

> The theory of international exchange and trade gives a basis for mutual cooperation and mutual benefit, and it applies to the essence of what states do day by day. When noticed, trading is dismissed as "low politics," pejoratively contrasting it with the "high politics" of sovereignty, national interest, power, and military force. However, it is possible for relationships among states to be entirely transformed or even reversed by the low politics of trade.
>
> (1986: xi)

The possibility of how the "low politics" of trade may be transforming the Sino-Indian relationship is one of the central themes of this book. As China and India continue to bolster their bilateral trade and investment, interdependence between the two will grow in the years to come. The importance of the neoliberal argument is that it shows that although states may first only cooperate with one another out of their own self-interest, this may grow to take on larger significance. As trade between two states (or more) grows and intensifies, so will mutual trust, which in turn will help make future expectations more predictable. With the predictability of mutual expectations come the prospects for sustained cooperation. As Axelrod (1984) has noted, actors are more prone to cooperate in continuously iterated games of Prisoner's Dilemma (compared to a "one shot" Prisoner's Dilemma game). This highlights one of the key differences between the neorealist and neoliberal positions—for neorealists, international relations interactions are characteristic of a "one shot" Prisoner's Dilemma game because of the uncertainty of the future; what the neoliberals have demonstrated though is that in international relations, actors often deal with one another over long time horizons and have repeated interactions. For this reason, they come to learn that the strategy of defection (and mutual defection, as is characterized by the security dilemma) is a suboptimal strategy.

According to Keohane and Nye (1977), institutions (conceptualized both informally and formally) help states coordinate their behavior and help states to achieve desired outcomes in particular issue areas. Institutions thus emerge in dilemmas of common interest that are characterized by Pareto suboptimal outcomes. Institutions can help coordinate action and produce Pareto optimal outcomes as individually oriented actions could lead to disastrous outcomes. It is in these specific circumstances that institutions can play an important role. As Axelrod and Keohane (1993) note, institutions can thus help mitigate the impact of anarchy. Institutions where there are mutual interests (Schelling's (1960) mixed motive games) provide a focal point for coordination. They reduce uncertainty. When time horizons are long,[5] stakes are regular and information is reliable, cooperation can be facilitated. Institutions help fill this role and create these favorable conditions. Institutions thus alter payoff structures for the actors involved. Institutions also serve to reinforce reciprocity, which delegitimizes defection, making it more costly.

This "market failure" approach directly relates to the arguments neofunctionalists have long made about the origins of the European integration process. The neofunctionalist approach to European integration is based on the work of earlier theorists such as Mitrany (1948), Haas (1958, 1968), Lindberg (1963) and Schmitter (1969, 1971). More recently, theorists such as Burley and Mattli (1993), Beukel (1994) and Gabriel (1995) have expanded upon the work of these earlier theorists. The foundations of the neofunctionalist approach lie in Durkheim's (1893) notion of functional differentiation. For Durkheim, functional differentiation was the source of modernization. Sectoralization, segmentation and specialization within society resulted in an increase in efficiency. In turn, this created an increase in the mutual interdependence of sectors. Functional differentiation thus forces the cooperation and coordination of the various sectors of society. Based on this logic, functionalists therefore assume that society is pluralistic with multiple inter-est and preference structures. These competing social and political groups within society form a relationship of *complex interdependence*, yet in the process try to realize their preferred roles.

Economic interdependence and international trade

Keohane and Nye (1977: 7) contend that "dependence" refers to a state of being determined or significantly conditioned by external forces but contend that "interdependence" consists of "situations characterized by reciprocal effects among countries or among actors in different countries." Interdepen-dence is therefore a relative concept, ranging from relationships of pure symmetry to pure dependence, and can be broken down into two types: *sensi-tivity* (the extent to which the immediate effects of external action are felt); and *vulnerability* (the relative cost of adopting alternatives/substitutes in the longer-term) (ibid.: 10–13).

Having established the relationship between power (emphasized by realists) and interdependence (emphasized by liberals), Keohane and Nye juxtapose two polar opposite yet complementary models of world politics: political realism and complex interdependence. Since conditions of world politics can always be situated somewhere in-between the two extremes, the task is not one of developing a theory that is universally applicable, but rather, of select-ing the model that corresponds best with world politics in a given issue area or geographical region, at a given point in time. In their application to empir-ical cases in oceans and money, Keohane and Nye (ibid.: 139) find that the "traditional" political realist models are becoming "less useful" and that "new theories . . . will frequently be needed for understanding reality and framing appropriate policies."

In analyzing the nature of the Sino-Indian economic picture, the potential for the "low politics" of trade to transform a previously conflictual relation-ship will be explored in this book. It will be argued that China and India have just started on the road of interdependence. As Keohane and Nye dis-covered in their case studies of US-Canadian and US-Australian relations, the power structure model emphasized by neorealists was becoming less rele-vant. Though power and interest still figured in the relationships (thus the title *Power and Interdependence*), economic interdependence started to take on a logic of its own and undercut neorealist arguments in important ways. This book will argue that this process of economic deepening is just begin-ning to unfold in China and India and will serve to moderate competition and rivalry. In the Sino-Indian case, the beginning of this process is especially surprising because both states fought a bitter war in 1962 and should be expected to be commercial rivals. However, as the economic analysis will demonstrate, despite the overlapping nature of the Chinese and Indian econ-omies, there are key sectors where trade is flourishing. Second, the prospects for enhancing intra-industry trade also look promising. As China and India continue to engage one another in the realm of low politics, it is indeed possible that this basic coordination will spill over into other arenas and provide incentives for further deepening and integration.

Deviating slightly from Keohane and Nye's (1977) model, the approach taken here will parallel more closely Richard Rosecrance's (1986) arguments concerning economic interdependence. Whereas for Keohane and Nye there are differences between "sensitivity" interdependence and "vulnerability" interdependence (turning back on the former has less costs than turning back on the latter), according to Rosecrance, all trade produces vulnerability interdependence. As Rosecrance (1986: 145) notes:

> Any tie can be broken. In this respect all ties create "vulnerability inter-dependence" if they are in the interest of those who form them. One could get along without Japanese cars or European fashions, but eliminating them from the market restricts consumer choice and in fact raises opportunity costs. In this manner, trade between industrial countries may be equally important as trade linking industrial and raw material producing countries.

Whereas for Keohane and Nye, China and India have a basic level of sensitivity interdependence, for Rosecrance, this would have implications of vulnerability.

Overall, though, the key point stressed by neoliberal scholars is that in contrast to neorealists, they emphasize how states can learn to cooperate and change their policies. As Rosecrance (ibid.: 61) notes:

> [States] do not incessantly repeat the old behavior and the old errors . . . what is most striking is the detachment of international capitalism from the particular state: it serves no individual national interest but seeks instead . . . to redistribute production and funds in ways that serve its *own* interest."

As Rosecrance (ibid.: 39, 156–159) also notes, since the cost of war has continued to rise with technological change and the prospect of nuclear exchange, economic interchange becomes a more viable and attractive option. Now that both India and China are nuclear powers with relatively modern militaries, the cost of war since the 1962 border war has definitely increased. Thus, the attractiveness of trade and engagement is self-evident in many respects.

Sociological transformation and "soft" realism

Neoliberal institutional arguments directly relate to sociological theories of communication. As the economic forces of interdependence are beginning to undercut concerns for relative gains and strategic balancing, the Sino-Indian relationship also shows initial signs characteristic of peaceful change. According to Adler and Barnett:

> [T]here is emerging a transnational community of Deutschian policy-makers, if you will, who are challenging the once nearly hegemonic position of realist-inspired policy-makers and offering an alternative understanding of what is possible in global politics and a map of how to get there . . . departing significantly from realist-based models to understand the present and future security debates . . . others have noted that the realist paradigm is better realized in theory than in practice, that states are not as war-prone as believed, and that many security arrangements once assumed to derive from balancing behavior in fact depart significantly from realist imagery.
>
> (1998: 4)

Accordingly, many international relations theorists such as Deutsch (1957) have suggested that states can overcome the security dilemma. One of the ways this is possible is through mechanisms of communication. As Norbet Wiener notes (in Deutsch, 1966: 77): "communication alone enables a group to think together, to see together, and to act together." As Adler and Barnett (1998: 7) continue: "through transactions such as trade, migration, tourism, cultural and educational exchanges . . . a social fabric is built not only among elites but also among the masses, instilling in them a sense of community." What these theorists suggest directly relates to the neoliberal argument of the transformative effects of low political engagement.

The Sino-Indian relationship, it will be demonstrated, is beginning to show the signs of peaceful change. China and India have started transitioning towards creating "dependable expectations of peaceful change" (ibid.: 34). As Adler and Barnett note of "tier one" conditions that precipitate peaceful change:

> [B]ecause of exogenous or endogenous factors states begin to orient themselves in each other's direction and desire to coordinate their relations . . . There is no expectation that these initial encounters and acts of cooperation produce trust or mutual identification; but because they are premised on the promise of more pleasant numerous interactions, they provide the necessary conditions for these very possibilities. In general, states have an incentive to promote face-to-face interactions, dialogue, and policy coordination for any number of reasons; such developments can, at the least, allow states to achieve Pareto superior outcomes, and, at the most, provide the context for the development of new social bonds.
>
> (ibid.: 38–39)

In the case of the Sino-Indian relationship, both China and India are beginning to recognize that enhancing trade and deepening interaction are preferable to rivalry and conflict. China and India are in the process of reinterpreting their social reality (ibid.: 40)—that is from one of conflict, epitomized by the 1962 war and the triangular Cold War dynamics of Sino-Pakistani-Indian relations, to one of mutual gain. The territorial uncertainties left by (British) imperialism on both India and China and the war that this resulted in were stabilized in the 1980s and 1990s with numerous confidence-building mechanisms and the creation of the Line of Actual Control on the Sino-Indian border (Sidhu and Yuan, 2001). The Cold War dynamics of US-Soviet balancing and the impact this had on regional powers such as China and India appear less relevant today. Though the Pakistan issue will remain a key irritant, the Sino-Indian relationship has normalized and appears poised for deepening after Pokharan II nuclear tests.

As Adler and Barnett (1998: 50) conclude in their study, the initial conditions precipitating peaceful change start a path-dependent process (that is difficult to turn back on) towards dependable expectations of mutual cooperation. As they (ibid.: 51) conclude, the desire to capitalize on trade and economic interaction will naturally encourage the development of international institutions. At the same time, however, the very economic associations encouraging economic interchange and coordination will create pressures to produce order and security. Though it is far too early to tell in the case of China and India, with the processes that this book highlights (deepening economic, energy and diplomatic interchange), we may be witnessing the initial steps toward a Sino-Indian cooperative framework.

The theoretical base of the book then relates more closely to arguments made by traditional realists (before the "neo" turn of the 1970s). In the work of Morgenthau (1948), Carr (1939) and Niebuhr (1950) one sees a subtler version of realism. While acknowledging the key role of power and interest in international relations, Morgenthau entertained the role that institutions and norms play in establishing world peace. According to Morgenthau, long-lasting peace can only be achieved through "transformation." The steps towards this transformation are made through the politics of "accommodation" whereby international conflict can be managed and mitigated through a revival of diplomacy and mutual understanding. According to Niebuhr, the intensification of day-to-day interaction is the key to developing mutual trust and resolving international conflict. Finally, Carr's discussion of "peaceful change," in line with Frederick Sherwood Dunn's[6] (1937) initial insights on the topic, highlights how a middle ground between idealism and realism is necessary and that the key to resolving international conflict lies in negotiation and bargaining. The "soft" realism employed in this book, therefore, is closer to the richer analyses of earlier realists. With the Sino-Indian relationship, we are seeing the beginning of the politics of accommodation, the building of mutual trust and exchange. This is taking place in the low politics of economics and trade but also at higher official levels between political and military elites.

The methodological outlook, organization and structure of the book

Methodology

The research question that this proposal seeks to address is: "What is the nature of the Sino-Indian security relationship in the Indian Ocean region and is it in the process of transformation?" In most cases a research question will consist of answering a "why" question. However, as some analysts have pointed out, answers to "how" and "what" questions are equally legitimate in social scientific enterprises (Wendt, 1987: 512; Price and Reus-Smit 1998: 277). The differences in these questions stem from what Wendt refers to as differences between constitutive and causal analysis. For instance, positivists assume that the only legitimate question that can be asked is the causal question of "why?" Interpretivists, on the other hand, maintain that the unique nature of social life makes the epistemology and proper practice of social science fundamentally different from that of the natural sciences. The two, however, are apples from the same tree. As Wendt notes, "answers to why-questions require answers to how- and what-questions, and so even positivists must engage in at least implicit constitutive analyses" (Wendt, 1999: 85; also Keat and Urry, 1982: 31; Foucault, 1982). Nonetheless, constitutive theories also have to be judged against empirical evidence if possible, as not all interpretations are equally valid. Thus, as Wendt notes, constitutive inquiry faces the same epistemological problem as causal inquiry, "how to justify claims . . . whether constitutive rules or causal mechanisms from what we can see" (Wendt, 1999: 85). It is for these reasons that King, Keohane and Verba contend that there is no fundamental epistemological difference between so-called Explanation and Understanding (King *et al.*, 1994; Hollis and Smith, 1990).

There are, however, significant methodological differences between causal and constitutive theorizing (that reflect the different kinds of questions that they seek to answer). So as Hollis and Smith note, there are always "two stories to tell" in social inquiry (in Wendt, 1998). The differences, however, cannot be perceived as distinctions between causation and description. As King, Keohane and Verba (1994) note, "descriptive inference" and "causal inference" have the same fundamental purpose, which is explanatory or what they refer to as scientific inference. Non-causal explanation, for instance (some of) the activity of historians, does not explain why an event occurred, but explains what it was in the first place; this is done by classifying and synthesizing events under a concept such as revolution, hyperinflation, and so on (Dray, 1959; Wendt, 1999: 86). Thus as Wendt concludes, "theories which answer 'what?' or 'how-possible?' questions 'explain' the world."

In another sense, answering "how" and "what" questions is an important end in itself. This is because without good descriptions of how things are put together and what is happening, any explanations will probably be limited or false. In addition to providing a basis for causal explanation, constitutive theory is also valuable insofar as it shows that there are multiple ways to put a phenomenon together. In this way, recognizing the importance and contribution of constitutive questions will make for better all-round social science. As Wendt puts it: "If all observation is theory-laden, then constitutive theory gives us the lenses through which we see the world" (1999: 87).

According to King, Keohane and Verba, good research projects pose "a question that is 'important' in the real world" (1994: 15). The project here is consequential in this sense because the nature of the bilateral relationship between the world's two most populous states (which are also nuclear powers) "significantly affects many people's lives" and could "help predict events that might be harmful or beneficial" (ibid.: 15). A better understanding of the nature of the relationship between China and India can surely be considered to have "real world" significance.

The methodological approach to be adopted will be interpretative in nature. Following King *et al.*, the book will be concerned with inference. The research question here is constitutive in nature. Yet notably it is still concerned with "explanation" in addition to "understanding." In determining what the nature of the Sino-Indian relationship is in the IOR, an important explanation of how this relationship can be characterized will be offered. The argument that will be made is that existing neorealist arguments cannot explain emerging empirical discrepancies and can be fruitfully augmented with neoliberal and constructivist approaches. Before examining the content of the chapters in this book in the next section, it is worthwhile linking the methodology employed here to the theoretical issues raised earlier. These issues are best addressed by framing this analysis in terms of the fundamental point of social scientific inquiry.

According to Peter Hall, the mainstream position is that:

> [S]ocial science is an effort to identify the causal factors (or variables) that tend to produce a particular kind of outcome. One begins such an inquiry by formulating a set of theories that identify the relevant causal factors and how they operate, along with a rationale for their operation generally couched as deductions from more general contentions about the world based both on previous observations and on axiomatic premises. From each theory, the investigator then derives predictions about the patterns that will appear in observations of the world if the causal theory is valid and if it is false, with special attention to predictions that are consistent with one theory but inconsistent with its principal rivals so as to discern which among a set of competing theories is more likely to be valid.
>
> (2003: 391–392)

As King *et al.* (1994) suggest, the researcher should then seek as many and as varied a set of observations as possible and check if these observations are consistent with the relevant theories involved.

The relevant international relations theories that could possibly provide insight into the Sino-Indian relationship were presented earlier as a continuum ranging from holism and individualism, on the one hand, and idealism and materialism, on the other. In explaining the Sino-Indian relationship, neorealist-oriented theories and accounts have long dominated the Sino-Indian literature. This book, however, seeks to question the accuracy of neorealist accounts of Sino-Indian relations and whether recent developments in the Sino-Indian relationship are consistent with the assumptions of neorealism. In seeking to make "as diverse a set of observations as possible" (Hall, 2003: 2392), understudied (and importantly linked) areas within the Sino-Indian relationship are chosen as points of analysis—maritime security, economics, energy and very recent elite dialogue. Since the focus of this book is on testing the accuracy of neorealist explanations of Sino-Indian relations in the contemporary issue areas noted above, the appeal of a qualitative methodology becomes apparent. This is because the only case in this book is the Sino-Indian one. Thus, rather than testing the validity of neorealist theories more generally in world politics, this book hones in on the (traditionally dominant) neorealist account of the Sino-Indian relationship. While examining a single case, a detailed look at a diverse set of observations within that case (also known as process tracing, Bennett and George, 1997) can be a fruitful way to determine which theory's predictions and assumptions the case in question conforms with.

The central contention made in this book is that the diverse (yet linked) observations made in the Sino-Indian case do not strictly conform to neorealist predictions. However, rather than rejecting neorealist explanations all together because of their inconsistency with the observations made in the areas of maritime security, economics, energy and recent elite dialogue, this book points towards theoretical pluralism (an appeal to "soft" realism and theories of neoliberalism and peaceful change). If neorealist theories were correct, one would generally expect Sino-Indian maritime rivalry, economic factors to be secondary to security considerations, competition in securing energy supplies and signs of tension and rivalry in elite dialogue (if there is any meaningful dialogue to begin with). This book, however, descriptively tracing recent developments in these four issue areas, finds that strict neorealist explanations are implausible.

Organization and structure of the book

The chapters in this book, excluding Chapter 1, are correspondingly arranged according to the four issue areas of observations noted above. In the field of maritime security (Chapter 2) it is discovered that although China and India have undoubtedly embarked upon ambitious naval modernization programs and are developing overlapping spheres of interest, this does not necessarily point towards competition and rivalry.

As many Sino-Indian neorealists focus on growing Sino-Burmese and

Sino-Pakistani naval cooperation as well as Sino-Indian naval moderniza-tion, this book focuses on maritime security. Though other non-maritime security issues such as nuclear and border relations are also undoubtedly important and examined in this book to a lesser extent, an analysis of mari-time security has several advantages. First, the issue of maritime security bridges over into an analysis of Sino-Indian energy policies. Energy policies in turn are the link between economic issues and issues of maritime security. Second, post-Cold War Sino-Indian maritime security is an emerging field within the study of Sino-Indian relations.[7] Instead of focusing on the better covered nuclear and border issues,[8] this book seeks to make a contribution to the literature on Sino-Indian maritime relations.

Even while reviewing the Sino-Indian neorealist arguments, attempts will be made to "update" these lines of argument with a discussion of recent developments in Sino-Indian maritime relations that could be interpreted through a neorealist lens. For instance, China's so-called "String of Pearls" strategy is discussed in some depth, as well as developments in Sino-Pakistani and Sino-Burmese naval and military cooperation in 2005 and 2004. The same is done for India's South Asia and "Look East" policy. Furthermore, an attempt is made to link official Chinese and Indian naval doctrine to Sino-Indian maritime activity in the IOR. Indeed, there are few comprehen-sive examinations of Sino-Indian naval doctrine and maritime activity.

Specifically, Chapter 2 will be organized by examining: (1) China's naval strategy and naval forces; (2) the IOR as an expanding zone of Chinese interest; (3) India's naval strategy and forces; (4) the Indian Navy's evolving role in the IOR; and (5) alternative interpretations of Sino-Indian activity in the IOR. The "updated" neorealist accounts of Sino-Indian competition in the IOR will be discussed. The closing section of Chapter 2 will challenge these neorealist accounts of Sino-Indian relations by offering a reinterpreta-tion of the same events. In this section it will be argued that China's maritime activity in the IOR may be non-threatening in nature and may reflect con-cerns unrelated to India. Moreover, it will be held that India's acceleration of its "Look East" policy should be contextualized as something more than a response to increasing Chinese presence in the IOR.

Chapter 3, in contrast to neorealist expectations, explores the emergence of economic interdependence between the Chinese and Indian economies (preceded by a look at the path towards Chinese and Indian economic liberal-ization). It specifically examines the growing institutional dynamics of Sino-Indian trade and the growth in Sino-Indian trade in goods, trade in services, and bilateral investments. Moreover, the areas where trade could be expanded are explored. This chapter concludes that Sino-Indian trade has been growing at a very impressive rate in the past few years and that there are substantial gains to be realized from further economic integration. Both India and China have long-term goals to create a free trade arrangement with ASEAN; coupled with long-terms plans to enhance Sino-Indian trade, there are signs, as Swaran Singh (2005a) notes that (Asian) politics are increasingly being driven by economics. Chapter 4 will thus show the potential that the "low" politics of economics have to transform the Sino-Indian relationship. In this way, these arguments will serve to moderate neorealist accounts of the Sino-Indian relationship.

Chapter 4 traces China and India's energy concerns and policies. However, instead of being poised for competition and rivalry over securing energy supplies, as neorealism would predict, Chapter 4 concludes that China and India have learned to coordinate their energy strategies.

Finally, Chapter 5, in contrast to neorealist expectations explores the growing elite consensus between India and China. It traces the emergence of a "political will" to transform the relationship and to realize the gains possible from bolstering trade. It will be argued that there is a growing interchange and communication between China and India's top politicians and military officials. This chapter will contend that China and India are in the process of reinterpreting their relationship in a more friendly and positive light. This relates to arguments concerning peaceful change as discussed by Adler and Barnett (1998). Military and political cooperation continue to reach new heights when both China and India declared the year 2006 to be the year of "Sino-Indian Friendship." Both China and India share many of the same vulnerabilities in the IOR (terrorism and piracy) and have significant incentives to coordinate their maritime policies. China can help protect Indian shipping and commerce in East Asia and India can reciprocate in the Indian Ocean. Chapter 5, however, does acknowledge the continuing irritants in the Sino-Indian relationship (the Pakistan and border issues) and how the Sino-Indian relationship can be contextualized in the global balance of power.

First and foremost though, in Chapter 1, the post-independence history of the Sino-Indian relationship is examined. This chapter is crucial especially to those unfamiliar with the history of Sino-Indian relations because it puts the entire book and the chapters that follow it in their appropriate context. By historically tracing the evolution of Sino-Indian relations, an appreciation is gained of both the source of neorealist theorists, insights and of how other theories may begin to shed light on the ever-changing Sino-Indian relationship. The origin of neorealists, applications to the Sino-Indian relationship can be firmly traced to the collapse of Panchsheel in the 1950s, the emergence of Cold War dynamics in Asia and to the Sino-Indian Border War of 1962. However, the possibility of applying theories of interdependence and peaceful change can be traced back to the normalization achieved throughout much of the 1980s and 1990s and consolidated in the first years of the second millennium following India's nuclear tests.

1 The history of Sino-Indian relations

Sino-Indian relations after World War II

India achieved independence on 15 August 1947 after a long and nonviolent nationalist movement. China attained independence on 1 October 1949 in what was the culmination of the Chinese Civil War (1945–1949). There was a brief period of cooperation from 1949–1957 where diplomatic relations were formally established (1 April 1950) and high-level visits were exchanged. India was the first non-socialist country to establish formal diplomatic relations with the PRC. India also strongly advocated the PRC's presence in the United Nations Security Council and consistently voted in the PRC's favor until 1962 (Swamy, 2001: Appendix IV). In 1954, the two states signed an agreement on Trade and Intercourse between the Tibet region of China and India and had an Exchange of Notes. India thus signed away all its inherited privileges in Tibet by virtue of earlier pacts (see, for instance, Ganguly, 2004: 105–120). The Five Principles of Peaceful Coexistence (Panchsheel) and the Bandung Conference were highlights of Sino-Indian cooperation. However, the cooperation was not to last. By the late 1950s, serious differences between the two states had begun to surface, particularly over the undemarcated border. The unresolved border issue would lead to war by 1962.

Colonial legacy was in many ways responsible for the India-China border dispute. The 1913–1914 Simla Conference, which was attended by representatives from British India, Tibet and the Republic of China, resulted in the conclusion of a vague agreement. Opaque references were made to watersheds and the natural boundaries between British India and Tibet. Later these references were utilized in the creation of the controversial McMahon Line. Although Chinese representatives were involved, the central government in Beijing never formally signed the agreement. Furthermore, though Tibet signed the agreement, the Nationalist Kuomintang government under Chiang Kai-shek as well as the Communist Party under Mao Tse-tung later failed to recognize the agreement's legitimacy and sought to restore Chinese borders to former historical levels in the early nineteenth century.

In 1950, the People's Liberation Army (PLA) of China advanced into Lhasa and brought Tibet under Chinese control. The *de facto* takeover became *de jure* when the Dalai Lama accepted the seventeen-point agreement of May 1951 with China. This nullified any Tibetan claim to independence (Sidhu and Yuan, 2003: 12). For India, with the Chinese takeover of Tibet, the buffer zone provided by the Tibetan plateau and the Himalayan frontier disappeared (Garver, 2001b: Chapter 3).

The Indian leadership was caught off guard with these developments but in response quickly implemented a two-prong strategy. First, Nepal, Bhutan and Sikkim were incorporated within India's defensive boundaries. Furthermore, Indian administration was extended into the Tawang tract (a monastery region beyond the McMahon Line). Second, Nehru tried convincing the Chinese to maintain a relationship characterized by suzerainty over Tibet. However, the latter strategy failed and by the 1954 Panchsheel Agreement, India, realized that Chinese occupation of Tibet was a *fait accompli*. Subsequently, India attempted to use the positive momentum generated by the Panchsheel Agreement to reach a conclusion on the contentious border issue (Sidhu and Yuan, 2003: 13). Border talks between India and China failed in 1954 and relations steadily deteriorated. Even India's army chief as Sidhu and Yuan note, "admitted that Nehru was aware of the Chinese threat but realized that there was very little they could do militarily" and continued to seek a diplomatic solution (ibid.: 13).

In 1958, in a letter to Nehru, Chinese Premier Zhou En-lai suggested that both India and China should "temporarily maintain the status quo" (GOI, 1959: 54). However, Zhou maintained that boundary disputes between India and China existed; that there existed a line of actual control (LAC) exercising administrative jurisdiction on both sides; that the two sides should observe the current LAC (which by default was the McMahon Line) pending a final resolution to the dispute; and that both sides should withhold patrolling close to the disputed areas to ensure peace (Liu, 1994: 20–26).

While Sino-Indian relations continued to deteriorate, revolts broke out in Tibet over Chinese rule in the late 1950s. The revolts culminated in March 1959 where the Dalai Lama, disguised as a soldier, fled from Lhasa. Having been assured of asylum by Nehru, he reached India on 31 March 1959, and set up the government-in-exile in the northern Indian border town of Dharamsala. The Chinese were outraged and immediately implicated the US and CIA involvement in the affair. As one analyst has noted:

> In the Chinese eyes, political asylum given to the Dalai Lama and the Tibetan rebels and the warm welcome Nehru himself extended to the Dalai Lama at this moment were at least an unfitting reception, if not a provocative act.
>
> (Liu, 1994: 24)

The tensions over Tibet brought the status of the Panchsheel Agreement into question. It indicated the significance of the unresolved status of borders in the Ladakh region of Indian Kashmir and in the North East Frontier Agency

(NEFA, now the Indian state of Arunachal Pradesh) north of Assam and East of Myanmar (*Documents* . . . 1960: 24; Saigal, 1979: 19). China had already occupied the Aksai Chin plateau of Ladakh and built a road through it, connecting its Tibetan region with that of Xinjiang. Correspondingly, India launched "Operation Onkar," a strategy designed to establish military posts along the McMahon Line to be completed by July 1962 (Saigal, 1979: 19).

Armed clashes then occurred in two separate regions, first in Longju (in the eastern sector) and then in Kongka (in the western sector) in 1959. Negotiations in April 1960 to attempt to settle the increasing tensions failed. Shortly thereafter, the Indian army implemented its "forward policy," pushing northward. Then, in October 1962, war broke out between the two states.[1] PLA troops ousted Indian troops from their post in Dhola in the eastern sector, which was beyond the McMahon Line (on the Chinese side, and established as a part of the forward policy under Operation Onkar). The better-prepared PLA forces overwhelmed Indian troops in both the eastern and western sectors.

In the Ladakh theatre India was essentially routed and by mid-November China was in possession of all the territory that Beijing had previously claimed. In the NEFA, the Indian defense effort completely broke down. The morale of the troops was completely crushed and the army leaders were disgraced. China had reached within 40 miles of Tezpur and 100 miles from the Digboi oil fields. Then, suddenly, on 21 November 1962, the PLA unilaterally withdrew to where the Chinese government thought the territorial boundaries with India should be (Praval, 1990: xi; Sidhu and Yuan, 2003: 15). Although the Indian government strongly opposed China's point of withdrawal, they could do little but appeal, at the least, for a reversion to the status quo ante. However, the war was far more consequential for India for other reasons. The war did not change the status quo of the border but "for all intents and purposes, India had lost the war and was forced to accept both territorial loss and national humiliation on a grand scale" (Sidhu and Yuan, 2003: 15). The scale of the defeat and the psychological impact that it had on India cannot be underestimated (ibid.: 17). From a military standpoint, Indian forces proved completely incapable of defending India's borders. As Sidhu and Yuan (ibid.: 17) note, "The outward sense of optimism that had characterized defense and foreign policy making at the political level between 1947 and 1962 never returned." Though the United States, Britain and even the Soviet Union criticized Chinese actions, they were all unable or unwilling to commit themselves militarily against the Chinese. India thus made the shift towards developing an indigenous conventional military capability that could deal with the Chinese threat and preserve Indian territorial integrity. After China successfully tested its first nuclear bomb on 16 October 1964, there were additional incentives for India to commence its own nuclear program (Thomas, 1993).

From 1962 until 1976, tensions between China and India remained high as both sides fought their own Cold War. As a result of India's huge defense efforts following the 1962 border war, the threat of overt conflict slowly receded. However, the process of normalization still loomed large, despite the fact that both sides had informally accepted the cease-fire line of 21 November 1962 as the LAC (Liu, 1994: 176–177). Both sides deployed hundreds of thousands of troops in the remote boundary regions and infrastructure improvements were made on both sides (i.e. construction of roads, airfields, etc, see Mansingh and Levine, 1989). One of the most consequential developments of the 1962 border war was the emergence of important new security dynamics. India and the Soviet Union emerged on one side and China, Pakistan and the United States on the other (Mansingh and Levine, 1989; Sidhu and Yuan, 2003: 18).

What started as ideological disputes between Mao and Khrushchev culminated in the Sino-Soviet split by the mid-1960s. Moscow accused Beijing of pursuing a reckless foreign policy agenda and Beijing in turn accused Moscow of becoming ideologically soft towards the West (Athwal, 2004). The Sino-Soviet split coincided with increasing Indo-Soviet cooperation, best embodied by the 1971 Friendship Treaty and with Sino-US rapprochment. This resulted in Kissinger's famous trip to Beijing in 1971 (N.S. Singh, 1986; Malik, 2002).[2]

The Sino-Pakistani partnership emerged primarily as the outcome of the Sino-Indian border war and quickly began to take the form of an anti-India alliance. Pakistan and China reached a boundary agreement on 3 March 1963 on their common border, which both parties agreed had not been delimited and demarcated. Moreover, during the 1965 Indo-Pakistani War (fought mainly over Kashmir), China sided with Pakistan and accused India of suspicious military activity in Tibet (Vertzberger, 1983: 38–40; Rose, 2000: 226). During the 1971 war between India and Pakistan, which led to the formation of Bangledesh, Sino-Pakistani cooperation took place at both the diplomatic and military levels. In April when India began backing a guerilla movement in East Pakistan, Premier Zhou offered his support to Pakistan's dictator General Yahya Khan, contesting that "should the Indian expansionists dare to launch aggression against Pakistan, the Chinese government and people will, as always, firmly support the Pakistani government and people in their struggle to safeguard state sovereignty and national independence" (Vertzberger, 1983: 47). Such statements, coupled with news of Kissinger's secret visit to Beijing in July were the primary factors pushing India to sign the Indo-Soviet Friendship Treaty on 9 August 1971 (Hersh, 1983: 452; N.S. Singh, 1986: 87–89). As one analyst has observed, "Sino-Indian animosity after the 1962 war soon evolved into a dependent antagonism ... Any attempts to improve relations between New Delhi and Beijing were constrained by the Sino-Soviet antagonism and the Indo-Pakistani confrontation" (Mansingh and Levine, 1989; Sidhu and Yuan, 2003: 18).

Though in rhetoric, Chinese support for Pakistan appeared deep in both 1965 and 1971, the level of their actual military commitments was quite calculated. As Rose has noted, in both the 1965 and 1971 wars, China "merely provided Pakistan with a reasonable deterrent against India's much larger and technologically superior military" (Vertzberger, 1983: 52; Sidhu and Yuan, 2003: 21). In other words, China did not want to give aid to the extent that it would enable Pakistan to carry out offensive military operations against India. As another analyst has also commented, "China wanted a policy that would demonstrate all-out support for Pakistan without going beyond a certain limit of actual commitment to military involvement" (Vertzberger, 1983: 52).

Relations between India and China began to take a positive turn in the 1970s when in 1976, India and China finally exchanged ambassadors again. Though Prime Minister Indira Gandhi was prepared to improve relations with China by 1969, the Chinese did not respond until 1976 (ibid.: 56). Despite warnings from Soviet Premier Alexei Kosygin, the Indian government under Morarji Desai continued to make overtures toward China (Liu, 1994: 126; Swamy, 2001: 101). The Desai-led Janata government sought to distance New Delhi from Moscow by improving relations with Beijing. In turn, the post-Mao Deng Xiaoping government realized that the Indo-Soviet relationship was closely tied to Indo-Chinese hostility. Therefore an improvement in Sino-Indian relations would serve to distance New Delhi from Moscow. Coupled with US military defeats in Vietnam and the subsequent US "retreat" from Asia, the Chinese felt that an improvement in Sino-Indian relations would frustrate Soviet attempts to fill the vacuum created by the US withdrawal and encircle China (Mansingh and Levine, 1989: 36; Liu, 1994: 124–125).

In February 1979, India's Foreign Minister Atal Bihari Vajpayee strategically visited China during the Sino-Vietnamese War (or Third Indochina War) and then in June 1980, Deng Xiaoping suggested to Indian journalists that a resolution to the border issue could be based on a mutual recognition of the status quo: Indian acceptance of Chinese control of Askai Chin and Chinese recognition of Indian control of territory in the eastern sector. For the first time as well, as one analyst notes, "China also departed from its previous position on Kashmir, declaring it to be a bilateral issue between India and Pakistan instead of unequivocally backing the latter" (Sidhu and Yuan, 2003: 22; also Garver, 1996: 323–40). Despite counter-pressure from Moscow in the final year of the Leonid Brezhnev period (1964–1982), the process of Sino-Indian normalization continued in the pattern of: regular summit meetings between heads of state and government, high-ranking military and nonmilitary officials and with the institutionalization of confidence-building measures (CBMs). This ongoing process has been highly significant and led to the 1993 Agreement on the Maintenance of Peace and Tranquility and the 1996 Agreement on Confidence-Building Measures.

The period, however, was not without its tensions. For instance, in December 1986, India granted statehood to Arunachal Pradesh, formerly NEFA, an act that was seen by China as an attempt to impose the controversial McMahon Line (one of the causes of the original 1962 border dispute, Liu, 1994: 142). On the other hand, Chinese movements in western Ladakh across the LAC prompted protests from New Delhi. Border tensions began to heat up once again to the point where India mobilized troops (as a part of Operation Chequerboard in Sumdorong Chu in the eastern sector), making the prospect of war ever more real (Garver, 1996). There was also China's rapidly developing nuclear missile program and reports about the supply of nuclear and missile technologies to Pakistan (Sidhu and Yuan, 2001: 23).

As the Cold War drew to a close, the prospects for Sino-Indian détente also improved. Mikhail Gorbachev's reforms brought Moscow and Beijing closer and also meant that the "India" card was becoming less relevant in Sino-Soviet relations. Though Prime Minister Rajiv Gandhi insisted on Chinese sovereignty over Tibet and emphasized India's policy of noninterference, China was still concerned about renewed nationalist sentiment in Lhasa and moreover the links between Tibetan nationalist groups and right-wing Hindu parties (Mansingh, 1994a: 299).

Prime Minister Rajiv Gandhi's visit to Beijing in December 1988, the first since Nehru's in 1954, was a definitive moment in Sino-Indian relations. During the visit, the two states established a framework for cooperation. India accepted China's position that bilateral relations (especially economic) could be expanded and improved before the resolution of the border issue. And China accepted India's position that a joint working group headed by deputy foreign ministers be created to settle the border dispute with an acceptable time frame. Sino-Indian ties reached a new high in 1996 when Jiang Zemin became the first Chinese president to pay an official visit to India. During this time, both India and China agreed to reduce troops along the LAC and signed the Agreement on Confidence-Building Measures. In this period of cooperation, increasing institutional links were established not only at the military level but also within the strategic, journalistic and political communities. Research and scholarship opportunities increased markedly between the two states and an agreement on bilateral cooperation in science technology and space was signed (ibid.: 296).

The biggest change to Sino-Indian relations from the 1980s through to the 1990s was the large increase in bilateral trade. It increased from $117.4 million in 1987 to $700 million in 1993–1994. It now stands at $13.4 billion (CIA World Fact Book, 2004). Though both states export similar goods such as carpets, garments, textiles, industrial components and handicrafts, there are areas where each state enjoys comparative advantages and where trade can be expanded. As basic infrastructure continues to improve in both states (e.g. telecommunications, shipping lines and banking channels), the prospects of enhancing trade also increase (Mansingh 1994a: 295; Sidhu and Yuan, 2003: 25).

Politically, China made an implicit shift in this period to acknowledge India's superior position in South Asia. For instance, there was a noticeable weakening in the verbal support for Pakistan in the ongoing Kashmir dispute (Garver, 1996: 337–343). Moreover, in 1987, when India invaded Sri Lanka to quell Tamil insurgents, China shifted from a previous pro-Colombo position to a neutral position in the Indo-Sri Lankan confrontation. Similarly, China did not condemn the Indian economic blockade of Nepal in 1988 in response to Chinese weapons sales to Kathmandu even though it was negatively affecting Sino-Nepalese exchange rates (ibid.: 337–343; Rose, 2000: 226–227). Thus as Sidhu and Yuan note, "China had essentially acquiesced to New Delhi's dominant role in South Asia" (2003: 26). This would all change, however, when India conducted its Pokharan nuclear tests in 1998.

In May 1998, India conducted five nuclear tests in the Pokharan desert and brought international attention and concern to the subcontinent. In a letter to US President Clinton, Prime Minister Atal Bihari Vajpayee explicitly linked India's official nuclearization to a threat "on our borders" by "a state which committed armed aggression against India in 1962" (*New York Times*, 1998: A14). Though, the "Chinese threat" was explicitly mentioned as the motivation for developing nuclear weapons, this had always been a background factor from the beginning of India's nuclear program. The option to construct nuclear weapons was left open by India in the early days of its nuclear energy program in the 1950s (Abraham, 1999; Perkovich, 1999). According to Beaton and Maddox, by mid-1963, with the completion of the CIRUS plutonium reactor and the Trombay plutonium plant, India kept the nuclear option open in case it became a political and military necessity (Beaton and Maddox, 1962: 141). For a long time, however, Nehru opposed the construction of any nuclear bomb despite it being left as a background option. Even in the aftermath of war with China in 1962 and the possibility of the development of a Chinese nuclear bomb, Nehru argued, "It will not have the slightest effect on India if they have a test tomorrow ... We are not going to make bombs" (quoted in Mirchandani, 1966: 22; see also Lall, 1962: 66).

Following Nehru's death, the debate within and outside the government on the nuclear weapons question intensified (Sidhu and Yuan, 2003: 27). China's successful test in 16 October 1964 also caused a slow but discernible shift in Indian policy on the bomb. From a no-bomb policy, the new Lal Bahadur Shastri government in the sixty-ninth session of the Congress Party's conference in January 1965 contested that it could not "say anything about the future" with regard to the nuclear option and that the preexisting Indian policy would be reconsidered if China succeeded in stockpiling nuclear weapons and advancing missile technology. Also in 1965, the secretary of the Congress Parliamentary Party, K.C. Pant, returning from meetings from the UN General Assembly, noted that China could occupy a permanent seat on the UN Security Council and that India would only be able to clinch a seat on the permanent council if it achieved (nuclear) parity with China (Ray, 1967: 140).

Shastri thus launched a dual strategy. First he sought nuclear guarantees from the great powers and, second, commenced the subterranean nuclear explosion (SNEP) and the peaceful nuclear explosion (PNE) projects. This eventually led to the Indian PNE in the Pokharan Desert on 18 May 1974.

Though Prime Minister Indira Gandhi did not make the connection to the Chinese threat explicit, the Ministry of Defence, in its annual report, made note of China's stockpiling of nuclear (150) and thermonuclear weapons (with a capacity to make forty weapons of 20 kilotons annually). Particular concern was expressed about China's medium-range ballistic missiles (DF-3 with a 2,800 km range) and their ability to reach targets all-over India (GOI, 1971: 1–2; 1973: 7).

India's nuclear weapons program thus originally began with the Chinese threat in mind. However, as the program continued, domestic factors also became important. As Sidhu and Yuan note, "New Delhi considers its nuclear and missile capabilities to be symbols of international prestige . . . [and] . . . political leaders have . . . exploited this to enhance their own standing in domestic politics" (2003: 29). In addition, Pakistan's alarming nuclear and missile development provided a huge impetus for India to go nuclear. Pakistan accelerated its nuclear program after its humiliating defeat and dismemberment in the 1971 Indo-Pakistani War (Thomas, 1986, 1993; Thomas and Gupta, 2000: 2). As Prime Minister Zulfikar Ali Bhutto noted, Pakistanis were willing to "eat grass" to match India's nuclear capability (Thomas and Gupta, 2000: 2). By the 1980s, Indian analysts were almost entirely convinced that Pakistan had put together a functioning and effective nuclear weapons program with the help of China (Palit and Namboodri, 1982). Leading up to the Pokharan II nuclear tests, India thus saw itself responding to developments in its strategic environment (Garver, 2001b: 216–242; Sidhu and Yuan, 2003: 29). Furthermore, the Bharatiya Janata Party (BJP) felt that the tests would help buttress their national political strength. The indefinite extension of the Non-proliferation Treaty (NPT) in 1995 and the impending entry into force of the Comprehensive Test Ban Treaty (CTBT) by the end of 1999 were also important factors leading to Pokharan II. The collapse of the Soviet Union and the ascendance of the United States caused some to think that the bomb would be required to conduct an autonomous foreign and security policy (Singh, 1998). This is because many in India felt that the Soviet Union could no longer be relied upon for India's nuclear security. There was the fear then that India would be left vulnerable in the face of conflict with the world's nuclear powers.

The combination of the Chinese threat and the increasing Pakistani threat was especially highlighted in Vajpayee's letter to Clinton as well. In addition to Vajpayee's letter, India's Defence Minister, George Fernandes made a series of polemic public comments about China being India's "number one threat" (Perkovich, 1999: 415; Sidhu and Yuan, 2003: 30; Swamy, 2001: 102).

Beijing's initial response to the tests, reported in the *Xinhua News Agency* remained restrained and simply expressed concern. However, when the second round of tests were conducted on 13 May and when the *New York Times* published Prime Minister Vajpayee's letter to President Clinton with specific reference to the Chinese threat, China reacted angrily and strongly ("China's Statement . . ." 1998: 7). China was therefore more upset about being labeled as the primary motivation for India developing a nuclear capacity than at the tests themselves *per se*. Despite being vocal in support of the UN Security Council Resolution 1172, China never considered sanctions as the United States did. In the international arena the Chinese appeared to care more about the implication that they were responsible for or being perceived of as a threat than India's actual nuclearization.

Following the Chinese reaction, however, India began to moderate its "China-threat" rhetoric. Domestically, left-leaning Indian political parties were highly critical of Vajpayee's letter and Fernandes' comments. Many politicians and political analysts lamented that the BJP government was needlessly amplifying Sino-Indian tensions. Indian Foreign Minister Jaswant Singh's June 1999 visit to China would prove to be a key turning point in Sino-Indian relations. The visit took place during the 1999 Indo-Pakistani Kargil Crisis. The visit not only emphasized Chinese neutrality in the dispute but it demonstrated that both sides were willing to open a security dialogue to progress relations. Chinese Foreign Minister Tang Jiaxun reciprocated the visit in July 2000. This signaled the return of high-level exchanges between the two states. Li Peng, Chairman of the National People's Congress, visited India in January 2001, Premier Zhu Ronghi visited India in January 2002 and Prime Minister Vajpayee visited China in 2003 (Singh, 1999; Garver, 2001b). Economic, scientific and technological cooperation resumed and important border negotiations on the alignment of the LAC took place with the JWG in 2001, 2002 and 2003 (Sidhu and Yuan, 2003: 33).

Conclusion

This chapter has examined the modern history of Sino-Indian relations. The end of British imperialism left India and China with territorial uncertainty and a largely undemarcated border. In the early post-independence period there was a brief period of optimism where it appeared that China and India might forge a cooperative relationship. However, these hopes quickly faded and both India and China found themselves caught up in the politics of the Cold War. The Sino-Soviet relationship began to deteriorate rapidly following Khrushchev's de-Stalinization speech in 1956 and India's position of non-alignment, in reality, brought it closer to the Soviet Union. Border tensions between India and China finally gave way in the Fall of 1962 in the Sino-Indian War. The brief but bitter war had a tremendous psychological impact in India and to a lesser extent in China. By the early 1970s, in the global struggle for balance of power, China found itself aligned with Pakistan and the United States and India with the Soviet Union. Sino-Indian relations did not begin to normalize until Deng Xiaoping succeeded Mao Zedong. Under Deng, China began to liberalize its economy and in the 1980s Sino-Indian relations began the process of normalization, culminating in the 1993 Agreement on the Maintenance of Peace and Tranquility and the 1996 Agreement on Confidence-Building Measures.

In the post-Cold War period, India began to liberalize its economy and bilateral trade between India and China began to increase markedly. The border issue (and the related Tibet problem), however, still remained unresolved and Sino-Pakistani nuclear and missile cooperation continued to be a major irritant. India's Pokharan II nuclear tests also proved to be a major setback. Prime Minister Vajpayee's June 2003 visit to China was a key turning point and helped bring Sino-Indian relations back on the right foot. With both China and India continuing their development and with relations once again normalized, it is interesting to see where the Sino-Indian relationship is currently going and where it may go in the future. The following chapters of this book try to deal with these questions by primarily focusing on developments in Sino-Indian relations in the past few years. The next chapter will examine the geostrategic importance of the Indian Ocean and China and India's naval development and strategy.

2 The Indian Ocean and China and India's naval strategy and modernization

Introduction

A.T. Mahan, the influential naval strategist, argued in 1890 that "whoever controls the Indian Ocean will dominate Asia." As Mahan continued, "This ocean is the key to the seven seas. In the twenty-first century, the destiny of the world would be decided on its waters." Whether Mahan's prophecy will prove to be true remains to be seen. However, it is indeed the case that the Indian Ocean has become an instrumental body of water in terms of economics and security for its littoral states and even those states beyond its reach.

Commenting on the geographic unity of the Indian Ocean Region (IOR), K.M. Panikkar described its structure as being "walled off on three sides by land, with the southern side of Asia forming a roof over it . . . [giving it] . . . some of the features of a landlocked sea" (1946: 18–19). The Indian sub-continent, in addition, pervades the Ocean named after it and divides it into the Arabian Sea and the Bay of Bengal. The IOR is separated from the rest of mainlaind Asia by a distinct set of geographical features, ranging from the Arabian Desert to the longest chain of mountains in the world (comprising the Ararat, the Elburz, the Hindukush, the Pamirs, Karakoram, Kuen Lun, the Himalayas and the mountains of northern Burma; Kaushik, 1987). On the African side, the countries facing the Indian Ocean from South Africa to Ethiopia are divided from the rest of the continent by desert, dense jungle and the Great Rift Valley and its large lakes. The Ethiopian highlands in the north-east of the region come forward between the desert and the Red Sea. The Burmese-Thai border mountains, the Malay Peninsula and the chain of Indonesian islands divide the Indian Ocean from the Pacific Ocean. Australia forms the south-east pillar of the Indian Ocean and is separated by a distance of 4500 miles from South Africa, the south-western pillar.

Given the geographical structure of the Indian Ocean, with landmasses on all three sides, there are only three major entry points—all of key strategic importance. The south-east entry point is the straits of Malacca; the south-west entry point is around the Cape of Good Hope and the final north-west one is the Suez Canal. There are a few other routes, through the straits of Sunda, Lombok and Makaasar and around Australia (Cape York in the north-east and Base strait in the south-east) but these waters are often more difficult to navigate or cause for a longer journey. The major east–west sea-lanes from the Indian Ocean pass through the Strait of Malacca in the east and the Gulf of Aden and the Suez Canal in the west. These two "choke points" as well as the Strait of Hormuz (connecting the Persian Gulf and the Gulf of Oman) comprise the three major strategic spots in the Indian Ocean.

The Cape and the Australian routes are also important for really large supertankers, as they are broader gateways for Pacific–Atlantic ocean traffic. However, the traffic is not as high or as concentrated compared to the choke points discussed above. For instance, more than half the oil exported through the Straits of Hormuz, 15 million barrels per day (b/d), passes through the Strait of Malacca. States such as Japan, South Korea and China rely on the safe transit of ships through these sea-lanes (Majeed 1986: Chapter 1; Kaushik, 1987: 4; Das, 2001: 317). Over 50,000 vessels transit the Strait of Malacca per year and the Strait handles more than 11 billion barrels of oil per day (compared to the Suez Canal, where approximately 20,000 ships transit per year and 3.8 million b/d. "World Oil . . .," 2004). Suffice to say that any disruption at any of these instrumental choke points would cause major problems for the international economy.

In the past, the colonial powers—the Portuguese, the Dutch, the French and the British—realized the importance of these key strategic features of the Indian Ocean and vied for control. After discovering the Cape route, the Portuguese eventually established a presence in Goa and seized control of key points in the Indian Ocean. They gained control of the Red Sea and the Persian Gulf (at Socotra and Ormuz) as well as the Malacca Straits. Portuguese supremacy ended with the Dutch takeover of Malacca in 1641. After decades of struggle between the colonial powers, the British eventually gained hegemony in the Indian Ocean. They drove the Portuguese from Ormuz in 1822, acquired the Strait of Malacca in 1759, defeated the Dutch at Trincomalee in 1781, defeated the French at Mauritius in 1810, acquired Singapore in 1819 and seized important islands like the Maldives, Seychelles, the Chagos Archipelago and finally Aden in 1839. With the opening of the Suez Canal in 1869, the British completed the " 'most absolute hegemony of all times' in the Indian Ocean" (Kaushik, 1987: 14). Little has changed with regard to the contemporary strategic importance of the Indian Ocean and its choke points.

In terms of natural resources, the Indian Ocean is of great international importance. Its littoral states contain more than two-thirds of the world's oil reserves, 35 percent of the world's gas reserves, 60 percent of uranium, 40 percent of gold and 80 percent of all diamond deposits. Japan imports almost 90 percent of its oil from the IOR, Italy 85 percent, Britain 60 percent, Germany 60 percent and France 50 percent. Other than oil, many important industrial raw materials are located in the IOR. These include lithium, beryllium, circonium, thorium, coal, iron, copper, manganese, tin, bauxite, chromite, nickel, cobalt, vanadium and phosphates (ibid.: 6). As one analyst notes, "40 out of the 54 types of imported raw materials used by American industry are supplied by the Indian Ocean region" (ibid.: 6). In addition, the Indian Ocean itself is rich in various marine resources. The continental shelves (roughly 4 percent of the entire Indian Ocean region) contain enormous amounts of mineral deposits such as nickel, cobalt and manganese, much of which remain untapped. Furthermore, recent geological surveys are revealing the presence of gas and oil deposits both in Myanmar and Bangladesh and off their coasts (Muni and Pant, 2005).

For the two countries in question, China and India, the Indian Ocean is also of great importance. For China, the second largest oil-importing country, the Indian Ocean and the transit of oil from West Asia through the Strait of Malacca are increasingly a top priority. Currently over 80 percent of the oil China imports transits the Strait of Malacca (USA, 2005: 33). Moreover, close to 25 percent of Chinese exports to the Gulf region and to Europe transit the Malacca Strait (Mathur, 2002: 554, K.R. Singh, 2004: 198). It is projected that by 2015, 75–80 percent of India's oil needs will come from the Persian Gulf. Overall, almost 90 percent of India's foreign trade transits the Indian Ocean (Mohanty, 2004; Das 2005). (see figure 2.1).

The growing energy concerns for both India and China have provided additional incentives to continue with naval modernization. Energy security, SLOCs and naval strategy are inextricably linked. The geostrategic

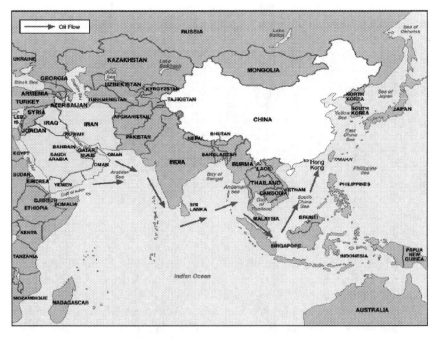

Figure 2.1 Oil flow through the Indian Ocean.

Source: United States (2005).

significance of the Indian Ocean as well as the geostrategic importance of the Indian Ocean have to be considered in concert with Chinese and Indian naval policies for a full understanding of the security dynamics in the IOR.

China's naval strategy and naval forces

China's naval strategy

China has only begun to pay serious attention to its naval forces in the past two decades. Jiang Zemin, China's former president and chairman of the Central Military Commission (CMC) emphasized strongly that China "must strive to establish a modern navy with a strong, comprehensive combat capacity" (*Xinhua*, 1999, FBIS-CHI–99–0421). Such remarks demonstrate the realization that China's offshore national security concerns—Taiwan, the South China Seas, the Indian Ocean and SLOCs are problems that necessitate maritime power. The Indian Ocean's incorporation into China's security sphere has grown alongside China's demand for energy resources. As China becomes more reliant on overseas energy to fuel its economy, which in turn fuels China's military modernization, China has become more concerned with ensuring the safe passage of its merchant marine through the Indian Ocean. In this sense, in the face of international conflict, foreign naval domination of the Indian Ocean could pose a threat to China's security.[1] A 1996 statement by a PLAN strategist best sums up the PRC's central concerns:

> The ocean is not only the basic space for human survival, but also an important theater for international political struggle ... The better people can control the sea, the greater they have the sea territorial rights [that have] become inseparable from a country's sovereignty.
> (Wanjun, 1995, cited in Cole, 2001: 9, also Downing, 1996a)

The PRC drew three primary lessons from this historical experience: (1) a strong naval force is needed for protection of the land; (2) a nation not understanding the importance of the ocean is a nation without a future; and (3) a major sea power incapable of defending its sea territorial rights will not be a major sea power for very long (Wanjun, 1995, cited in Cole, 2001: 9, also Holmes and Yoshihara, 2005).

The People's Liberation Army Navy (PLAN) was hailed during the fiftieth anniversary of the PRC for the advancements it had made. As was stated in the October, 1999 address:

> The Chinese navy has traversed a 50-year journey of struggle ... It started from scratch [and has] equipped itself with missile fast attack craft, missile destroyers, missile frigates, naval missiles, naval fighter bombers, strafers, antisubmarine patrol planes ... and has accomplished important scientific studies and experiments. [It has steamed from the

Arctic to] the Antarctic, . . . successfully conducted an experiment on the underwater launch of a carrier rocket from a nuclear submarine.

(Zuzhi, 1 October 1999, in FBIS-CHI–99–1005)

There was no PLA Navy when the PRC was proclaimed in 1949. However, the Chinese Communist Party (CCP) believed that China's eighteenth- and nineteenth-century humiliation had been greatly facilitated by invasion from the sea. Immediately following the Communist revolution, the CCP realized that the PRC needed to be defended from at least two would-be aggressors: the Kuomintang (KMT) regime in Taiwan and the United States. Thus the PLAN was officially established in May of 1950. In 1953, Mao Zedong wrote, "We must build a strong navy for the purpose of fighting against imperialist aggression." Echoing this sentiment, Deng Xiaoping called for "a strong navy with modern combat capability" and in 1997 Jiang Zemin pushed the Navy to "build up the nation's maritime Great Wall" (Chun-ming, 11 April, in FBIS-CHI–99–0418).

In general terms, the period 1953–1957 was characterized by several attempts to modernize various branches of China's defense sector, including the navy. Real naval expansion though came in the 1970s with the launch of China's "four modernizations program" (*sihua*) in 1975 and after 1978 when naval and air forces were specifically singled out for modernization (Kondapalli, 2004). In this period, China became more assertive, seizing islands from the control of Vietnam and the Philippines in 1974 and 1988. China also became increasingly competitive with Japan in its exclusive economic zone (EEZ) and confrontational with Taiwan. China's naval expansion was solidified in the 1990s in combination with the collapse of the USSR and its withdrawal from Cam Ranh Bay and the US withdrawal from Subic Bay.

China's naval strategy has correspondingly evolved alongside its growing naval capabilities. China's initial strategy was to maintain a level of basic coastal defense. However, by the early 1980s Admiral Liu Huaqing, often called China's Mahan, increasingly employed the concept of "offshore defense" (*jinyan fangyu*), which eventually gave way to the incorporation of a full-fledged blue-water strategy (Goldman, 1996). As early as 1988, the foundations of China's blue-water strategy were spelled out. Chinese Naval Commander, Admiral Zhang Lianzhong identified three main defense perimeters and highlighted the importance of using naval forces to protect these lines. As Zhang noted,

[T]he exterior perimeter is conceived as encompassing the seas out to the first chain of islands. This region will be defended by conventional and nuclear submarines (some of which will be armed with anti-ship missiles), by naval medium-range aircraft and by surface warships. The submarines will play a dynamic role to ensure defence in depth, including the laying of mines in the enemy's sea lines of communication. The middle defence perimeter extends 150 miles from the coast and comes within but, in most cases, does not reach the first chain of islands. Anti-ship aircraft, destroyers and escort vessels will carry the main burden in this area. The interior defence perimeter extends to 60 miles from the coast. This will be the theatre of operations for the main naval air force, fast-attack boats and land-based anti-ship missile units.

(Zhang Lianzhong, cited in Downing, 1996a)

John Jordan has similarly commented on the three-ringed modern structure of China's naval strategy. In the first ring, a "maritime militia" protects the coastal areas and defends ports and harbors with missiles. The second ring is defended by fast patrol craft with surface-to-surface missiles or torpedoes and sub-chasers armed with anti-submarine rocket launchers and depth charge mortars. Frigates and destroyers would defend the line just beyond the inner defensive perimeter. Finally, submarines and long-range bombers would maintain the defense of the outer perimeter (Jordan, 1994; also see Liao, 1995). Moreover, as Lewis and Xue note, the operational guidelines of the Chinese navy in controlling the entire defense perimeter called for quick reaction, swift maneuverability in vast sea areas and combined combat operations (*kuaisu fanying, guanfan jidong, zhengti zuozhan*, Lewis and Xue, 1994: 323).

Originally, Admiral Liu Huaqing noted that the defense area to be safe-guarded by the PLAN had a range of 200 nautical miles. This was soon modified to 600 nautical miles, underscoring the long-range requirements of PLAN (Liao, 1995: 8–10). The control of the Spratly Islands in the South China Sea by PLAN effectively enhances this range to 1000–1500 nautical miles from the mainland coast (Liao, 1995: 14; Downing, 1996a: 130; Cole, 2001: 10). This jurisdiction roughly coincides within the scope of green water naval strategy and the "first island chain" (*diyi daolian*). It encompasses areas from Vladivostok in the north to the Strait of Malacca, including the Japanese Ryukus islands, the Philippines and the South China Sea (Downing, 1996a: 130, Kondapalli, 2004: 3). The blue-water capability (*yuanyang haijun*) co-incides with that of the "second island chain" (*di'er daolian*), generally encom-passing the Kuriles in the north and the Bonin and Mariana Islands and Papua New Guinea in the south (Lewis and Xue, 1994: 229–230; Downing, 1996a: 130; Zhan, 1994). China has therefore steadily shifted its naval strat-egy from a defensive Gorshkov style[2] to one increasingly incorporating Mahanian concepts of power projection and sea control (Ahrari, 1998: 31–36).

As Holmes and Yoshihara (2005: 25) have noted:

Mahan's influence on Chinese strategic thought was palpable . . . at a symposium on sea-lane security in the spring of 2004. Scholar after scholar quoted Mahan at the symposium, attesting to his influence. And almost without exception, they quoted the most bellicose-sounding of Mahan's precepts.

As Chinese naval strategists have noted of Mahan (1890: 138):

> command at sea . . . [meant] . . . that overbearing power on the sea which drives the enemy's flag from it, or allows it to appear only as a fugitive; and which, by controlling the great common, closes the highways by which commerce moves to and from the enemy's shores.
>
> (in Holmes and Yoshihara, 2005: 25)

Mahan's thinking had a circular logic to it: foreign commerce was necessary to ensure economic vitality; overseas bases were necessary to support commerce; and a battle fleet was necessary to defend bases and the flow of trade—trade that in turn supplied the revenues necessary to fund the navy (Mahan, 1890: 71). According to Mahan, powerful naval forces could be used to crush the battle fleets of rival nations to gain control of strategic waterways and ensure dominant power access to the sea-lanes and the commerce they conveyed. For Mahan, then, the command of the sea was inextricably linked with commercial, geographic and military considerations. As Holmes and Yoshihara note, "Commerce and thus national prosperity, hinged on sea power, as embodied in commercial and naval shipping and control of critical geographic nodes" (Holmes and Yoshihara, 2005: 25).

With China's preoccupation with economic development and its growing dependence on seaborne commerce for oil and other natural resources, the appeal to Mahan is understandable. Mahan insisted that armed conflict could be avoided and was detrimental to seaborne commerce. Nonetheless, his writings highlighted the zero-sum nature of the seas. As one analyst notes:

> Central to the theory of sea power was the expectation of conflict. When a nation's prosperity depends on shipborne commerce, and the amount of trade available is limited, the competition follows, and that leads to a naval contest to protect the trade. (Baer, 1994: 12)

In Chinese strategic naval circles, it is not uncommon for analysts to make comments such as "one can only guarantee smooth sea traffic and eventually gain sea domination by annihilating the enemy" and "who controls the seas controls the world" (Xingwang Wang, 2002; Xie, 2001, cited in Holmes and Yoshihara, 2005: 25). The following text from two leading naval officers at PLAN's leading research institute is worth quoting at length to demonstrate this logic:

> The seas have become the new high ground of strategic competition [including] rivalry over ocean islands, rivalry over sea space jurisdiction, rivalry over marine resources, rivalry over the maritime strategic advantage, [and] rivalry over strategic sea lanes . . . The seas are a key national security defense [and] remain of crucial strategic value, . . . not only a

protective screen, [but also] providing invaders with a marine invasion route . . . .Militarily, the naval battlefield is both a springboard for attack and a natural screen for defense. The seas are of crucial importance to a country's prosperity [and] honor [because]: . . . Maritime development will become the major means by which certain countries achieve their political aims; [and the Asian] region will become one of the priority regions of maritime strategic competition [as] one of the regions controlling the world economy . . . .Certain countries are acting to illegally seize maritime rights and interests, even to the extent of doing all possible to internationalize maritime disputes between countries . . . Establishing a Chinese maritime strategy has become a task of top importance [as we look] to the seas for our future survival space.

> (Youqiang and Rongxing, 20 May 1997, in FBIS-CHI–97–19, cited in Cole, 2001: 12–13)

Beginning with Liu Huaqing, who commanded PLAN for much of the 1980s, China moved to a strategy that pursued Mahanian sea power with "Chinese characteristics" (Holmes and Yoshihara, 2005: 28). Liu Huaqing formulated three phases to develop PLAN into a world-class sea power by the year 2040. In the first phase (from the 1980s to 2000), the focus was on training and enhancing existing formations as well as the renovation and improvement of conventional naval vessels. The primary objective during this phase was to deter regional threats and to fight battles quickly and at low risk. In the second and current phase (2001–2020), the emphasis is on the continued modernization of China's naval forces, with special emphasis on submarines and the construction of several light aircraft carriers of 20,000–30,000 tons. In addition, several warships are to be purchased to supplement the carrier task force in order to improve the strength of the fleet and to bolster PLAN's offshore combat capability. By the end of this phase, the PLAN is to have major ocean-going capabilities with the projection of force in and outside the Western Pacific. By the end of the final phase (2021–2040) the full extent of blue-water capability is suppose to be realized which will turn the PLAN into a force capable of power projection and surveillance around the world (Kondapalli, 2004: 4).[3]

Though the IOR and its SLOCs have taken on increasing importance for the PRC, Chinese naval efforts have been directed first to concerns in the China seas (East and South). The PRC, for instance, remains wary of US "gun-boat diplomacy . . . under the cover of so-called security globalization [and anti-terrorism]" (*Guozheng*, 1999, in FBIS-CHI–99–0602). In the Asia-Pacific region, the United States is alleged to be using the new defense arrangements with Japan and theater missile defense to "prepare the ground for future military intervention," and with "Eurasian strategy" to position the United States for a "one superpower-dominated 'U.S. century'" (ibid.). Theater missile defense is also described as another US instrument to actively push its interventionist strategy through a two-flank encirclement of China and Russia. The US is accused of desiring control of Taiwan because it is China's "most direct door to the Pacific," and the Spratlys, since they offer China "a strategic base closest to the Strait of Malacca" (*Donhang*, 1999, in FBIS-CHI–99–0604 and PRC, 2004).

The underlying theme behind the PRC's perspective is the threat posed by the United States and a cooperative Japan to Chinese security. This perspective reflects a broader aspect of the Chinese security perspective. As General Zhang Wannian, the vice chairman of the CMC has argued, China is "threatened by hegemonism and power politics, by militarism, and by foreign military intervention in Taiwan . . . our guard [must not be lowered]" (Hui-wen 1 April, 1999, in FBIS-CHI–99–0414).

A closer look at PLAN

Structure and organization

Traditionally, in the nineteenth century the Chinese Navy had been divided into four fleets: one based in Canton (modern-day Guangzhou), another in Fuzhou, Fujian, the southern fleet near Shanghai and the northern fleet in Port Arthur, Manchuria (Wright, 2000). Each fleet was responsible for defending a specific geographic region from attack or invasion. In essence, the southernmost provinces were treated as separate entities from the central and northern sections of the country in the structure of the navy. The traditional structure of the navy as one analyst notes, "in addition to emphasizing domestic and coastal security . . . helped ensure that these forces could not combine to challenge the central government" (Elleman, 2002).

Following World War II, the Nationalists unified the navy only to realize the dangers inherent in a unified Chinese navy (the Nationalist navy defected wholesale to the communists in 1949). The PRC's decision to reintroduce the traditional fleet structure (northern, central and southern fleets) indicates that domestic unrest is still on Beijing's mind. The CCP through the CMC retains full authority over PLAN and its policy (thus PLAN is structurally subordinate to the PLA). Moreover the naval commanders of the North, East and South Sea Fleets act only as deputy commanders under commanding PLA generals in their respective regions. The North Fleet, based in Qingdao, focuses on the Korean Peninsula, Japan and US forces. The East Sea Fleet, based in Shanghai is responsible for Taiwan. The South Sea Fleet, based in Zhanjian, is focused on Vietnam and the Philippines as well as disputed territories in the South China Sea. There are certain obvious disadvantages that come with such a fleet structure that relate to logistics and training (Kondapalli, 2001). Furthermore, a divided fleet is in theory weaker than one that is unified. Recent reports also suggest that regional rivalries in PLAN continue to persist as Northern Fleet Commanders reassigned to the Southern Fleet caused some unrest (Elleman, 2002).

PLAN's modernization

For many years China's navy remained an antiquated force consisting of naval equipment and weapon systems built in the 1950s and the 1960s. Serious efforts to upgrade the status of the navy, however, did not materialize until the post-Mao period. Admiral Liu Huaqing was one of the leading proponents of naval modernization in the 1980s. He established four main goals for the Chinese Navy: electronization, automation, ballistic missile development and nuclearization. This would affect all types of naval equipment in China's inventory and would demand further research and development as well as acquisition from abroad. As Kondapalli notes, "By the 1980s, several types of naval equipment were either built or a large-scale modernization of the equipment was initiated" (2004: 6). This included the development of the dual–100mm ship-borne gun weapon system; the *Duihai*-1 missile-gun escort; the replacement of the *Shangyou*-1 two-mount dual rotary launcher by the eight-mount fixed launcher, the *Duihai*-2 missile-gun escort; and the Yingji-8 anti-ship missile, featuring minimum altitude sea-skimming ability, strong penetration capability and high target finding abilities and greater explosive power (*China Today* . . . vol. 1, 1993: 170–171; Kondapalli, 2004: 6).

The modernization process of naval equipment also included the enhancement of electronic counter-measures and combat command automation of the first generation of Chinese destroyers. In addition, there was extensive retrofitting of speedboats as well as improvement in torpedo, escort and vessel equipment (*China Today* . . . vol. 1, 1993: 139). More specifically, the 053 H2 missile frigates, the 051G destroyers and the SY-2 ship-borne missile systems were targeted for upgrading (ibid., 171). The Seventh Five-Year Plan and the so-called "strategic transformation" (*zhanlue zhuanbian*) of 1985 outlined the general parameters by which naval equipment was to be developed in the 1980s and emphasized the importance of technological upgrading. In short, given the lack of PLAN's attack capabilities, the five-year plan sought to develop second-generation missile destroyers, multi-function frigates, conventional-powered submarines, anti-ship missiles and underwater systems. Despite these efforts, by the 1990s, the Chinese Navy still lagged behind its strategic competitors in the region—namely South Korea, Japan and Taiwan (Cole, 2001).

More recently, at the fourth plenum of the Fifteenth Party Congress from 19–22 September 1999 there was another push to redouble PLAN's modernization ("Work Division . . .," 1999). The deliberation called for the development and testing of a new "generation of weaponry" (ibid.). Also in October of 1999, China reportedly concluded a five-year $20 billion arms deal with Russia as part of a program for the creation of "a powerful comprehensive combat force" with "rapid reaction capacity, emergency field repair ability and defense readiness" (*Xinhua*, 1999, in SWB FE/3559 G/11; *Tai Yang Pao*, 1999 in SWB FE/3691 G/3–4; "Hong Kong . . . 2000).[4] From 1999 onward, reports indicate that China has indeed embarked on naval modernization on a massive scale.

Chinese shipyards at Dalian and Shanghai have recently completed two indigenously built 052C-class ships and in total will commission six into service in either the 052B or 052C-class ("China Installs . . ." 2003).[5] The 052C warship is equipped with an advanced integrated air defense system, apparently similar to the US Aegis phased radar display, which has a capacity to engage many targets simultaneously. The 052C is also equipped with eight HQ9 surface-to-air missiles (SAMs) with a long vertical range of 90 km (Anzera, 2005). Destroyers of the 052C-class will also have the ability to conduct long-range surface warfare using two different kinds of surface-to-surface missiles (SSMs): the HN3, a type of cruise missile with a range of 2500 km and capable of carrying conventional or nuclear warheads; and the YJ12, a supersonic missile with a range of 200 km. Coupled with a new depth sonar system, the 052C greatly enhances PLAN's major areas of weakness—air defense and anti-submarine warfare ("New Generation . . .," 2004; Bussert, 2004; Chi, 2004).

The rest of China's surface fleet, consisting of 20 destroyers and 43 frigates is being consistently upgraded as old obsolete ships are being rapidly decommissioned. The Chinese Navy is increasingly reliant on recently purchased Russian *Sovremenny*-class destroyers in this regard. Two of these destroyers were purchased from Russia in 2000 for $840 million and an additional two were ordered in 2002 (to arrive in 2006) for an estimated $1.4 billion (Homes and Yoshihara, 2005: 38). The *Sovremenny* was designed in the 1970s by the Soviet Union to specifically counter US carrier groups and their air defense systems. Each of these destroyers carry advanced surface-to-surface anti-ship missiles (SS-N–22) dubbed the Sunburn. The "sea-skimming" missile is specifically designed to penetrate the defenses of carrier groups and is armed with Moskit anti-ship missiles, carrying a 300-kg conventional warhead with a range of 120 km (Kondapalli, 2004: 9; Holmes and Yoshihara, 2005: 38). The US Navy has still been unable to solve the "sunburn problem" as the missile can reach speeds of Mach 2.5. The Chinese purchases were likely influenced by the result of the 1996 Taiwan Strait Crisis where two US carrier battle groups appeared in a show of force to deter Chinese aggression.

There are also the Chinese *Luhai*-class *Shenzhen* destroyers, launched in 2001 and 2002, in some circles dubbed the "China Aegis." Like the newly developed 052C-class destroyers, these ships were fitted with advanced integrated defense radar systems similar to Aegis. Much of the key equipment for these ships was imported, for instance, gas turbines from Ukraine, electrical systems from Germany, torpedoes from Italy and Kamov Ka-28 helicopters from Russia. This ship also carries C–802 anti-ship cruise missiles and several short-range SAMs ("China Launches . . .," 1999; Sae-Liu, 1999). As Holmes and Yoshihara note, since anti-air ships "are indispensable to open-ocean warfare, the *Luhais* could also further China's blue-water aspirations, allowing this platform to perform double duty" (2005: 39). With the 052-class ships, the *Sovremennys* and the *Luhais*, the core strength of China's surface fleet, China has greatly improved its defense capabilities and has seriously improved its sea-denial capability.

In addition, PLAN has also carried out the upgrading of the SAM system on its two *Luhu*-class and 16 *Luda*-class destroyers (Kondapalli, 2004: 9). Eight *Jiangwei*-class guided-missile frigates have also been armed with anti-ship cruise missiles. Additionally, the newly launched *Jiangwei*-III frigate has incorporated Russian gas turbine technology in AL31ST and has also incorporated new generation 100 mm twin stealth guns ("China Builds . . .," 2003; "Design Concept . . .," 2003). China has also developed fast missile-armed patrol boats, designed to fight in coastal waters, and these were recently unveiled. The boats reportedly carry four anti-ship missiles and can reach speeds of 50 knots (Chi, 2004; Global Information System Naval Staff, 2004). The presence of these craft would also enhance China's sea-denial capability.

Currently China does not appear fully committed to the development of a serious carrier capability despite approving the construction of two aircraft carriers with an initial commitment of 250 million *yuan* ("Beijing to Buy . . .," 1999: 56). Instead Beijing appears to be more interested in continuing to study the design features of foreign aircraft carriers. For instance, in 1985, China purchased the retired aircraft carrier *Melbourne* from Australia. Then in March 1998 a Macao company bought the former Soviet carrier *Varyag* from the Ukraine. In August 2000, Tianma Shipbreaking of Tianjin purchased the decommissioned *Kiev* for $8.4 million and in September of the same year China bought the carrier *Minsk* from South Korea for $5 million (Lee, 2002; Storey and Ji, 2004). Recent reports also indicate that PLAN leased a carrier from Australia to study its design (Sakhuja, 2005b). In terms of naval aviation, China made a $2 billion purchase in 1999 of 30 Russian Su-30 ground-attack fighters to go along with dozens of previously purchased Su-27 air-superiority fighters (Kondapalli 2004: 11; Holmes and Yoshihara, 2005: 39). Although China has continued to struggle in its production of its indigenous multi-purpose fighter, the J-10, one study indicates that by the end of 2005 China will have over 150 of these three impressive fighter aircraft in addition to the large inventory of third-generation fighters (Fisher, 2003: 144).

The anti-submarine warfare (ASW) capabilities of the PLAN have also been recently bolstered with the acquisition of 8 French Super Frelon Z-8s with surface search radar (with an Italian Whitehead torpedo). Moreover, the Dauphin II license-built Z-9C has been equipped with Thomson-Marconi Sonar HS-12 dipping sonar technology. Other ASW platforms include several Shaanxi SH-5 flying boats with Doppler search radar (capable of carrying depth charges, torpedoes and 4 C-101 supersonic anti-ship missiles; Sengupta, 1999: 30–34). Using such technology the Chinese Navy has been aggressively carrying out marine surveying and surface and underwater mapping in the South and North China Sea but also as far out as the Philippine Sea and the Indian Ocean. As Kondapalli has noted, PLAN has "boasted that it has made grand navigation totaling 2.9 million kilometers, surveyed 6,500 islands, explored 14,000 navigational obstacles and prepared over 2,300 marine maps, including digital marine maps useful in military targeting" (Kondapalli, 2004: 12; also Han *et al.*, 2003).

China's underwater force is also growing rapidly and is quickly becoming formidable (Goldstein and Murray, 2004; Glosny, 2004). In total, China has 57 tactical submarines, consisting of 51 diesel submarines (SS) and six nuclear-powered attack submarines (SSN). In addition to four Kilo-class submarines purchased from Russia in the 1990s, China also added eight more Kilo-class submarines in 2002 at the cost of $1.6 billion, to be delivered by 2007 (Goldstein and Murray, 2004: 166). Furthermore, as many as ten indigenous *Song*-class submarines are currently under construction at various Chinese shipyards as well as some entirely new Chinese *Yuan*-class diesel submarines (ibid.: 162–170). This will complement PLAN's nine existing *Song*-class boats and will continue to replace the 30 aging *Romeo*-class submarines. China is also in the midst of developing Type 093 and 094 SSNs and ballistic missile class submarines (SSBNs) and will likely deploy several of these in the years to come. Currently, China deploys five *Han*-class nuclear submarines and one *Xia*-class of the Type 093 or 094 (Glosny, 2004: 132). With close to 300,000 naval personnel, China is quickly becoming one of the world's leading naval powers.

The IOR as an expanding zone of Chinese interest

As the Chinese economy continues to expand, the importance of the Indian Ocean and its SLOCs become ever more important. As noted earlier, 80 percent of China's oil and most of its natural resources transit the Indian Ocean and through the Strait of Malacca. Moreover, many Chinese exports have to transit the same SLOCs in the reverse order to make it to various international markets. Commenting on the importance of these waterways for China, President Hu Jintao called China's reliance on the highly trafficked Strait the "Malacca Dilemma" (USA, 2005). Chinese analysts have been quite clear about their desire to protect these routes in the Indian Ocean. As one analyst notes, China's exploding foreign trade means that its "dependence on strategic ocean passages through the Indian and Pacific Oceans will greatly increase" (Yijian 1999, cited in Garver, 2002: 12). As a result, the PLAN will need to ensure the protection of SLOCs for the safe transit of strategic resources such as iron ore and petroleum (Garver, 2002: 12). It is inevitable that the Indian Ocean and its littoral will be a major scene of great power activity and involvement as India, China and other states rely on these SLOCs (ibid.: 13).

Beijing has been quick to emphasize in the Mahanian sense that the rise and decline of great powers rest not only on their domestic economic and political capabilities but also on the "control of the supply routes for overseas resources" (Zhang, 2001, cited in Garver 2002: 13). They are thus cautious of

India, as it is "situated in the region of the world where resources were most abundant and where the strategic interests of [the various powers] are greatest and most concentrated" (Zhiyong 2001: 9–10, cited in Garver 2002: 13). Thus, China is wary of what it labels India's desire to control the Indian Ocean and at last dominate South Asia as a first-rate international big power.

For some theorists, the security of China's sea-lanes in the Indian Ocean, and Chinese strategy in South Asia (including its maritime strategy) are also strongly influenced by the thorny Tibet issue. As one analyst notes, "Beijing has been chronically concerned about the stability of its control over that vast, mineral-rich, and strategically located region" (Garver, 2002: 5). Correspondingly, in China, there is constant concern as to whether India is engaging in pro-Tibetan and anti-China scheming. Thus, in an effort to keep India from pursuing such activity and in countering India should such activities become a reality, China continues to support a strong and independent Pakistan.

From the Chinese perspective, Tibet was the fundamental cause of the 1962 war.[6] According to Chinese records of that conflict, the primary objective of Indian policy was to expel Chinese authority from the region and to convert Tibet into a buffer zone between the two states (Yan, 1993: 27–28; Garver, 2002: 8). After the 1962 war, India cooperated with the United States even more closely in surreptitious operations in Tibet. Furthermore, since 1960, the Indian government has allowed the Dalai Lama to organize and maintain quasi-governmental structures in India. Consequently the Tibetan exile community is able to use India as a base of operations for its pro-independence activities.[7] Moreover, following the 1962 war, India organized several Tibetan military organizations (the ITBP and the SFF) that operate under Indian command and with Indian training, arms and support.

Beijing's main fear is that India may once again in the future cooperate with the United States in a Tibetan rebellion against Chinese rule. The Chinese worry that India may gamble to erase the humiliation of the 1962 defeat and restore the Tibetan buffer lost in 1951. In this context, a strong and loyal Pakistan becomes the key constraint to such a threat. The existence of a robust and hostile Pakistan presents India with a two-front threat: Pakistan in the west and China in the north and north-east. As a result, India cannot concentrate its forces on either front and it weakens its ability to deal with either potentially hostile party. Thus, for Beijing, the existence of this two-front threat minimizes the possibility of Indian intervention in Tibet. According to Garver (2001b, 2002), this explains China's long-standing support for Pakistan's conventional and nuclear weapons programs as well as its support for Pakistani missile development in the 1990s. In relation to the IOR, it also explains heavy Chinese backing of an ambitious maritime access project in Pakistan's Baluchistan province in the past few years. Although China's primary naval matter of concern relates to the Taiwan issue and gaining control of the waters around China in the first and second-island chains, the importance of the Indian Ocean is certainly growing. According to some analysts, recent Sino-Pakistani and Sino-Burmese naval cooperation, as well as China's relations with other IOR littoral states provide clues as to what the future security environment of South Asia will look like.

China's "String of Pearls" strategy

In January 2005, the United States Department of Defense prepared an internal assessment report on China's future military plans based on the findings of the consultancy agency Booz, Allen and Hamilton (see Kondapalli, 2005a). According to the report, China was involved in a long-term geostrategic strategy of constructing military bases and facilities in areas close to crucial SLOCs and choke points. Termed China's "String of Pearls" strategy, the document noted Chinese involvement in the South China Seas, Thailand, Cambodia, Myanmar, Bangladesh, Pakistan, Africa, the Suez Canal, Venezuela and the Panama Canal. Although some of these activities have been widely reported for a long time, such as Chinese constructions in the Woody Islands (in the disputed South China Seas), the "String of Pearls" document was one of the first to look at China's energy, trade and security policies in a holistic manner and draw everything together (Dutta, 2005). Thus, it is worth taking a closer look at Chinese activities, especially as they pertain to the IOR.

China's "String of Pearls" stretches from its own Hainan Islands to the disputed Woody Islands in the South China Seas. It involves proposals to construct a canal across the Kra Isthmus in Thailand (to bypass the vulnerable Straits of Malacca); 2003 agreements with Cambodia and plans to improve Sihanoukville; military and naval cooperation with Myanmar; a proposed container port at Chittagong in Bangladesh; and the Sino-Pakistani jointly constructed naval base at Gwadar, Pakistan. Chinese companies are already operating at Port Said, near the Suez Canal and at the Panama Canal (Kondapalli, 2005a).

On the Hainan Islands, China has recently completed the Sanya naval base and hopes to place its new Type 094 SSN submarines there once they are completed. China has also established an air-refueling base at Zhanjiang, near Hong Kong, aimed at enhancing the air force's long-range aviation capabilities (particularly the Su-27, Su-30, J-10 and J-8 aircraft). China has also upgraded military airstrips on the Woody Islands.

China's involvement in the resurrection of a proposal to build a canal across the Kra Isthmus has also drawn attention. The idea was originally conceived in 1677 but it was not until 1993 that the project resurfaced under a proposal made by the Thai government. The "Kra project" has an estimated bill of $23 billion and the contract has reportedly been given to a firm based in Hong Kong, the Phuket Pass Project Company Limited (ibid.). Reports indicate that the project will commence as soon as the China Three Gorges project is complete sometime this decade (because of the shortage of qualified engineers and personnel). If successfully completed, China would greatly reduce its "Malacca dilemma" as ship traffic could be rerouted through the Gulf of Thailand (Nanda Kumar, 2005; Saghal, 2005; Swaran Singh, 2005b).

Some reports indicate that China has become increasingly interested in the Bangladeshi port of Chittagong and in constructing airfields in Bangladesh (Berlin, 2004: 245). China has offered Bangladesh (as well as Pakistan) nuclear power plants as well as low-cost financial capital in an effort to improve relations. China appears to have its eye on Bangladesh's immense natural resources, including its huge natural gas reserves, estimated at 60 trillion cubic feet and rivaling those of Indonesia (Niazi, 2005a). Bangladesh's close proximity to Myanmar, a key Chinese ally, would make its gas reserves accessible to China. Bangladesh is also a doorway to India's troubled north-eastern region, including the state of Arunachal Pradesh, where China has territorial claims.

India's relationship with Bangladesh remains bogged down with border problems and the continuous influx of millions of Bangladeshis into the north-eastern state of Assam.[8] India's access to Myanmar's vast gas reserves also hinge on Dhaka and whether it will allow the transit of a pipeline through Bangladesh (a fact not lost on Beijing; Niazi, 2005a). If China succeeds in duplicating its relationships with Myanmar and Pakistan, more and more naval cooperation between it and Bangladesh can be expected in the years to come. The Bangladesh-China Defence Cooperation Agreement concluded in December 2002, and Hasan Mashhud Chowdhury's (Bangladesh's Chief of Army Staff) recent visit with Zhang Dingfa, the Commander of PLAN in September 2004 may indicate what lies ahead ("Chinese Navy . . .," 2004).

Realizing Sri Lanka's strategic location in the Indian Ocean, Beijing has also been active in fostering closer ties with Colombo. Much like with Bangladesh, China has offered Sri Lanka low-cost capital financing for many development projects and Beijing continues to deploy economic incentives to draw Colombo closer. Recently China and Sri Lanka came to an agreement for the construction of a bunkering facility and oil tank farm at Hambantota. The contract was drawn up for China's Huanqiu Engineering Corp. and calls for the construction of ten oil tanks and four pipelines. The infrastructure will help Sri Lanka service the hundreds of ships that transit the sea-lanes just south of the island, many of which are Chinese (Mohan, 2005a).

Some Indian analysts are growing increasingly anxious about China's growing influence in Sri Lanka. As one notes, referring back to remarks made by Napoleon, "if China acquired control over the northeastern Sri Lankan port of Trincomalee, Beijing would be in a position to convert the Bay of Bengal in to a veritable Chinese lake" (Maitra, 2005). India's position in Sri Lanka remains hamstrung by the prolonged conflict by the Sinhalese majority and the Tamil minority in Sri Lanka. India, having a Tamil-majority state (Tamil Nadu), has to move cautiously in mediating the ongoing dispute in Sri Lanka.[9]

Reports also continue to surface that China has come to a secret arrangement with the Maldives for the construction of a submarine base there (Bansal, 2005a; Kondapalli, 2005b; Subramanian, 2005). Much to the annoyance of New Delhi, China continues to push for representation in the

South Asia Association for Regional Cooperation (SAARC), which includes Bangladesh, Bhutan, India, Maldives, Nepal, Pakistan and Sri Lanka. All the other member states in addition to agreeing over China's autonomy over Tibet, support Beijing's entry into SAARC (Niazi, 2005a).

Sino-Burmese maritime cooperation

Throughout the 1990s, Chinese firms were involved in modernizing and constructing numerous facilities along Myanmar's coasts in the Andaman Sea and the Bay of Bengal (Garver, 2001b). Chinese businesses undertook, for instance, the modernization of the harbor, wharf and cargo handling facilities in costal cities such as Sittwe, Bassein, Mergui and Yangon (Myanmar's naval bases are also located at several of these harbors which are dual use, civilian and military; Berlin, 2004: 246). At Hainggyi Island, south of Bassein, Chinese companies constructed a new harbor and military base. Chinese companies also constructed radar and electronic monitoring operations on Ramree Island, Cocos Island and at Zadetkyi Kyun Island (off the southern tip of Myanmar's portion of the Kra Isthmus). PLA personnel were known to rotate through the Cocos Island facility and intelligence gathered from the sites was presumably shared by China and Myanmar (Garver, 2001b: 16). The facility on Zadetkyi Kyun was one of two Earth satellite stations maintained by China outside of PRC borders and importantly the electronic monitoring facilities at this location (and also on Ramree and the Cocos) enable the PLAN to keep tabs on Indian military activity in the vicinity.

Overall, China has established at least four known electronic listening posts along the Bay on Bengal, in the Andaman Sea at Manaung, Hainggyi, Zadetkyi Island and the strategically important Cocos Islands (as they are just north of India's Andaman Islands, Sharma, 2001: 82, Kondapalli, 2005a). There are also reports that Chinese technicians have been spotted at the naval bases at Monkey Point (near Yangon) and Kyaikkami, just south of the port city of Moulmein. There are also Chinese-built radar stations on Saganthit Island near Mergui in south-eastern Myanmar (Sharma, 2001: 82). Naturally, India is concerned about such developments.

The most ambitious Chinese project in Myanmar was the building of an integrated transportation system linking China's Yunnan province with Kyaukpyu port on the northern end of Ramree Island (also known as the Irrawaddy Corridor). Numerous roads were built from Yunnan to Lasio, Bhamo and Mandalay in northern Myanmar. Plans were also laid out to dredge the upper Irrawaddy between Bhamo and Minbu to build new barge-loading facilities at those two cities. From Minbu, a new highway was also to be constructed across the Yoma mountain range. With this in place, a new causeway-supported highway could then be pushed across the 50 km of marsh and tidal plain separating Ramree Island from the mainland proper. At Kyaukpyu, a new modern port has been constructed to accommodate ocean-going ships picking up and delivering cargo transiting the road–river line to Yunnan. Finally, a new deep-water port has been developed at Thilawa, 25 miles south of Yangon. This new harbor can accommodate large ocean-going ships and a rail line to be built northward over an existing bridge over the Bagon River to Yangon is also proposed ("Southwest China . . .," 2001). In 2001, it was estimated by the navigation bureau of Yunnan province that over 200,000 tons of freight was moving annually over the various Irrawaddy corridor routes (equivalent to the carrying capacity of 21-meter gauge railways. Udai Bhanu Singh, 2005).[10]

Recently, in 2004, China reached an agreement with Myanmar to construct a 1250km pipeline connecting the deep-water port of Sittwe to Kunming, the capital of Yunnan province. At ports like Hainggyi, Kyaukpyu and Mergui, China will be able to berth larger displacement vessels and recently China also expanded the Mandalay and Pegu airfields to receive heavy transports. The Kunming Initiative, launched in 1999 as a sub-regional cooperative effort between Bangladesh, China, India and Myanmar, was meant to expand infrastructure projects so that interior land-locked provinces like Yunnan and Sichuan could have maritime outlets through Myanmar.

Regular high-level exchanges between China and Myanmar have also continued to take place. Recently, in July 2004, Premier Wen Jiabao hosted Burmese Premier Khin Nyunt. Both parties emphasized the "Baopuo" friendship and the continuing economic and political cooperation between China and Mynamar ("Wen Jiabao Holds . . .," 2004; "Burma to Promote . . .," 2004).

Sino-Pakistani cooperation

In 2001, China began backing the construction of an ambitious maritime access project in Pakistan's Baluchistan province. Also known as the Gwadar Project, it involved the construction of a new deep-water port at Gwadar. Pakistani leaders had discussed the development of a port at Gwadar for many years. However, the project became more urgent following the 1999 Kargil Crisis. During the crisis, Indian submarines, frigates and destroyers deployed quickly just outside the Karachi harbor. This particular harbor carries nearly 90 percent of Pakistan's trade, including a large percentage of its oil imports (Garver, 2001b: 17). Also as the homeport of the Pakistan Navy, Pakistani elites became quite concerned that the entire navy was bottled up by the quick Indian naval concentration in 1999. Pakistani dependence on Karachi was thus revealed as a major vulnerability of Pakistan. Though Pakistan had implemented some temporary measures following the crisis such as the utili-zation of Ormara harbor as a naval base (called Jinnah Naval Base) and the acquisition of anti-submarine frigates from China, it was not until March 2001 that plans for the creation of a new port at Gwadar were revealed. The Gwadar Project was seen as a way to make the Pakistani Navy a powerful force that could contest regional navies. Accordingly, the government of Pakistan labeled the port area a "sensitive defense zone" (Niazi, 2005b).

Plans to fast track the Gwadar Project were initiated during the US (and allied) invasion of Afghanistan. Beijing was already wary of the US presence in the Persian Gulf and was increasingly alarmed by the US presence in Central Asia. The Gwadar deep sea port was conceived as a way for China to help protect its ships transiting the Persian Gulf. Gwadar's close proximity to the Strait of Hormuz and Iran was seen as a key geostrategic advantage (Bansal, 2005a; Dutta 2005; Kondapalli, 2005b; Sakhuja 2005a). As Niazi (2005b) notes, "The convergence of Sino-Pakistani strategic interests has put the port project onto a fast track to its early completion." Correspondingly, China's Vice Premier Wu Bangguo was flown to Gwadar to lay its foundation on 22 March 2002.

The first phase of the project was completed in December 2004, three months ahead of schedule and has seen the construction of three functioning berths. The three berths have lengths of 602 m, 4.5 km dredged to 11.5 to 12.5 m as well as one 100 m service berth and related port infrastructure ("Presidents of Pakistan . . .," 2004). The port will be able to handle bulk carriers weighing up to 30,000 tons and container vessels weighing up to 25,000 tons. The cost of the first phase was$248 million ($198 million pitched in by China and $50 million by Pakistan). The total cost of the project is approximated at $1.16 billion. China has already contributed over $200 million to the construction of 653 km Markan Coastal Highway, linking Gwadar to Karachi (Niazi, 2005b). The second phase of the project will feature the construction of nine more berths and terminals and will also be heavily financed by China. The new terminals will be able to handle ships in the 200,000-ton category. The Gwadar Project also calls for the development of 18,600 hectares of land, which includes 400 hectares in phase's I and II for port development, an export processing zone of 74 hectares, a special industrial zone of about 4,000 hectares and a 1,000 hectare oil refinery (ibid.).

When completed in 2007, Gwadar will be one of the largest and most strategically located deep-sea ports in the world. If work continues at its current pace, the Gwadar port will be complete by March 2007. The project involves 450 Chinese engineers and over 600 Pakistani engineers. Of particular interest is how the deepening of the port has been expanded from 11 m, to 14 m and now to a reported 19 m. Generally speaking, most large displacement vessels only require ports to be 11 m deep for berthing (Bansal, 2005a; Kondapalli, 2005b). As Kondapalli notes, "Increasing the depth of this port further indicates to a long-term plan of China in the naval sphere" (2005a: 3). Ports as deep as 19 m would only be useful for very large aircraft carriers and nuclear submarines. China and Pakistan have also been holding joint military and naval exercises of late. For instance, in October 2003, frontline battleships, seaplanes, carrier-borne helicopters and two battleships held naval exercises off the coast of Shanghai (Chu, 2003).

Based on the picture painted above, some analysts of Sino-Indian relations, most prominently John Garver, have argued that China and India are involved in a realist struggle of power balancing (Garver, 2001b, 2002; Malik 2001;

Lee 2002; Mohan, 2003).[11] This Asian power struggle is said to be increasingly characteristic of what Robert Jervis famously described as a "security dilemma" (Jervis, 1978). Such arguments directly relate to China's status as a rising power and its efforts to enhance its influence in South Asia. India is seen as the reactionary power and has responded to Chinese efforts of encirclement with counter-encirclement evidenced by its "Look East" policy (Garver, 2002). In linking China's growing energy concerns to its security policies, many other analysts have characterized China as a "revisionist" power, with a desire to alter the current international status quo. The international system and security are characterized in zero-sum terms and China's increasing competitiveness is perceived to be dangerous as it may give way to regional or international conflict (Salameh, 1995–96; Calder, 1996; Rachman, 1996; Bernstein and Munro, 1997; Munro, 1999; Brown *et al.*, 2000; Kane and Serewicz, 2001).

With reference to Chinese activities in Myanmar and China's rapid establishment of logistical points, Garver (2002) notes that India's geographic advantages *vis-à-vis* China in the IOR are diminishing. The PLAN will be able to compete with the Indian Navy on more equal terms in the region. Furthermore, there remains the possibility that Myanmar may emerge as a Chinese security partner on India's eastern flank as Pakistan is on India's western flank. If this were to occur, then India would face security challenges on all of its borders which all linked to China in one way or another. Moreover, in the event of a future Sino-Indian war, India's ability to defend its north-east border would be greatly jeopardized if PLA forces were able to secure transit through Myanmar. In addition, if Chinese air and naval forces had access to facilities along Myanmar's coast and enjoyed logistic support running over roads through Myanmar, coupled with forward logistic bases on the Bay of Bengal, the Chinese could pose serious threats to India in the face of conflict. Thus, when the prospect of PLA utilization of the Irrawaddy Corridor is coupled with similar utilization of the Gwadar complex, India's security is seriously diminished (Garver, 2002).

The Gwadar Project is seen as strategically significant for two major reasons. First, the Gwadar complex substantially diminishes India's ability to blockade Pakistan during a war. It would also significantly assist China's ability to supply Pakistan by sea and by land during a war. Pakistan's ability to sustain a war against India is greatly enhanced by the Gwadar complex and diminishes the possibility of India isolating Pakistan from outside support in the event of a war. Second, the project fits in line with Pakistani ambitions of making Pakistan the main corridor for trade and transport with the Central Asian Republics and the outside world. What this all means in terms of Chinese interests is that a stronger Pakistan helps maintain a balance of power in the region, which is perceived to be essential to Chinese security (Garver, 2005). Stronger transport links to the sea via countries friendly to China also facilitate the economic development of China's western regions. Furthermore, the PLAN will also have a new point of access and

will likely be able to utilize the Gwadar complex should this military require-
ment materialize. Thus, in supporting the project, China is trying to influence
events far outside its own borders and in the process is deepening its rival's
sense of in security (Garver, 2002, 2005; Malik, 2001). Coupled with increasing ties to Bangladesh, Sri Lanka and possibly the Maldives, China's "String
of Pearls" strategy, from the realist point of view, is a classic case of a rising
power asserting its influence in the international arena.

India's naval strategy and naval forces

India's naval strategy

When the British left India in 1947 the newly formed states of South Asia had
to basically build their naval capacities from scratch. To be sure, the British did
leave some vessels and training establishments behind, however, they were
totally inadequate for a country of India's size and strategic location (Singh,
1981: 326; Singh, 1992: 39–40). As one analyst notes "two-century old con-
scious imperial policy had ensured that at the time of independence, the indigenous sea power of the new big state was virtually non-existent" (Singh, 1986:
13). The long British rule also had another major effect: it negatively influenced the evolution of naval planning and strategy even after independence.
As S.S. Khera notes:

> Throughout the 1950s, and until 1962 no one, neither the Government of
> India, nor the top military commanders, appeared ever to have made up
> their mind as to what should be the strength of the Indian Army, the
> Indian Navy and the Indian Air Force, nor even as to what kind of army,
> navy or airforce the country should have.
>
> (1968: 39)

Such indecisiveness is what led to the reliance upon Britain. Up until 1958,
British officers continued to head the Indian Navy, and the Indian Navy was
conceptualized as part of a wider Commonwealth naval presence in the IOR.
Though Nehru wanted India to play a larger role and envisaged it as an
independent naval power that would be able to hold its own against Asian
neighbors, the reliance on Britain and British planning had its consequences.
As Major General Sukhwant Singh has noted

> Unfortunately, the politicians and bureaucrats went about achieving it
> [naval power] the wrong way. Considering that the development of naval
> power was a long-term process requiring the help and cooperation of an
> established navy, they hitched the wagon to Britain, a declining power,
> and thus reduced the Indian Navy to a junkyard of British discards for a
> decade and a half.
>
> (Singh, 1981: 327)

After 1958, when British officers no longer headed the navy, the Indians were compelled to take their own decisions and plan for future contingencies. At that time Pakistan had already expanded its navy with the help of the United States and the British. There was no other immediate neighbor with whom India had an adversarial relationship. However, Pakistan's overall naval capacity was still limited (taking into view the task of defending the two wings in the East and the West as well as the long sea-lane that connected them). Thus, until 1962, the Arabian Sea remained the focal point of the Indian Navy's possible theater of operations (K.R. Singh, 2002: 61). However, with the 1962 Sino-Indian border war, the situation began to change. India's maritime threat perception came to encompass the Bay of Bengal region and led to the strengthening of naval presence in the Andaman-Nicobar Islands. Furthermore, during the early 1960s the Indonesian Navy had been acquiring large numbers of ships from the USSR and bolstering their naval presence. Relations with Indonesia had begun to deteriorate during this period (for instance, Indonesia put forward claims to islands in the Nicobar group) and India began to fear a united Pindi–Jakarta–Beijing axis. It was not until the Indo-Pakistani War of 1965 and the death of Nehru though that India began to chalk out an independent role for its navy in the emerging security environment.

The second phase of India's naval policy marked the transition from the British legacy towards the creation of a balanced navy with blue-water capability.[12] The Indo-Pakistani War of 1971 was a major landmark within this period as well as the changing international equation in the IOR (expansion of the US presence, rapid growth of Iranian naval power in the Arabian Sea, etc.). The impetus for change, however, stemmed from the 1962 Sino-India conflict. Analysts began to call for the creation of a two-fleet navy with a fleet on each coast (Bindra, 1980). The Eastern Fleet Headquarters was correspondingly established at Vishakhapatnam in November 1971 (on the eve of the 1971 war). During this period, the era of long British hegemony was also ending. The British Prime Minister formally announced in 1968 that Britain intended to withdraw from the East of the Suez by 1971. This was followed by the famous UN General Assembly Resolution in December 1971 declaring the Indian Ocean as a Peace Zone. Such developments motivated many in India to argue that India should take appropriate measures to safeguard its legitimate interests in the light of the rapidly changing regional and international security environment (Singh, 2002: 66). Many felt that the vacuum that could be created with the British departure should be filled by India in an effort to "maintain the balance of power in the Indian Ocean" (Kamath, 1954). The British withdrawal, in conjunction with the 1971 war, created what has been termed the "Enterprise Syndrome." This refers to a shift from maritime strategy oriented towards escort duty and limited sea control capability (mostly *vis-à-vis* Pakistan) to the creation of a capacity for long-range ocean surveillance by air and a limited sea-denial capability (*vis-à-vis* great powers as well). Indian maritime strategy thus widened in scope and a great power presence in the area became the central future ambition (Singh, 2002: 77). By the end of this period, India had acquired four submarines, one escort carrier, two cruisers, oil ships, replenishment ships, destroyers and frigates to form the base of its blue-water fleet.

The third phase is of great significance because of the end and the beginning of the "New" Cold War and the increasing international focus on Asia. During this phase, US strategy aimed at a rapid escalation of forces for regional intervention. The Iranian Revolution with its threat of exporting radical Islam, the Afghan Crisis leading to the Soviet military intervention, and the drawn-out Iran–Iraq war provided the legitimacy for the bolstered US military presence in the region as well as a new strategic link-up between the US, China, Pakistan and Saudi Arabia. This new strategic environment provided Pakistan with a new opportunity to be strategically at the forefront in dealing with Afghanistan and Central Asia.

Naturally, India was uncomfortable with the emerging security dynamics in Central and South Asia. India's policy of negotiated settlement of the Afghan problem as well as its sympathetic position towards the Kampucheans during the Kampuchean Crisis (perceived to be in support of Vietnam, which invaded as the result of Khmer Rouge atrocities) was seen by outsiders to support the USSR. In response, the Chinese initiated a great diplomatic offensive in South Asia, one of the goals of which was to isolate India (Singh, 2002: 82). This was primarily by way of supplying large quantities of weapons, including warships to India's neighbors in South Asia.

These geo-political developments led India to come naturally closer to the USSR. It also forced India to reconsider its maritime doctrine and weapons requirements. Though maritime strategists such as K.M Panikkar have underlined the key role of the Indian Ocean in determining Indian security, the urgency of this reality was not realized till after the 1970s during the period of the "New" Cold War (Rasgotra, 1991). As Indira Gandhi proclaimed in her opening address on September 4 1980, "Today we find it [the Indian Ocean] churning with danger" (Tellis, 1985: 1192). As Admiral Tahiliani put it, India's central position straddling the Indian Ocean confers on it a special overseeing role ranging from the Cape of Good Hope to the Strait of Malacca (Tahiliani, 1981, cited in Singh, 2002). This new threat perception of the strategic environment and the new self-appointed role in the Indian Ocean provided further rationale for realizing the creation of a blue-water navy capable of sea denial at a projected range (ibid.: 83).

Recently, on 26 April 2004, the Indian Navy, for the first time in its history released its "Indian Maritime Doctrine." The 135-page document was made public on 23 June 2004. The doctrine clearly outlined India's intentions of becoming a "blue-water" navy and outlined the desirability of force projection beyond the Indian shores. One of the primary themes of the new naval doctrine is to give the Indian Navy an enhanced role in light of India's overall aspiration to great power status. One of the ways this is envisioned is by "nuclearizing" the Indian Navy and placing within it India's credible second-strike capability. India's Nuclear Doctrine of August 1999 emphasized the need for a nuclear triad. The current Indian Maritime Doctrine simply revises the earlier defense doctrine and highlights the desirability for situating the most powerful component of the nuclear triad in the navy. As Kazi (2004: 55) has noted, "It marks a definite shift from coastal defense to three vital issues: strategic concerns in the East, power projection, and littoral warfare to aid the land forces in a conflict."

In many ways, India's new naval strategy can be interpreted as an aggressive strategy aimed at developing a credible nuclear deterrent. For a long time, the Indian Air Force (IAF) and the Indian Army had a clearly outlined role within the Indian military and especially within India's nuclear framework. The new naval doctrine has now given the Indian Navy a key strategic role in launching nuclear weapons in the face of a nuclear war. As a second-strike is more preferably launched from the high seas rather than from land and is more attractive below the surface, submarines have also implicitly taken on an important role in the context of India's new naval doctrine. As one analyst has noted:

> The Indian government is in covert talks with the Russians to lease two *Akula*-class nuclear submarines (that have both longer undersea duration and ability to fire nuclear weapons) and has, for nearly two decades, been engaged in making its own nuclear submarine coded Advanced Technology Vessel.
>
> (Sujan Dutta, 2004)

The importance of maritime reach and naval force projection has been appreciated for many years since independence and continuously emphasized by those within the Indian Navy. However, it was not until recently that the Indian Navy received serious attention for realizing India's great power ambitions. This has partly to do with India's improving economy and the resulting growing budgetary allocations assigned to military expenditure.

The evolving geostrategic significance of the Indian Ocean also has played a role in the impetus for modernizing the Indian naval forces. Given India's heavy reliance on the safe transit of trade through the Indian Ocean, the need for an adequate naval presence to protect SLOCs could never be clearer. As India is predicted to encounter serious energy shortfalls in the years to come, it clearly cannot afford to have its maritime links to the Persian Gulf obstructed (Ashraf, 2004: 60). The increasing number of joint naval patrols between the Indian Navy and the United States (and other navies) following 11 September 2001 attests to the growing role that the Indian Navy will play in the Indian Ocean. The creation of the Far Eastern Naval Command at Port Blair in the Andaman and Nicobar Islands also highlights the importance of monitoring the nearby Strait of Malacca (ibid.: 61).

As was discussed in the third phase, there has been a steady abandonment of the Indian Navy's inward-looking focus towards more of an extra-regional one. The doctrine specifically calls for the development of capabilities to deal with "conflict with an extra-regional power" and to protect "persons of Indian origin and Indian interests abroad" (Saikat Dutta, 2004). The latter goal, though quite ambitious, is taking on increasing significance, as there are large Indian populations in many of the Indian Ocean littoral countries. For instance, as many as 3.5 million Indian workers are located in the Persian Gulf region alone and remit close to $10 billion dollars annually to the Indian economy. It is only natural for India to want to ensure stability in such areas so that workers and their remittances can flourish (Das, 2005: 68).

Correspondingly, the new Indian Maritime Doctrine also calls for the Indian Navy to increase its presence in the designated areas of the Arabian Sea and the Bay of Bengal. This is to "safeguard mercantile, marine, and sea-borne trade and secure India's coastline, island territories, and offshore assets" (Ashraf, 2004: 61). In these areas, the Indian Navy's primary objective would remain "sea control" in addition to "sea denial" to hostile navies. The doctrine is also cautious of Pakistan's growing naval presence, citing Pakistan's recent acquisition of French AGOSTA-90B type submarines and expresses concern for China's increasing "ocean-going" ambitions in the IOR (Mohanty, 2004: 94).[13] Moreover, the doctrine also looks East, noting that submarines are already in service in Singapore, under construction for Malaysia and planned for in both Thailand and Myanmar. There are also appeals to enhance international cooperation to combat terrorism, piracy and weapons and drug trafficking in the IOR.

Although there may be a significant gap in what the new Indian Maritime Doctrine seeks to do and what the Indian Navy is actually capable of doing, the long-term vision of the Indian Navy is nonetheless clear. The Indian Navy, in short, aspires to have capabilities in line with those of other major powers in the international system. The maritime doctrine of the Indian Navy notes that the focus of naval power has clearly shifted from controlling SLOCs and fighting major sea battles to dominating the littoral while reiterating the continuing importance of sea control and sea denial (ibid.: 94). In the years to come, this may come at the cost of raising the suspicions of India's neighbors about its hegemonic aspirations in the region.

A closer look at the Indian Navy

Structure and organization

There is general agreement within international security communities that India is a major regional superpower and a major Asian land power. India has a fairly well trained army of one million with over 4,000 tanks and an equal number of artillery. Its paramilitary forces, numbering more than one million, are second only to China's ground forces but are considerably more mobile and modern ("India Outlines . . .," 2004; Margolis, 2005: 66). The Indian Air Force (IAF) is also equipped with new Russian and French aircraft, and recently simulated air combat trials between US F-15s and Indian Su-30s left India as the clear victor (Margolis, 2005: 66). India's fast-pace nuclear development has also challenged the international and Asian status quo. Current estimates place India's nuclear stockpile at between 35 and 90 bombs with large stockpiles of weapons-grade uranium and pluto-nium as well as the existence of many nuclear reactors capable of producing more fissile material. India's Prithvi short-range missiles and Agni II medium range missiles can easily deliver nuclear warheads across Pakistan and to many parts of China. The recently deployed Agni III missile is able to reach Beijing.

Since Pokharan II, many international scholars have turned their attention to India's nuclear program and many of these developments are by now well known. However, India's evolving naval development has received far less attention, and it is this area that will now be examined.

The Indian Navy is divided into three main commands: Headquarters (HQ) Western Naval Command at Mumbai, HQ Eastern Naval Command at Vishakhapatnam and HQ Southern Naval Command at Kochi. Other bases include HQ Far Eastern Sub-Command at Port Blair, HQ Naval Aviation at Goa and Arakonam. In addition, several bases are under construction and near completion at Calcutta, Chennai and Karwar (Mohanty, 2004: 96–97). The naval base at Karwar, code-named "Project Seabird" will be the most impressive and will likely be one of the central command centers of the future Indian Navy (Berlin, 2004; Sakhuja, 2005a, 2005b).

The Naval Headquarters (NHQ) of the Indian Navy is located at New Delhi with the Chief of the Naval Staff (CNS, currently Admiral Madhavendra Singh) as the head. The Chief of Naval Staff has four Principal Staff Officers (PSOs) including: the Vice-Chief of Naval Staff (VCNS), the Deputy Chief of Naval Staff (DCNS), the Chief of Personnel (COP) and the Chief of Material (COM). The VCNS primarily monitors policy planning and research and development. The DCNS basically handles all aspects of naval oper-ations, such as surface, submarine, airborne and diving. The COP is in charge of human resources and the COM is in charge of providing material support for the Navy's ships and submarines.

The operational command in the Indian Navy is exercised through two operational control systems—Flag Officer Commanding-in-Chief (FOC-in-C) East and FOC-in-C West. These authorities are responsible for all operations along the eastern and western seaboards respectively. The FOC-in-C South has training responsibilities but no operational ones.

Traditionally the overwhelming emphasis in Indian defense expenditure had always been placed on the Indian Army and Air Force (primarily the result of the air–land battle dynamics between those hostile to India, Pakistan and China). Although there were temporary surges in naval expend-iture during the mid-1950s, the early 1960s and later the mid-1980s, the Indian Navy at best could only procure no more than one-eighth of the defense budget. Recently, however, India has been steadily increasing its naval expenditure as a proportion of its defense budget. In 2004, naval spending was tripled to 18 percent of the defense budget (Mohanty, 2004: 95; Margolis, 2005: 66). This reflects the increasing role of the navy in India's overall military strategy (especially as its usefulness was demonstrated in the 1999 Kargil Crisis).

India's naval modernization

India recently purchased the ex-Soviet 44,500-ton carrier *Admiral Gorshkov* and four Tu-22M long-range naval bombers/strike aircraft for $2.5 billion (Margolis, 2005: 66). Moreover, India is also planning on building six or more French diesel submarines. An additional $1.5 billion has been set aside to purchase 40 nuclear-capable MiG-29K interceptor/strike fighters for the aircraft carrier group. As Margolis has noted, "The true cost of India's expanding nuclear programs and other secret defense projects, like the ATV and a new 32,000–35,000-ton light carrier, do not appear in the grossly understated $16.5 billion annual defense budget" (ibid.: 66). An additional 15–20 MIG-29Ks are also sought for the light carrier that is currently under construction ("Indian Navy Will . . .," 2004).

The purchase of *Admiral Gorshkov*, which was delayed by eight years of intense negotiations with Russia, was made more urgent as the retirement of India's sole remaining aircraft carrier, the 28,700-ton *Viraat* approaches in 2007.[14] The Indian-built light aircraft carrier that is currently in the works is geared to be ready by 2008–09. As Chief of Naval Staff Admiral Arun Prakash contended:

> By 2015–20 the Indian Navy will be a three-aircraft carrier force—one carrier on either coast and one in reserve—with adequate surface and subsurface combatants, robust reserves and sound logistical support for blue water operations and visibility wherever national interests dictate.
>
> ("Indian Navy Will . . .," 2004)

In the near future, New Delhi plans to control the Indian Ocean with two carrier battle groups backed by nuclear submarines with the support of long-range, shore-based naval aviation, with communications and targeting provided by a plethora of specialized Indian-made satellites.

As noted earlier in discussing India's evolving maritime doctrine, submarines have increasingly taken an important role in India's security equation. India is reportedly spending one billion dollars this year on a secret project with Russia to build a nuclear-powered submarine based on the Soviet *Charlie* I-class design.[15] Though New Delhi denies the existence of such deals, reports continue to surface about India's top-secret Advanced Technology Vessel (ATV) program (Bedi, 2004). The ATV program was first formulated in the 1970s under PM Indira Gandhi and has been maintained ever since by all subsequent governments at varying levels of interest. The Defence

Research and Development Organization (DRDO) manages the program with the support of the Navy and the Bhabha Atomic Research Centre (BARC). The central objective of the ATV program involves the indigenous design and construction of a nuclear power plant based on a pressurized water reactor (PWR), capable of generating up to 190 megawatts. The initial work on this project was taken up by Bharat Heavy Electricals Limited (BHEL) and has been rumored to involve Russian engineers. In recent years the ATV program has received a considerable boost after years of technical and political hurdles (Mohanty, 2004: 100; www.indiadefence.com).

In 2004, another deal with Russia saw the lease-purchase of two Type 971 *Akula* class nuclear-powered attack submarine (SSN) submarines (to be in operation by 2006; Margolis, 2005: 66).[16] The double-hulled *Akula*, first commissioned between 1986 and 1992, has advanced acoustic silencing technologies. The submarine also comes with the sophisticated MGK-503M Skat (Shark Gill) sonar suite for automatic target detection, complemented by formidable Molniya-M/Pert Spring Satellite Communications (SATCOM) sensors.[17] Armed with Novator Tsakra (SS-N-15) "Starfish" and Novator SS-N-16 "Stallion" missiles, the *Akula* is a powerful weapon in anti-submarine warfare (ASW). The *Akula* is also a potential menace for surface units with powerful PJ-10 BrahMos Anti-Ship Cruise Missiles (ASCM).[18]

The "sea-skimming" BrahMos (whose guidance system is currently being enhanced by Indian software engineers) has a range of 300 km and can reach speeds of up to Mach 2.8. Moreover, the *Akula* is also armed with the RK-55 *Shkval* heavy torpedo, reportedly capable of crippling "even a 100,000-ton carrier with a couple of successful hits" (Majumdar, 2005). It is thus no surprise that the *Akulas* will form the strategic arm of the Indian naval fleet and greatly contribute to India's ASW capabilities.

More recently in September 2005, India also secured the purchase of six French *Scorpene* Type-75 submarines (based on French nuclear submarine designs). The Indian Navy has hopes that the boats, the first to be commissioned in 2012, can be adapted to nuclear propulsion. The stealthy *Scorpene* is difficult to detect and is armed with powerful anti-ship missiles and wire-guided torpedoes. In total, the six French *Scorpenes* will come with 36 SM *Exocet* submarine missiles, most notably useful in surprise attacks on surface fleet vessels. In a statement issued by the Indian Navy it was noted that "the induction of the *Scorpene* class submarines will provide the much desired impetus to the Indian Navy's underwater might and will go a long way in securing India's maritime interests" ("India to Build . . .," 2005).[19]

India also deploys 19 conventional submarines, including ten Russian Kilo-class diesel boats, four German T-209s, and five Soviet period Foxtrots (in reserve). The newly leased Russian *Akulas* will spearhead the Indian Navy's impressive underwater naval force.

In terms of surface warfare, India has eight modern destroyers (five of which are Soviet *Kashins*), 16 frigates and many fast attack crafts and boats that are supported by a squadron of Harrier ground attack fighters and eight long-range Tu-142F Bear reconnaissance bombers (Margolis, 2005: 67). Three Russian-made *Talwar*-class stealth frigates that are armed with long-range BraHmos cruise missiles will be delivered to the Indian naval forces by the end of 2005, with the possibility of three more in the near future (Namoodiri, 2004). There are also plans to develop several improved *Godvari*-class frigates indigenously (Project 16A) with weapon and ship system upgrades (www.indiadefence.com). India is thus one of the world's top naval powers behind the United States (first tier), France, the United Kingdom, Russia (second tier), and Japan and China (third tier).

India has also been steadily working on building heavy space boosters with Russian help, namely in the Polar Satellite Launch Vehicle (PSLV) series. Moreover, there are continuing reports that India is developing a 7,000-mile-ranged ICBM named *Surya*. There are also other reports that indicate that India is working on the development of submarine-launched ballistic missiles (SLBMs) code-named *Sagarika* and *Dhanoush* that may be operational by 2010 with the new ATVs designed to carry them (Margolis, 2005: 67).

The Indian Navy may also benefit from recent improvements in Indo-US relations. Since the Pokharan II nuclear tests of 1998, the international community has been forced to recognize India as a key strategic player in international relations. The incoming George Bush administration has been quick to see India as a strategic counterweight against the rise of a potentially hostile China. In the Bush administration's controversial *National Security Strategy Report* of September 2002, India was for the first time listed as a key global power. Thereafter, in late 2004, US Secretary of Defense Donald Rumsfeld visited India to discuss bilateral relations and security cooperation. More recently in March of 2005, US Secretary of State Condoleezza Rice, highlighting the growing strategic importance of India, arrived in New Delhi first.

There continue to be some outstanding issues between the US and India though. For instance, India's controversial $22 billion pipeline deal with Iran to supply 5 million tons of gas per year for 25 years to meet India's growing energy needs has been a sore point with the United States.[20] Continuing American-Pakistani security cooperation, such as the proposed sale of F-16s and the labeling of Pakistan as a "major non-NATO ally" in 2004 has continued to irk India. Furthermore, despite the "landmark" July 2005, Indo-US agreement on civilian nuclear cooperation and general agreements on defense coordination, many within Indian circles are still waiting for the full gamut of sensitive technology transfer from the US. Although the Bush government lifted some bans on sensitive technology in September 2004 within the framework of the Next Steps to Strategic Partnership (NSSP), many security experts in India feel that the US, despite how warm India becomes (such as declaring support for Ballistic Missile Defense, BMD) will not share advanced technology with them.[21]

In the other areas covered by NSSP, civilian space technology, high technology commerce and missile defense, the United States has moved more cautiously. Bans on space technology and equipment, placed on India after Pokharan II, have recently been lifted and the India Space Research Organization was removed from the list of organizations where all technology transfer was prohibited. However, transfer of civilian space technology is being determined on a case-by-case basis and the US has been slow to initiate the next phase of NSSP, which calls for the easing of export licensing policies.

One of the US fundamental concerns remains the proliferation of advanced technology and therefore export control laws still remain tight. Moreover, India remains committed to not signing the Non-proliferation Treaty (NPT) and the Comprehensive Test Ban Treaty (CTBT) (Nanda, 2004). To address Washington's concern, however, India has agreed to place an export-control attaché in New Delhi (as has been placed in Abu Dhabi, Moscow, Hong Kong and Beijing).

There are other signs, however, that technology transfer may continue to intensify. For instance, there are plans for the joint production of civilian satellites and of other dual use technology items. There have also been recent joint military exercises. Moreover, India's support of BMD may actually be paying dividends. Delhi's support of Washington's national missile defense was largely responsible for the US giving the nod to Israel for the sale of Phalcon radars for India's Airborne Warning and Control System (AWACS) (Bedi, 2005). Previously, in a similar deal between Israel and China, the United States denied permission ("Indo-U.S. Ties . . .," 2004). Recently as well, India voted against Iran, some speculate under US pressure, in support of the European resolution in the run up to the vote at the International Atomic Energy Agency (paving the way the way for Iran's nuclear activities to be referred to the UN Security Council) ("EU3 to Call . . .," 2006).

It is also important to realize that the United States and India, both "vibrant democracies" remain engaged in an active security dialogue and wish to continue improving relations. In September 2005, a US defense team briefed Indian officials in New Delhi on the Patriot PAC-III anti-missile system and on sensitive technologies of the F-18/A and F-16 fighter jets (advanced radars, electronic warfare, engine and weapons systems). As Lieutenant General Jeffrey B. Kohler noted, the briefing "is part of the US commitment to develop a strategic partnership with India and sharing classified details of the Patriot missile system is one of its elements" ("Pentagon Briefs India . . .," 2005). The possible sale or leasing of US P3C-Orion naval spyplanes as well as F-16 and F-18/As was also discussed at the meeting.

In October 2005, the US and Indian Navies participated in joint "Malabar" naval exercises where both the P3C-Orions and the F-18/A were fielded. In November 2005, F-16 Fighting Falcons were involved in joint air exercises with the Indian Air Force in Kalaikunda (West Bengal) (ibid.). The proposed deal for the Patriot anti-missile system, 126 combat aircraft and up to 12 P3C-Orions would be one of the largest military deals signed by New Delhi at an estimated $6 billion (Bedi, 2005).

Currently much of India's naval prowess can be attributed to its purchases from abroad, especially from Russia. Since the early 1960s there has also been a shift towards reducing the navy's dependence on foreign help. Although this policy has not been allowed to be at the expense of the Indian Navy's overall combat efficiency, a turn towards indigenous development is nonetheless discernible. For instance over the past four decades, India's three major shipbuilders, Mazagon Dockyards Limited (Mumbai), Goa Shipyard Limited and Garden Reach Shipbuilders and Engineers (Calcutta) have built nearly 100 surface ships and two submarines. Private companies such as ABG, Larsen and Toubro (Gujrat), Tegma (Chennai) and Anderson Marine (Goa), working in conjunction with state-controlled companies and shipyards (such as Hindustan and Cochin) have also contributed to the fleet strength of the Indian Navy (especially in the construction of patrol vessels and fast interception craft).

Overall, the Indian Navy includes some 55,000 personnel as well as 7,000 naval aviation personnel, one marine commando force as well as an army brigade assigned for amphibious operations. In addition, there are also over 40,000 civilians employed by the Indian Navy.

The Indian Navy's evolving role in the IOR

Presently, the Indian Navy's primary mission is to be prepared for a possible confrontation with Pakistan. The Indian Navy's usefulness was particularly evident during the 1999 Kargil Crisis. The Indian Navy was able to effectively blockade the Pakistani Navy and prevent vital resources from reaching Karachi. In any new conflict, India's naval power could again be effectively used to rapidly eliminate Pakistan's Navy, which consists of eight obsolete destroyers and frigates and seven conventional submarines (Margolis, 2005: 67). Karachi and the new port under construction at Gwadar could also be easily blockaded again, cutting off supplies of fuel, munitions and other strategic goods. Though it has taken a long time for strategic thinkers in India to come to this realization, the India Navy could in fact prove to be far more decisive than the Indian Army or Air Force in any war with Pakistan (Pakistan's land and air forces are better trained and equipped). As one analyst has commented, "Pakistan could not fight for longer than a week in the face of an Indian naval blockade—unless the U.S. Navy challenged it" (ibid.: 67).

Many Indians believe that the appearance of a US carrier battle group in the Arabian Sea in support of Pakistan during the 1971 Indo-Pakistani War forced Delhi to halt its plans to launch a western offensive aimed at crushing Pakistan.[22] Those following this school of thought have long argued for the build-up of naval strength so that the United States could not intervene in Indian affairs again in the future.

India's evolving naval strategy (as alluded to earlier) has also been cautious of Chinese growing naval ambitions. China's decision to develop a blue-water navy caused some concern in strategic circles in India. As one analyst notes, "In coming decades, geopolitical tensions between the two uneasy neighbors and rivals easily could intensify as they vie for hegemony over South and Central Asia, Indonesia, and even the South China Sea, political influence, oil, resources and markets" (ibid.: 67).

For India, the IOR came to be perceived as an area of Indian influence similar to how the Americans perceive of Central America and the Caribbean (Hagerty, 1991; Tanham, 1992). Since the communist takeover in China in 1949, some Indian leaders, such as Sardar Vallabhbhai Patel, have been deeply concerned with Chinese moves towards the IOR (Mehrotra, 1997: 44–48). However, such perspectives did not become more dominant within elite security circles until the traumatic defeat suffered at the hands of China in the 1962 border war.

Since 1988, with the beginning of the normalization of relations, this realist view has modified according to some analysts but has not fundamentally changed (Garver, 2001b, 2002; Malik, 2001; Lee, 2002; Mohan, 2003). Simply put, for India, Chinese military activities in the IOR diminish Indian security. Chinese activities particularly in the past 15 years have amplified Indian security concerns. These Chinese activities fall into five central categories: (1) covert and overt assistance to Pakistan's nuclear and missile efforts, plus assistance in the development of Pakistan's military and military-industrial capabilities; (2) initiation of military relations, including an arms supply and intelligence exchange relation with Nepal; (3) initiation of dense relations with Myanmar, including military cooperation and involvement in the development of overland transport and maritime sectors; (4) growing People's Liberation Army (PLA) activity in the Indian Ocean, including ship visits and the establishment of electronic monitoring facilities; and (5) the cultivation of military relations with Bangladesh and attempts to establish normal relations with Bhutan (Garver, 2002).

The Indian response to the Chinese presence in the IOR

Realist-leaning Indian analysts, in the face of these Chinese efforts, attribute to Beijing, a strategy of encircling India (Kanwal, 1999; Mansingh, 1994a). In response to increasing Chinese presence in the IOR, many analysts argue that India has moved steadily towards its neutralization with its own actions (Garver, 2001b; Malik, 2001; Lee, 2002; Mohan, 2003). In February 2001, Indian Foreign Minister Jaswant Singh formally opened a 165-km road in north-western Myanmar, built by India's Border Roads Organization. The road, stretching from Tamu just inside Myanmar across from Imphal in India's Manipur state, southward to Kalemo, opened a new channel of economic cooperation between India and northern Myanmar. This road helped to dilute and temper the dominant Chinese economic presence in northern Myanmar. Furthermore, it would also facilitate the Indian Army's movement in the event that it needed to sever links between Yunnan province and the Bay of Bengal.

More recently, in late October 2004, the Indian government officially opened its door to the Junta regime for a six-day visit. General Than Shwe, the head of Myanmar's military junta and his Cabinet delegation (industry, communications and energy ministers) was given the red-carpet treatment as he held talks with Prime Minister Manmohan Singh in New Delhi (Mukherji, 2004). The journey was especially noteworthy because it was the first such trip by a Burmese head of state for more than 24 years. In addition to agreeing on stepping up economic engagement between the two states, New Delhi emphasized the importance of Myanmar's cooperation in cracking down on anti-Indian rebels in the north-east. Since independence in 1947, anti-Indian rebel groups, using bases in Bangladesh, Bhutan and Myanmar have wreaked havoc on India's seven north-eastern states, killing more than 50,000 over the years ("Burma Strongman . . .," 2004). In the memorandum of understanding signed between the two states, the possibility of Indian IT companies from Banglore investing in Myanmar was discussed thoroughly during General Shwe's tour of the high-tech region ("Indian IT Companies . . .," 2004). Furthermore, Indian help on a proposed hydroelectric project in Tamanthi was also discussed. In return, India explored the possibilities of tapping Myanmar's vast natural gas reserves and the possibilities of creating a pipeline through Bangladesh (Nanda Kumar, 2005).

Following up on the high-profile Burmese visit to India, in November 2004, Prime Minister Manmohan Singh went to Myanmar to lay the foundation of the $18 million Imphal-Tupul rail project. In the same month, Delhi gave its approval to a rail project that would connect Manipur with Mandalay. The project will be undertaken after plans to extend the track from Jiribam (currently Manipur's only railhead) to Imphal (via Tupul in the Tamenglong district) are completed (Thokchom, 2004). Praising Prime Minister Singh's initiatives, Manipur's Chief Minister Okram Ibobi Singh noted:

> In pursuance of its "look east" policy, the Centre [Indian Federal Government] has already decided to focus on improving infrastructure in the region, and a trans-ASEAN highway will pave the way for much stronger economic and social interaction with our neighboring countries.
>
> (ibid.)

Despite popular protests against the regime and continued outcry over the 1988 jailing of Myanmar's pro-democracy leader Aung San Suu Kyi (who was educated in India), the Indian government continues to normalize relations with Myanmar (Kumar, 2005). For a long time India continued to support the pro-democracy movement in Myanmar only to recently realize that the military junta was not going to leave and that China had made serious inroads in the country (Udai Bhanu Singh, 2005). Realizing the potential strategic danger of letting China dominate Myanmar, Delhi has acted promptly in reestablishing ties with Yangon. The recurring terrorist attacks in the north-east and the difficulty of developing the north-east without the cooperation of Myanmar pushed Delhi to make its turn-around.

Moreover, Myanmar is undoubtedly India's natural and only gateway to ASEAN.

In mid-2001, India's government established a joint command named the Far Eastern Naval Command (FENC), headquartered in Port Blair for the Andaman and Nicobar Islands. This new command would exercise joint command of air, naval and ground forces in the region (Garver, 2001b). Moreover, a new air base on Car Nicobar was set up for offensive and defensive operations. A new 11,500 ft-long airstrip was constructed at Port Blair to accommodate very large jet aircraft such as Boeing 747, which could be rushed to service for the rapid deployment of reinforcements. Maritime surveillance aircraft are also to operate out of the new command and many of the Indian Navy's most modern warships have been assigned to it. FENC, once fully developed by approximately 2012, will have a chain of small anchor stations and three main bases. In structure it will be similar to the US naval base at Hawaii. The base will spread from Narcondam to Indira Point and Car Nicobar will serve as the central link to all the various FENC stations (Maitra, 2005).

One of the reported tasks of this new command unit was to counter Chinese naval activity in the area. Indian security elites noticed increasing Chinese activity in the Bay of Bengal as well as the development of strong overland links between Yunnan province and the coast of the Bay. The Far Eastern Strategic Command has thus concentrated its efforts at strategic choke points in the region: the Six Degree Channel between Aceh and Sumatra and Grand Nicobar Island, the Ten Degree Channel between Nicobar and the southern Little Andaman Island, and the Preparis North and the Preparis South Channels lying between the mouths of the Irrawady and North Andaman Island (Garver, 2001b: 23; Maitra, 2005).

According to some analysts, India's immediate response to news of the Gwadar Project (signaled by Zhu Rongji's public pledge of support during his May 2001 visit to Islamabad) was to question Pakistan about China's involvement (Malik, 2001; Garver, 2002). Prime Minister Vajpayee with President Musharraf raised the issue in their July 2001 meeting. India was naturally concerned that the PLAN would have access to the facilities and enhance China's ability to offset Indian naval presence in the region. New Delhi received ambiguous replies from Islamabad and brought Washington on board in pressuring Beijing to limit its involvement. Beijing's response to this request, however, remains unclear.

According to some analysts, the long-term response of India has been to accelerate Prime Minister Narasimha Rao's "Look East" policy, initiated in 1995 to counter the Chinese presence in the IOR (Garver, 2001b, 2002; Chellaney, 2005; Mohan, 2005b; Sakhuja, 2005a). Under the leadership of Vajpayee, Jaswant Singh and George Fernandes, India began rigorously expanding relations with numerous South-east and East Asian states (Jaffrelot, 2003; Fu, 2004). India's security dialogue began first with Japan and Vietnam, two states extremely cautious and wary of Chinese security interests. Briefly, acceleration of the "Look East" policy also involved official visits, joint military exercises and security agreements with Indonesia, Singapore, South Korea, Philippines, Laos, Cambodia and Thailand (2000–2005).

The most dramatic element of the Indian policy has been its reach towards Taiwan. In January 2002, a major Taiwanese newspaper reported that Indian air force officials had secretly visited Taiwan and that India and Taiwan had begun to exchange military information. Moreover, Taiwan also began posting a military liaison officer to India (Lianhe Xinwen Wang, 2002). More recently, in November 2004, it was announced that the Taiwan Science Council would launch a new division in India. In recent years diverse science cooperation between India and Taiwan has encompassed fields such as seismology, nanotechnology, information education and social science. The new science division in India will focus on the exchange of technologies in the high-tech industries (Chiu, 2004).

Particularly disturbing for Beijing was the high-level exchanges between Taiwan and India during the November 2004 "India-Japan-Taiwan Trialogue: Prospects for Democratic Cooperation." Former Indian Defence Minister and current president of the United Party, George Fernandes as well as Jagdish Shettigar, the economic policy advisor of the BJP, were some of the noteworthy participants on the Indian side. The conference aimed to "promote awareness of potential areas of tripartite cooperation between India, Japan and Taiwan in the areas of economic growth and trade, high-tech industry, democratic development as well as other inter-regional issues of vital interest to each country" ("Former Indian Official . . .," 2004). Taiwanese Premier Yu Shyi-kun noted that there was ample room for bolstering economic and political ties between India and Taiwan. Bilateral trade between Taiwan and India increased to $1.5 billion in 2003 and was over $2 billion in 2004 (Wu, 2004). Specific emphasis was placed on bolstering Indo-Taiwanese ties in the fields of IT, high technology and food processing (Kuo, 2004). The premier noted that Taiwan supported both India and Japan's bids to become permanent members of the United Nations Security Council.

Alternative interpretations of Sino-Indian activity in the IOR

In contrast to the realist school, those in the liberal interdependence school argue that China's rise will coincide with its successful incorporation into the international system. This school emphasizes the intensification of Asian economic interdependence that will act to mitigate regional conflict (Paik, 1995; Roy, 1996). In terms of China's growing energy needs, rather than stimulating conflict and competition, energy security issues, according to this school will likely promote regional cooperation (Yergin *et al.*, 1998; Manning, 2000; Chang, 2001).

China's "String of Pearls" policy clearly has strategic elements to it that cannot be ignored. It does appear that China is systematically trying to increase its influence in areas of vulnerability such as the Strait of Malacca.

Moreover there is also evidence that the "String of Pearls" may be a grand strategic vision to establish Chinese influence in the world's other major "choke points" such as the Suez and Panama Canals.

For states around the world, including India and China, energy security is undoubtedly becoming more and more important in ensuring prosperity. The traditional concept of security and the distinction between high and low politics is increasingly less relevant in the modern world. The widening scope of security, to include both the interrelated areas of economics and energy, is a reality that states have had to come to terms with. In the realist conception of things, competition at the international level has grown to incorporate access to vital economic markets and resources. Thus, in one state's struggle to gain access to resources, another state's sphere of influence is penetrated, counter-measures are taken, to which there are more responses and so forth. This is the type of language in which conflicts like World War I are so often described. The question here is whether the Sino-Indian relationship can now be characterized as an evolving security dilemma and whether Sino-Indian activity can be explained in another way.

The strategically non-threatening motives for Chinese and Indian involvement in the IOR

Chinese cooperation with Myanmar is nothing new. China has been one of the few steadfast supporters of the Burmese military regime since its inception over four decades ago. Throughout the Cold War and after the collapse of the Soviet Union, China remained one of the most important trading partners of Burma. Thus it is not surprising that China remains deeply engaged with this neighboring state. China's primary concerns in its relationship with Myanmar relate to gaining access to vast Burmese gas deposits to promote the development of its own southern region (particularly Yunnan province) and to monitor its own ships passing through the Strait of Malacca.

Much as India's engagement with Myanmar has underlying concerns that emphasize Burmese cooperation in the development of its north-east region, the full potential of Yunnan cannot be realized without Burma on board (Udai Bhanu Singh, 2005). Myanmar's economic modernization is in the best interest of both India and China. For China, upgrading Burma's port facilities, which remained quite obsolete, is part of this process. Full access to the Bay of Bengal through Myanmar would be an obvious tactical advantage but this does not necessarily have anything to do with targeting India. Given China's geographical realities, it makes sense to explore alternative routes to transfer vital resources to the relatively under-developed southern and western regions of China. Access to hydrocarbons, given the projections of China's growing energy needs, remain very important in the national policy agenda. Myanmar, traditionally a Chinese ally, is a natural partner to help fuel the Chinese economy with oil and gas (Berlin, 2004: 245).

Moreover, the installation of electronic monitoring stations in the Coco

Islands may have more to do with monitoring Chinese ships as they transit the Indian Ocean. Although the stations do give China the opportunity to monitor Indian naval movements in the vicinity, their limited infrastructure do not pose any serious threats to the Indian Navy. The "Malacca dilemma," and the possibility of piracy, terrorism and/or blockades especially after 11 September 2001 are more immediate problems (Khurana, 2005a). In fact, Chinese activity in the Bay of Bengal is nothing new either. As early as 1962, Romeo-class submarines were known to frequent these seas (Kondapalli, 2005b). Recent reports may also suggest that Chinese facilities in Myanmar are being used to explore the possibility of untapped seabed mineral resources off the Burmese coast (Udai Bhanu Singh, 2005). Sino-Burmese cooperation therefore may not something overtly directed against India, as a strategy of getting the upper hand. China's primary goals likely have a domestic component.

John Garver (2005: 219–220), reversing previous claims, has recently noted that the Sino-Burmese partnership may be quite delicate. This relates to how the ethnic Burmese have been traditionally suspicious of China and could easily be riled up to support anti-China causes as well as how domestic political changes (to the left) could negatively affect Sino-Burmese relations. As Garver (ibid.: 220) concludes, "In sum, although China has significantly enhanced its position in South Asia via partnership with Myanmar . . . that partnership may well rest on fragile foundations."

Historically, China has played the "Pakistan card" before in its dealings with India. To this day many Indians resent Sino-Pakistani nuclear and missile cooperation, causing some extremists to support "the nuclearization of Vietnam as payback" (Karnad, 2005). It is important to realize though that Sino-Pakistani cooperation did not take off until after the 1962 Sino-Indian border war, in which India was not without blame. In recent years, despite the continued affirmation by top-ranking Chinese officials of Pakistan's ongoing status as a key "all-weather ally," Chinese support for Pakistan in its disputes with India has become less and less vocal. This has been especially evident in the Kashmir dispute where China made a shift from publicly supporting Pakistan throughout the Cold War to taking a more neutral stance.[23]

Recently released (US government) archival evidence suggests that anti-Indian Sino-US-Pakistani cooperation had much to do with India's non-aligned position (and President Richard Nixon's poor relationship and perception of Indira Gandhi, see Malik, 2002). Though the Sino-Pakistani alliance remains a key check to possible Indian misconduct with the Sino-Indian border and on Tibet, the contemporary dynamics of the Sino-Indian-Pakistani triangle are different than they were during the Cold War. Recent Indo-Pakistani dialogues have demonstrated that India and Pakistan have come a long way since Pokharan II in 1998. In September 2004, in New York, Prime Minister Singh and General Musharraf in what was characterized as a "landmark" meeting, agreed to intensify the dialogue on the contentious Kashmir issue and on cross-border terrorism ("No Drift in Policy . . .,"

2004). Indian aid to Pakistan in response to the October 2005 earthquake disaster has also been appreciated and there is renewed optimism that the two states can come to terms.

With reference to Gwadar, Chinese strategic intentions as Alok Bhansal (2005) has noted, may have more to do with the United States than India. Initially China was reluctant to finance the Gwadar Project because the Pakistani government had offered the United States exclusive access to two of its crucial airbases in Jacobabad (Sind) and Pasni (Baluchistan) during the US invasion of Afghanistan (Niazi, 2005b). China was also upset at Pakistan for allowing the US to construct listening posts in its war on terror in Pakistan's northern regions that bordered Tibet and Xinjiang (Niazi, 2005b). China successfully pressured the Pakistani government to remove US electronic gadgets from Gilgit (by threatening to pull out of Gwadar) that according to the Chinese were gathering information on China's Lop Nor nuclear testing sites (Kondapalli, 2005b). In addition, before moving on to fund the Gwadar Project, China got assurances from Pakistan that it had "sovereign guarantees" to use the proposed port facilities when completed. China's large energy interests in Iran run counter to the US interests in the region. The United States has a significant presence in the Arabian Sea and in the Persian Gulf, so Gwadar, which is in close proximity to Iran and the strategic Strait of Hormuz, could have more to do with future Chinese plans to monitor and counter US influence in the region (Zhang, 2005: 66). China's strategic outlook is generally more concerned with the US and its "hegemonism" than with India. China has and will continue to be apprehensive about the US presence in Central Asia, its overwhelming presence in the Indian Ocean and the capability gaps that exist between Beijing and Washington (Gill, 2005: 251; Swaine, 2005).

Given Gwadar's close proximity to the Persian Gulf, it is an ideal location to monitor ship traffic and to ensure the safeguard of Chinese energy interests in the region. Furthermore, with the roads constructed to Pakistan, vital resources can make it to Xinjiang province much more rapidly than if they were routed through the Strait of Malacca. Although the successful completion of Gwadar would undoubtedly give the Pakistani Navy a key tactical advantage, the need for such a port, to reduce dependence on Karachi has long been clear and discussed since the 1950s (Kondapalli, 2005b). Though it is understandable why Indians would be concerned from a geostrategic point of view, the Gwadar port along with Sino-Burmese cooperation has more to do with China's domestic policy agenda and the importance of energy security.

Lately the completion of phase II of the Gwadar Project has come under severe difficulties as the result of widespread unrest in the province of Baluchistan. Baluchistan nationalists have been in a protracted armed dispute with the federal government over accusations that the center is unfairly extracting resources from the province while giving the region little in return. The Baluchistan Liberation Army (BLA) and the Baluchistan Liberation

Front (BLF) are the two most active rebel groups and have been responsible for violent attacks on government officials and infrastructure in recent years. On 3 May 2004, BLA rebel forces killed three Chinese engineers working on the Gwadar port project. On 9 October 2004, two Chinese engineers were kidnapped, one of whom was killed on 14 October in a botched rescue operation (Niazi, 2005b).

Members of the East Turkestan Islamic Movement (ETIM) have also been fighting against the increasing "Hanification" of Xinjiang and have been implicated in attacks against the highly visible Chinese population in Pakistan. Some reports indicate that continued political turbulence in the region has halted Chinese financial support of the project and is causing delays (Bansal 2005a). As Niazi (2005b) notes, "The realization of economic and strategic objectives of the Gwadar port is largely dependent upon the reduction of separatist violence in Baluchistan and Xinjiang." Some have gone as far as suggesting that the United States has been supporting BLA rebels in an attempt to halt the construction of Gwadar and in destabilizing neighboring Iran (Bansal, 2005b).

The Sri Lankan government, while increasing cooperation with the PRC, has also been cooperating with the Indian government of late. A December 2003 agreement was reached between India and Sri Lanka that saw Indian help in reconstructing the important Palay airstrip on the Jaffna peninsula in northern Sri Lanka. In addition, a recent agreement was reached between India and Sri Lanka to cooperate on maritime surveillance with a particular concern for the Liberation Tigers of Tamil Eelam (Berlin, 2004: 243). Furthermore, India has also been involved in negotiations with Sri Lanka about the use of Trincomalee for economic and maritime purposes. The Lanka branch of the Indian Oil Corporation has recently taken over one million tons capacity at a tank farm at Trincomalee on a 35-year lease and Lanka IOC has also acquired over 100 gas stations all over Sri Lanka. As Berlin (2004: 243) notes:

> For many years, Ceylon Petroleum Corporation operated only 15 of Trincomalee's 99 storage tanks, limiting sales to 25 tons per ship and making the fuel expensive. But once Lanka IOC activates the tanks and brings in petroleum products from the Chennai refinery on the Indian mainland, Trincomalee oil will become not only cheaper, but also significantly more plentiful.

Sri Lanka and India are also currently involved in discussions to construct a pipeline between the Southern Indian cities of Chennai and Madurai and Colombo (which would essentially be a Trincomalee offshoot).

In short, Indian moves in Sri Lanka, as in Myanmar, are not necessarily related to China's activities in those states. India's Sri Lanka policy has historically been dominated by domestic politics and this will continue to be the case. Moreover, what is important to realize is that states such as Myanmar and Sri Lanka seek to encourage investment and economic stimulation from abroad. In Myanmar, for instance, Singapore, Japan and Australia have also made key investments. The regional perception of the Burmese government in fact, differs markedly from the European and American one, namely of a closed military dictatorship. The new military junta under General Shwe has tried to open its doors to outsiders and ASEAN states have responded by trying to engage Myanmar out of isolation. There is hope in Asia that over the long term, through engagement, Myanmar can be set on a positive track. Despite external pressure from the EU and the United States, most ASEAN states support Myanmar's upcoming chairing of ASEAN in 2006 (the EU and the US feel that it will legitimate the military regime). There is hope that as in Indonesia, a dual role for the military and politicians can emerge over time. Myanmar's younger generation is increasingly being sent abroad to study overseas and is bringing back new ideas for the military regime (Udai Bhanu Singh, 2005). It is within this wider context that Sino-Indian involvement in Myanmar and Sri Lanka as well as other states in South Asia should be perceived. Small states such as Sri Lanka are in need of economic partnerships and cooperative arrangements with as many states as possible. Both India and China have made moves to capitalize on this desire and to gain access to resources in these smaller IOR littoral states (such as gas).

Sino-Indian involvement in the IOR cannot be exclusively characterized in terms of a security dilemma. Although it may be easy to describe events in both Myanmar and Sri Lanka as a series of moves and counter-moves by China and India respectively, this does not represent the full picture. As of yet, there remains a lack of serious military or security intentions in China and India's engagement of these states. It must also be realized that overall, the Chinese Navy, despite the impressive modernization that is underway, is yet unable to project force at long distances. The Chinese Navy is not a blue-water navy and needs to develop for several decades before serious incursions can be made into the Indian Ocean. The primary weaknesses are the lack of long-range projection, amplified by the absence of an aircraft carrier group, lack of intelligence, surveillance and reconnaissance capabilities and major air-refueling problems ("China Emerges . . .," 2004: 38). Without logistical support, China cannot sustain any military operation in South Asian waters for any prolonged period of times and will continue to be outclassed by the Indian Navy, with its key geostrategic advantages in the Indian Ocean (Khurana, 2005c; Kondapalli, 2005b; Saghal, 2005; Sakhuja, 2005a).

Chinese foreign policy and PLAN will also remain heavily preoccupied with the Taiwan issue and most forces will be allocated to reflect this reality (PRC, 2004: Chapter 1). The Taiwanese and Japanese Navies are definitely forces to be reckoned with in the Taiwan Strait and in the East China Sea. Recent studies have suggested that PLAN would have its hands full and would likely lose in a current naval engagement with the Taiwanese Navy (Glosny, 2004; Goldstein and Murray, 2004). Japan also has clear interests in protecting Taiwan and has a formidable navy that cannot be ignored

(Elleman, 2002). Japanese foreign policy is also becoming increasingly assert-ive under the Koizumi-led government. The Indian Ocean, and especially the Arabian Sea and the Persian Gulf have witnessed creeping increases in Japanese naval presence (currently up to 36 warships) and will likely continue in the future as well. In this sense, Japan as well the United States, which has a major naval presence in the Indian Ocean, with its naval bases at Diego Garcia and Changi (through an arrangement with Singapore in 2000) and in the Pacific at Guam and Okinawa, will serve as major moderating influences for China. The US Navy has been playing this moderating role with the Indian Navy by conducting joint-naval exercises off the Indian west coast (Malabar) and jointly patrolling the Malacca Strait. In short, though China may at some point utilize its "String of Pearls" in Myanmar, Gwadar and elsewhere as key strategic cards in the international game of power balancing, there are few present indications that this is the case. China remains ham-strung by several factors discussed above to seriously threaten the Indian Navy and assert itself in the Indian Ocean. As Michael Swaine (2005: 267) notes:

> First, and foremost, Chinese forces are deployed to deter or defeat pos-sible threats or attacks directed against China's heartland, and especially its economically critical eastern coastline. The most likely sources of such threats include . . . Japan, South Korea, Guam and Hawaii.

At least in the short term, it is highly unlikely that China will become more aggressive for the other reason that it will play host to the Olympics in Beijing in 2008 and the World Expo in Shanghai in 2010. The last thing Beijing wants, barring a Taiwanese declaration of independence, is a major inter-national incident that would tarnish the global public opinion of the PRC and its modernization.

China's threat perception of India may indeed be quite limited. Despite Pokharan II, many scholars have concluded that India is simply not on China's "radar screen" (Cohen, 2001: 1; Shirk, 2004). China has not tradition-ally viewed India as a major international power. Instead Beijing has focused its attention on Japan and the United States. As Shirk (2004: 75) notes:

> India has many more experts on China than China has experts on India. Indian journalists, intellectuals, businesspeople, and the informed public are avid China-watchers, while their Chinese counterparts follow devel-opments in Taiwan, Japan and the United States with much greater interest than developments in India.

Shirk (ibid.: 89–90) also goes on to note:

> India's nuclear tests and its hostile rhetoric toward China did not provoke any serious rethinking of Chinese military posture toward its neighbor;

China continued to accord the Indian threat low priority ... My own interviewing indicates ... that Chinese military posture continues to be focused overwhelmingly on Taiwan and the United States, not India. Other experts in Chinese security policy draw the same conclusion based on their own interviews with military analysts and officials in Beijing.

This supports the argument that China's maritime objectives in the IOR and its so-called "String of Pearls" strategy may indeed have little to do with India and more to do with domestic Chinese interests (securing energy supplies, protecting SLOCs and sending resources to China's western provinces) and the United States.

Moreover, proponents of the "China Collapse Theory" would argue that internal pressures in Xinjiang, Tibet, the growing wealth disparities accompanying economic modernization and continuous stress on the Communist Party (from the liberalization/authoritarian dichotomy) will keep Beijing preoccupied with internal matters for many decades (Kondapalli, 2005b). As one analyst rightfully pointed out, China, as well as India and other Asian states, are still in the process of state building, a process that has long been completed in the West and will continue to consolidate for many decades to come (Bhalla, 2005). Furthermore, some analysts have commented on the defensive nature of China's grand security strategy. As Gill (2005: 247) notes

> In spite of dramatic changes in the global security environment, Beijing continues to pronounce its adherence to the proposition that the overall tendency of world affairs is toward "peace and development," increasing multipolarity and economic globalization, and a general easing of tensions.[24]

Within this international environment, China's security strategy has sought: (1) to maintain a stable domestic environment capable of dealing with external political, military, economic and cultural threats; (2) to manage Beijing's growing prosperity while allaying the fears of neighboring states through engagement in mutually beneficial interactions; and (3) to circumvent US hegemony in a peaceful and non-confrontational manner (Gill, 2005: 248; Scobell, 2002).[25] As Jiang Zemin (quoted in Gill, 2005: 248) made clear in a foreign policy speech delivered in Geneva in March 1999:

> The world is undergoing profound changes which require the discard of the Cold War mentality and the development of a new security concept and a new international political, economic, and security order responsive to the needs of our times ... The core of the new security concept should be mutual trust, mutual benefit, equality and cooperation ... To conduct dialogue, consultation and negotiation on an equal footing is the right way to solve disputes and safeguard peace.

As will be discussed in the chapters to follow, China appears to be willing to improve its relationship with India economically, politically and in many other areas. As Swaine (2005: 279) concludes, "China seems far more interested than it once was in furthering good relations with New Delhi, maintaining domestic stability, improving its overall military capabilities, and handling security problems along its eastern and southeastern borders."

Reinterpreting India's "Look East" policy

Realists have often mischaracterized India's "Look East" policy as a direct response to increasing Chinese presence in the IOR (Garver, 2001b, 2002; Malik 2001; Lee, 2002). India's "Look East" policy, however, is more correctly perceived as a longer-term trend, first initiated by Prime Minister P.V. Narasimha Rao in the early 1990s as India's foreign policy evolved out of non-alignment (Jaffrelot, 2003). India's initial interests in ASEAN were Japan-oriented. ASEAN was seen as a natural gateway to improving relations with the Japanese. According to J.N. Dixit, India's late influential Foreign Secretary, "Japan was identified [in the early 1990s] as one of the most important sources of both investment and technology by the Government of India" (Dixit, 1996: 254, cited in Jaffrelot, 2003: 46).

As India liberalized its economy, looking East and emulating the success of the Asian Tiger economies appeared to be an attractive option. India's economic reforms met with the approval of the ASEAN countries as it was granted "sectoral dialogue partner" status in 1992 (for tourism, commerce, investments, science and technology). By 1995, at the fifth ASEAN summit, along with China and Russia, India was granted full dialogue partner status. However, with the defeat of the Congress government in the May 1996 elections, some feared that India's burgeoning relationship with ASEAN would be put on the back burner by the leftist Gowda government. However I.K. Gujral, the first Minister of External Affairs to attend an ASEAN conference (July, in Indonesia), reaffirmed the importance of the Indo-ASEAN relationship. The Indian government stated that:

> We see the full dialogue partnership with ASEAN as the manifestation of our Look-East destiny. This is because we are geographically inseparable, culturally conjoined and now more than ever before, economically and strategically interdependent and complementary . . . What the Look-East policy really means is that an outward looking India is gathering all forces of dynamism—domestic and regional—and is directly focusing on establishing synergies with a fast consolidating and progressive neighborhood to its east in the mother continent of Asia . . . [India] would work with ASEAN as a full dialogue partner to give real meaning and content to the prophecy and promise of the "Asian century" that is about to draw upon us.
>
> (*The Times of India*, 25 July 1996, cited in Jaffrelot, 2003: 47)

India's full dialogue partnership status also made it an *ex-officio* member of the ASEAN Regional Forum (ARF), which dealt with security issues. Undoubtedly, for the ASEAN states, India's growing involvement in Southeast Asia was welcomed as a possible counterbalance against an increasing Chinese presence and assertiveness in the region. Chinese claims to the Spratly Islands in the South China Sea and hostile reaction to the Taiwanese elections of 1996, leading to the Taiwan Strait Crisis made several ASEAN states wary of Chinese domination. Singapore, for instance, which once considered the modernization of the Indian Navy as a possible threat, concluded an agreement with India in 1996 on military cooperation, with much of the focus on naval elements such as anti-submarine warfare (Jaffrelot, 2003; Fu, 2004). Likewise, India signed a Memorandum of Understanding with Malaysia on defense cooperation.

From the Indian perspective though, enhancing economic relations have always been at the forefront of engagement with ASEAN members (Dutta, 2005; Nairayan, 2005; Swaran Singh, 2005a). Since 1992, India has been actively pursuing this agenda bilaterally with official state visits to Indonesia in 1992, Singapore, Thailand, Malaysia, Vietnam in 1993, Singapore in 1994 and Malaysia in 1995 (many of these trips were reciprocated). Most notably on each visit there was an impressive delegation of Indian economic specialists and businesses. Thus, while some may emphasize recent Indo-ASEAN engagement as a response to budding Chinese involvement in South Asia, the process of events has actually been more fluid. China's involvement in South Asia and correspondingly, India's involvement in ASEAN of late, are nothing new. India's acceleration of its "Look East" policy in recent years was related to the desire to improve relations with the international community following the backlash to Pokharan II in 1998 (Jaffrelot, 2003; Fu, 2004). Despite joint naval and military exercises with many ASEAN states, the primary character of India's engagement with this organization remains economic, rather than security-oriented. Moreover, much of the defense and naval cooperation between India and ASEAN remains focused on protecting SLOCs and combating terrorism and piracy (Khurana, 2005a).

Prime Minister Manmohan Singh, commenting on the state of Indo-ASEAN relations at the third India-ASEAN summit in 2004, noted that:

> It is inevitable that we seek to take the India-ASEAN relationship to a higher level where we envision an Asian economic community, which encompasses ASEAN, China, Japan, Korea and India. Such a community would release enormous energies. One is captivated by the vision of an integrated market spanning the distance from the Himalayas to the Pacific Ocean linked by efficient road, rail, air and shipping. It would account for half the world's population and it would hold foreign exchange reserves exceeding those of the EU and NAFTA put together . . . We believe the Indian economy can absorb up to 150 billion dollars of foreign investment in the infrastructure sector over the next 10 years.

Our requirements of capital [for] infrastructure are very large. The requirements of our airports and railways alone amount to over 55 billion dollars in the next 10 years . . . As we look East and you look West, it is natural that we look at each other in this enterprise of the restoring Asia to its rightful place . . . the heart of India-ASEAN relations is the economic one.

(Choudhury, 2004).[26]

In 2003, India's trade with ASEAN rose to $13 billion from $3.5 billion in 1991. India and ASEAN have set a short-term target of increasing this figure to $30 billion by 2007 (ibid.). Also at the India-ASEAN Summit at Vientiane, Laos, a partnership deal was reached in spheres covering, economics, science, technology, health and culture. The accord between India and ASEAN aimed to create a free-trade area by 2011 with five ASEAN members—Brunei, Indonesia, Malaysia, Thailand and Singapore and by 2016 with the rest—the Philippines, Cambodia, Laos, Myanmar and Vietnam. Prime Minister Singh said that the focus has now shifted from "Looking East Policy" to "Doing East Policy" (ibid.).

For India's elite policy makers, as Fu (2004: 42) notes, "a true multi-polar world is established around a cooperation security system, which they believe is the safeguard for peace." Thus, although power-balancing considerations may still persist in some circles, India remains committed to developing the "cooperation security option" (ibid.: 43). Following the end of the Cold War, ASEAN's role has clearly shifted for India. The creation of strong economic ties with ASEAN members will go a long way in promoting a cooperative multi-lateral security framework in East and South Asia. India has correspondingly stressed the implementation of a Free Trade Treaty with ASEAN and has promoted sub-regional cooperation with regimes such as BIMST-EC (Bangladesh-India-Myanmar-Sri Lanka-Thailand-Economic Cooperation), BCIM (Bangladesh, China, India and Myanmar) and Ganga-Mekong.

Steven A. Hoffmann (2004: 40), writing in 2001, noted that the mainstream strategic perceptions of China held that "China does not constitute a clear-cut, direct military threat to India in the near term" though the long-term future was more uncertain. Thus although over the long term, as China's power rises, there may be fears about China's intentions in South Asia and its dealings with IOR littorals, in the short term, there is optimism that Sino-Indian relations can progress. As Hoffmann (2004: 40) notes of the Indian strategic community's viewpoint of China, "the possibility exists for India and China to avert major future problems through diplomacy and other forms of appropriate action." So while China is not a threat in the traditional sense, there "exists a 'window of opportunity' through which China's evolution may be vectored in a cooperative framework" though it would be unwise for India "not to institute adequate precautionary measures to cater for a possible reversal of China's policies toward an assertive and even aggressive stance in [the] future" (Jasjit Singh, 1999: 238–239, cited in

Hoffmann, 2004: 40). By the end of the summer of 2003, following Prime Minister Vajpayee's landmark visit to China, it appeared that India was ready to seize this window of opportunity and that even long-term threat perceptions were beginning to moderate. As Hoffmann (2004: 64) notes

> [I]ncluded in it [the new government rhetoric] was a statement that the quality of the India-China relationship had been transformed by the two governments' joint process, over several years, of developing "all round" bilateral cooperation, while the differences between the two countries were being addressed simultaneously.

The key catalyst in the transformation of the Sino-Indian relationship was the rapid growth in economic trade. As Hoffmann continues:

> [T]he India-China economic relationship has improved so markedly in recent years and months, and now shows such promise for the future, that great Indian and Chinese governmental emphasis can be placed on it . . . bilateral difficulties in the strategic or security area can be viewed by both sides in the context of successful economic relations, so that diplomatic progress can thereby be better enabled.
>
> (ibid.)

Conclusion

This chapter has tried to demonstrate that both China and India are currently undergoing a significant transformation in their naval forces and naval strategy. The Chinese and Indian Navies are quickly becoming formidable forces, the former with an impressive submarine force and the latter with growing carrier-group and long-range capabilities. Though much of China and India's naval modernization has been acquired by purchasing naval equipment and technology from foreign powers, indigenous research, development and production have also been enhanced over the years. Both Chinese and Indian naval doctrine calls for the eventual development of full-fledged blue-water capabilities. With this backdrop, according to neorealists, there are reasons for concern that Sino-Indian relations may be spiraling into a security dilemma in the IOR—with China's "String of Pearls" and growing activity in South Asia (namely, Sino-Pakistani and Sino-Burmese naval cooperation) and India's acceleration of its "Look East" policy. However, as was revealed in the last section of this chapter, mutual threat perceptions between India and China remain quite low. China's primary security concerns are in East Asia and its involvement in the IOR may have more to do with the US and securing energy resources than with India. Moreover, India's "Look East" policy has been more fluid than sometimes portrayed by neorealist scholars and in general terms both India and China have always been actively engaged in the IOR.

In recent years, the Congress Party, under the leadership of Prime Minister Manmohan Singh, has picked up the momentum generated by Vajpayee and the BJP in the summer of 2003 and has continued to engage China economically and politically. As Sino-Indian economic relations continue to improve, mutual understandings have been developing to create dependable expectations of peaceful change. The emerging Sino-Indian trade relationship will be examined in the next chapter and the possibility of how this low political engagement can lead to further interchange and cooperation will be explored. Thereafter, Chapter 4 will highlight China and India's energy policies and how these policies are currently in the process of convergence. The final chapter will trace the emergence of a Sino-Indian political will or elite consensus committed to realizing the full potential of the Sino-Indian relationship. These developments will continue to abate India's long-term threat perceptions of China and indicate that exclusively neorealist accounts of Sino-Indian relations may be too narrow.

3 Chinese and Indian economic liberalization and the nature of the Sino-Indian economic relationship

Chinese and Indian economic liberalization

Both India and China began planning for national development in the early 1950s following Indian independence in 1947 and Chinese independence in 1949. China largely had a command economy structure until the late 1970s and although India adopted a mixed economy, state regulation of economic activity was fairly extensive until 1991. In the 1950s, both India and China were at similar stages of development. The World Bank noted that both states had similar per capita incomes in the range of $50–60 (World Bank, 1983). Both states also adopted similar strategies for economic development (Chen and Uppal, 1971; Swamy, 2003). Mao and Nehru had been influenced by the perceived success of the Soviet Union's rapid industrialization of a rural economy with little external assistance (Nehru had visited the Soviet Union in the late 1920s and was impressed by Soviet planning; Nehru, 1946). The development strategy of the Soviet Union was in many ways emulated by both India and China as they focused on investment in heavy industry in the 1950s.

Gregorii Aleandrovic Fel'dman first formulated this development strategy in the Soviet Union in the 1920s. As one analyst has noted, in this strategy "the share of investment devoted to augmenting the stock of capital in the equipment-producing (heavy industry) sector determined the long-run rate of growth of the economy: the larger this share, the greater was the growth rate" (Srinivasan, 2004: 224). China and India more or less followed this model and emphasized the importance of industrialization. Even before independence, Indian elites started to believe that rapid industrialization in the fashion of the Soviet Union was the only means to eradicate poverty in India (Viswesvaraya, 1934; Thakurdas et al., 1944). After independence, the government's industrial policy resolutions of 1948 and 1956 assigned the state the responsibility for developing major industries such as transport and communication. However, in some select sectors such as agriculture, a push was made for privatization.[1] In China, the communist leadership followed the Soviet lead and nationalized all private enterprises. Both states executed their industrialization programs through state controls on investment and on foreign trade. As Srinivasan notes, "Indeed, both economies followed virtually autarkic policies which imposed a heavy cost on both in terms of efficiency of resource allocation and forgone growth" (2004: 225). Furthermore, since neither China nor India had developed any capital goods industries by the early 1950s, they came to rely on a capital-intensive import substitution model where equipment needed for investment had to be imported. The emphasis on heavy industry therefore had a substantial impact on foreign exchange and investment resources, leading both states to rely on investment and import quotas rather than on the markets and fiscal devices for control. Eventually, however, both states moved away from this model of development. In China, the impetus was provided by the disasters of the Great Leap Forward (1958–1962) and the Cultural Revolution (1966–1976) and later in India by an acute macroeconomic and fiscal crisis beginning in the 1980s.

China's economic liberalization

China's economic reforms or "opening up" commenced in the late 1970s in the post-Mao period. China's leader Deng Xiaoping has fittingly described this period as the "second revolution" with the first one being China's political liberation in 1949 (Deng, 1993: 113; also see Harding, 1987; Chai, 2000).

China's economic reforms were in many ways a move in the opposite direction of the policies pursued under Mao, which emphasized "self-sufficiency." The first signs of China's opening up and reform came two years after Mao's death when Deng Xiaoping persuaded members of the Communist Party of China to shift the focus from ideological struggle to economic development (Baum, 1994). The experiments of the Cultural Revolution were soon perceived in elite circles as an unfortunate national disaster. This coincided with a move away from Mao's "self-reliance" policies and Zhou En-lai's Four Modernization policies. The new Chinese orientation was framed after the concept of *"duiwai kaifang,"* meaning "opening to the outside world" (FewSmith, 2001: 36; Reardon, 2002: 185; Seekington, 2002: 346–358).

De-collectivization occurred first in the rural sectors and Special Economic Zones (SEZs) were established in coastal cities. These were the first two priorities in China's opening up and results began to show in the early 1980s (Swaran Singh, 2005a: 27). The initial success led to the further implementation of modernization plans and a new drive towards accepting interdependence and its implications for Chinese foreign policy.

The first critical challenge to Deng's reforms was to come in the form of rapid price hikes and the popular resentment that followed. The combination of mass domestic unrest over political repression and lack of freedom would prove to be a disastrous recipe and culminated in the Tiananmen Square crisis of 4 June 1989. This popular disaffection was met with even more heavy-handed political repression. Deng's partial economic reforms were also strongly challenged in China in light of Gorbachev's comprehensive *glasnost* in the Soviet Union from the mid-1980s (Wei Wei Zhang, 2000: 127).

Correspondingly, Deng and his advisors categorized the global process of modernization into four different categories: (1) that of hard governments and hard economies (former Soviet Union); (2) that of soft states and hard economies (India); (3) hard governments and soft economies (the Asian Tigers); and (4) soft governments and soft economies (Western states). Of the four processes of modernization, Deng concluded that the third system was the most successful of all and therefore that only economic reforms were necessary. Political reforms were put on the backburner.

China's economic opening had a significant impact on its political profile. For example, China's modernization became more and more dependent on foreign direct investment (FDI) as well as foreign trade. This not only had an impact on China but also served to accelerate development in other developing countries such as India (Swaran Singh, 2005a: 28). In China, development was to be achieved through a dual policy initiative. The first was the shift in the allocation mechanisms from central planning to market forces. The second was the shift of development strategies from an inward to an outward orientation. As Singh notes, "When directed by a centralized single-party political leadership, these economic reforms were to produce spectacular expansion of the domestic economy" (ibid.: 28).

Over the years, China has been steadily improving its investment climate in an effort to attract FDI since the end of 1970s. There are three primary laws regulating FDI in China. These include: *The Law of Foreign Wholly Owned Enterprises of the People's Republic of China, the Law of Chinese-Foreign Equity Joint Ventures of the People's Republic of China, the Law of Chinese-Foreign Contractual Joint Ventures of the People's Republic of China* and *Catalogue for the Guidance of Foreign Invested Industries* (*Report of the India-China . . .*, 2004). Furthermore, China has also devised industrial and regional guidelines for FDI. Given China's export-led growth strategy, the government generally provides preferential treatment toward FDI. This has especially been the case since China's accession to the WTO.

The Catalogue of Guidance for Foreign Investment Industries primarily guides the industrial distribution of FDI in China. The Catalogue categorizes FDI schemes into four categories. These include: "encouraged," "allowed," "limited," and "prohibited." "Encouraged" plans include 262 categories, "limited" 75 categories and "prohibited" 34 categories. The major fields where FDI is promoted include: (1) agricultural moderization; (2) infrastructure; (3) high-tech fields like electronics and IT, biotechnology and aviation; (4) industrial renovation and upgrading; (5) recycling and environmental protection; (6) development projects in China's western regions; and (7) general export-oriented investment (ibid.).

In recent years, the Chinese government has also accelerated up the liberalization of overseas or outward capital investment. In 1999, China adopted encouraging measures on the investment of overseas processing trade (PRC, 1999). Afterwards, China progressively adopted a series of measures to loosen controls and enhanced its guidance on enterprise outflow investment.

For instance, the authority of the government to examine and approve out-flow investments has been deregulated and the profit remittance deposit has also been abolished (PRC, 2003).

Furthermore, in July 2004, China issued the *Catalogue of Countries and Industries for Guiding Outflow Investment (NO. 1)*. For the first time, China issued guidelines for the outflow of investment. Moreover, Article 2 of *The Regulation on the Approval Matters of Outflow Investment and Establishing Enterprises* stipulated that: "the State supports and encourages all kinds of enterprises of different ownership with comparative advantages to go out to invest and establish enterprises abroad" (In *Report of the India-China* . . ., 2004: 51).

China's burgeoning domestic economy was coupled with receptive and supportive external conditions that made China's foreign trade a leading force in facilitating China's economic and social transformation. China's FDI and foreign trade figures slowly grew until the end of the 1980s but then came to a virtual halt in the wake of the Tiananmen Square Crisis of 1989. It was not until the early 1990s that China's foreign trade and FDI began to grow rapidly and made China the second largest recipient of FDI in 1996. China's contracted FDI, for instance, grew from $3.49 billion in 1991 to $42.3 billion in 1996 (Dzever and Jaussad, 1999: xiv). This stimulated debate in the popular media about China's "overheating" and reflected global concern about China's rise (ibid.).

China has indeed come a long way economically since the days of Mao. In many respects China was formerly one of the world's most isolated econ-omies, trading barely 0.75 percent of global total imports and exports. It was under the leadership of Deng that China's foreign trade began to grow at an average of 15.5 percent and brought China from conducting $20.6 billion in foreign trade per annum to over one trillion in 2004 ("China's Foreign Trade" . . ., 2002).

The nature of China's "opening up" and economic reforms have made China's development increasingly dependent on FDI and foreign trade. Moreover, China's social transformation and political stability have come to be entwined with sustaining high growth rates on a regular basis. To fully understand and appreciate the long-term trends in and the impact of Sino-Indian economic engagement it is necessary to examine how China's opening up has taken place.

China's four reform phases

China's economic reforms can be succinctly characterized into four consecu-tive phases (Xiao-guang Zhang, 2000: 7). The first phase (1979–1984) began with a series of measures to promote exports aimed primarily at providing a boost to foreign exchange earnings in order to rejuvenate the worn-down Chinese economy following China's period of isolation in the Cultural Revolution of the 1960s. The policies adopted in this period included the decentralization of foreign trade, repeated devaluations of the *Renminbi* and the establishment of Special Economic Zones (SEZs) to encourage foreign trade and attract FDI. The reforms in this stage introduced the household responsibility system in place of agricultural communes. This entailed the free sale of output at market-determined prices except for a relatively small proportion delivered to the state at fixed rates (Leung and Chin, 1983; Srinivasan, 2004: 228). This also led to the formation of township and village enterprises and the replacement by taxes of surrender of profits by urban enterprises.

The second stage reforms (1984–1985) focused on urban areas and on state-owned enterprises. The reforms comprised the introduction of a variety of contracts on enterprise leasing and management responsibility systems and the creation of a shareholding system to facilitate mergers, leases and auctions as well as bankruptcy of enterprises. Moreover, the reforms in the second stage focused on the development of markets for production materials and capital, labor, information and technology. This entailed the drastic reduction of the role of mandatory plans so business enterprises were free to make their own investment decisions (Srinivasan, 2004: 228). In this period, then, foreign trade corporations in China were operating increasingly autonomously and the number of commodities that were subject to central planning was reduced. The economy was also further opened through the creation of the Hainan and Pudong SEZs.

The third (1988–1993) and fourth (1994–1998) stages of reforms focused on the creation of a socialist market economy. The fiscal contract system was replaced with a tax-sharing system. In addition, the central bank was given the authority to regulate the money supply and to supervise China's financial systems. State-owned banks were transformed into commercial banks in this period and legal and regulatory reforms were also implemented. In this period the two-tier system of foreign exchange (official and swap exchange) was unified, making the *Renminbi* fully convertible (Swaran Singh, 2005a: 32).

In recent years, China has continued to intensify its economy by making both internal and external adjustments. Two main challenges have been the impetus behind recent adjustments. The first was the so-called "overheating" of the Chinese economy during 1993–1994 that required a "soft landing." The second was the East Asian Financial Crisis of the late 1990s. Both of these challenges culminated in China revising its constitution in March 1999 with new laws providing a far greater role for China's private sector. The new laws also highlighted how the private sector was complementary and integral to the Chinese social system (Langlois, 2002: 100–101). Continued reforms in China's state-owned enterprises (SOEs), namely putting an end to the system of non-performing loans (on which SOEs thrived) have also been pursued. Both of these policies, however, have caused labor unrest and have caused a massive increase in worker demonstrations across the country (Cheng, 2004; Tanner 2004: 139).

Following the lead of Zhu Rongji and Jiang Zemin, China's fourth generation of leaders under Hu Jintao have sought to tackle corruption and increase the level of transparency at the governmental levels. The SARS epidemic of 2003 proved to be a key turning point. Initially, widespread fear about social panic and economic disaster encouraged efforts to censor information about the deadly disease. However, Hu Jintao dismissed both Beijing Mayor Meng Xuenong and China's Health Minister Zhang Wenkang, who erroneously argued that the disease was under control in China. Thereafter the new leadership accurately revised the figures on the number of SARS victims, discouraged travel, and threatened prison sentences for the violation of quarantine orders (Swaran Singh, 2005a: 34).

In dealing with corruption, the Chinese leadership has been quick to administer justice at the public level. For instance, Yang Bin, one of the wealthiest people in China was sentenced in July 2003 to an 18-year prison sentence for property fraud. Moreover, the Minister of Land Resources, Tian Fengshan was dismissed after a Hong Kong newspaper reported his "misuse of land" in his former political base of Heilongjiang Province. Correspondingly, China has also been more transparent in reporting matters such as industrial accidents and deaths, with over 11,000 alone in 2003 (Kraus, 2004: 148–152).

China has also increasingly become integrated in the international economy as it entered in the World Trade Organization (WTO). China acceded to the WTO on 11 December 2001, the culmination of decades of economic reform, transitioning the Chinese economy from a command economy to a market-oriented one. Fifteen years in the making, the WTO agreement focused on principles of market access, non-discrimination and transparency. In short, China committed to overhaul its trade regime and to open its domestic market for greater competition. What followed was a series of sweeping and often costly reforms that lowered trade barriers in almost every sector of the economy, provided national treatment and improved market access to goods and services imported from other states. In the first year of WTO membership China took substantial steps, enacting over one thousand laws to bring the trading system into compliance with WTO regulations. WTO accession left China with several major challenges. First, the role of the government changed as business enterprises received more autonomy. The agricultural and manufacturing industries faced severe challenges as foreign agricultural and industrial products hit the Chinese market.

Some states such as the United States though have continued to press China on fully complying in areas such as intellectual property rights and trading rights and distribution services (USA, 2004). The United States has also raised concerns that China's agricultural industry has to continue to enhance its predictability and transparency and deal with the ad hoc policies often pursued by customs and quarantine officials. Overall, though, China's entry into the WTO has drastically boosted the institutionalization of its external economic integration (Wang, 2003). China will continue to liberalize its economy and trading system within the confines of the WTO in the years to come.

China has also made genuine efforts in recent years at social and political integration with the rest of the world. It has signed the International Covenant on Economic, Social and Cultural Rights in June 1998 and the International Covenant on Civil and Political Rights in October 1998 (Kraus, 2004). Many "watchdog" groups such as Amnesty International, however, remain highly critical of China's human rights record.

India's economic liberalization

The Indian economic reforms of 1991 represented a clear and direct shift from the dysfunctional development strategy of the previous four decades (Srinivasan, 2004: 229). The pre-reform strategy emphasized import-substituting industrialization and the state played a major role in the economy. The foundations of this strategy were laid prior to independence in 1947 and had a wide range of support. There was no significant political support for reforms until 1991 when a serious macroeconomic and balance-of-payments crisis forced a reassessment of India's development strategy. At the earliest, unlike China, whose economic reforms can be traced back to the early 1970s China-US détente, India's reform process can only be traced back to the mid-1980s. Though coalition politics in India have severely interfered in India's modernization and, moreover, economic reforms were not the only locomotive for India's opening up, India had a long track record of foreign trade and investment before the economic crises of the early 1990s. For instance, while the Chinese economy remained generally closed until the Deng Xiaoping reforms in 1978, Indian industry had already witnessed a steady nine times growth in its FDI since 1947, from Rs. (Indian Rupees) 2.5 billion to Rs. 24 billion for 1978 to Rs. 317 billion by 1985 (Jing, 1998: 208–209).

Until the beginning of the early 1980s, India's macroeconomic policies remained conservative in nature. As Srinivasan notes, "Current revenues of the central government exceeded current expenditures so that there was a surplus available to finance in part the deficit in the capital account" (2004: 229). However in the early 1980s, loose fiscal controls turned current revenue surpluses into deficits, causing the government to borrow at home and abroad to finance not only investment but also current consumption. External borrowing was granted to India on concessional terms from multilateral lending institutions and in bilateral arrangements with major lending states. As the years passed, the Indian government also started to borrow abroad on commercial terms from both the capital markets and from nonresident Indians. In 1983–1984, out of the $22.8 billion of public and publicly guaranteed external debt, around 17 percent was owed to private creditors. Just before the macroeconomic crisis of 1990–1991, India's external debt had nearly tripled to $69.3 billion and over 30 percent was owed to private creditors (World Bank, 1996: Table 3.1a). This, however, did witness moderate liberalization, in the form of delicensing of some industries and allowance of flexible use of capacity through "broad banding." The relaxation of import restrictions also helped generate growth in this period. Thus the average rate of growth in terms of real gross domestic product (GDP) over the 1980s was 5.5 and 5.8 percent (GOI, 1999a: Appendix Table 1.2).

Domestic manufacturers benefited from very high levels of protection from competition abroad in this period. Various entry–exit barriers were the main characteristics of this industrial protectionism (Swaran Singh, 2005a: 37). This had a long-term negative impact on the competitiveness of the Indian business sector, however. As one analyst notes:

> Even now, the Indian government has not had very strong groundswell for undertaking reforms in core infrastructure sectors like energy where India has been projecting its success on the basis of interest shown by private investors. The progress, however, has been slow to say the least.
>
> (ibid.: 38)

Ever since the 1960s, there have been attempts at moderating the rigors and unintentional and distributional consequences of the control system. The earliest attempt occurred after an acute macroeconomic crisis in 1966, forcing the Indian government at the time to seek help from the International Monetary Fund (IMF) and the World Bank. For a period of several years, upon recommendation from these institutions, the rupee was devalued and controls on foreign trade were briefly relaxed. The problem at this time was that many within the Congress Party and within opposition circles were opposed to Prime Minister Gandhi's relaxation of controls (Veit, 1976; Frankel, 1978; Rudolph and Rudolph, 1987). The pressure from political circles, coupled with the World Bank's failure to deliver nonproject assistance aid in return for liberalization influenced PM Gandhi to abandon liberalization.

The second attempt at liberalization was not made until Rajiv Gandhi became the Prime Minister in 1984. Along with his team of economic advisors (many of whom were former World Bank economists), keen on releasing rigid controls, the Rajiv Gandhi government experimented with trade and investment liberalization. Still the competitiveness of domestic producers did not improve. Thus, domestic demand was being stimulated by fiscal expansion, financed by borrowing at home and abroad and by the monetization of fiscal deficits. This fiscal expansion would prove unsustainable and resulted in the 1990–1991 economic crisis. By 1990–1991, the gross fiscal deficit had expanded to over 10 percent of GDP of which 4.3 percent was for interest payments on domestic and external debt (World Bank, 2000: Annex Table 8.6).

Escalating fiscal deficits coupled with rising oil prices during the 1990 Gulf Crisis put pressure on Indian prices and the exchange rate. This in turn led to expectations of currency devaluation. Political instability in 1990, added to public perceptions about the inability of the government to manage the Indian economy. Nonresident Indians and external investors began to withdraw deposits and capital and the foreign exchange reserve dwindled. The prospect of default on short-term loans became a reality and India's international credit rating was downgraded. This crisis, which spiraled out of control by 1991, required a concrete response from the government. In the face of rapid Chinese economic growth and the collapse of India's Soviet ally, it was clear that something had to be done.

The economic reforms of 1991 focused on fiscal consolidation and limited tax reforms, removal of controls on industrial investment and on a reduction of import tariffs as a way of addressing the balance-of-payments crisis and macroeconomic instability. The rupee was also devalued and this was followed by a period of careful exchange rate management. The rupee was also made convertible for current account transactions (Srinivasan, 2004: 232).

India's so-called "New Industrial Policy," initiated on 24 July 1991, represented a significant shift from India's traditional foreign direct investment (FDI) policies. First, the Indian government abolished the industrial licensing system in all industries. In order to facilitate greater transparency in the FDI approval system and expedite their clearance, a system of automatic clearance was put into practice for FDI proposals fulfilling the conditions laid down, such as the ownership levels of 50 percent, 51 percent, 74 percent and 100 percent foreign equity allowed in sectors specified for each limit. The guidelines were laid down for this approval process as well. The Foreign Exchange Regulation Act (FERA) of 1973 was amended in 1993 and restrictions placed on foreign companies by it were lifted.

New sectors such as mining, banking, insurance, telecommunications, construction and management of ports, harbors, roads and highways, airlines, and defense equipment, have since been thrown open to private, including foreign-owned, companies. However, the extent of foreign ownership continues to be limited in many of these service sectors.

In an attempt to boost investor confidence and provide a big push for bilateral investment flows India embarked upon the path of concluding Bilateral Investment Promotion and Protection Agreements (BIPA) with other countries. Currently, BIPAs are in place with 46 countries and another 11 are in the process of ratification. India is also a member of the Multilateral Investment Guarantee Agency (MIGA). For settlement of investment disputes, India, though not a signatory to the International Centre for Settlement of Investment Disputes (ICSID) convention, does use the additional facility available for non-signatory states for settlement of Investor-State disputes. Nevertheless India does subscribe to the Arbitration Rules of the UN Commission on International Trade Law (UNCITRAL) and has incorporated the spirit of the same in its Arbitration Law.

India's policy governing overseas direct investment (ODI) has also been liberalized since the early 1990s. The Guidelines for Indian Joint Ventures and Wholly Owned Subsidiaries Abroad now provide for the automatic approval of outward FDI proposals up to a limit expanded gradually from $2 million in 1992 to $100 million in July 2002. In January 2004, the limit of

$100 million was removed and Indian enterprises are now permitted to invest abroad up to 100 percent of their net worth on an automatic basis (Swaran Singh, 2005a: 39).

Indian companies have been investing capital in a rising number of projects over the past few years with actual investments exceeding one billion dollars annually. The manufacturing sector accounts for nearly 55 percent of cumulative Indian outward direct investments with about 40 percent in services. Major areas of their operation are in pharmaceuticals, metal products, auto components, edible oil processing, fertilizers and chemicals, oil exploration and software services.

The nature of the Sino-Indian economic relationship

India's new Congress government under PM Manmohan Singh is seen in many circles to be a positive force for economic reform. PM Singh is one of the primary architects of India's current phase of economic reforms and opening up. As the Finance Minister to PM Narasimharao in the early 1990s, Singh was the brains behind that government's New Economic Policy and structural adjustments. Since writing his PhD thesis at the University of Cambridge on the benefits of international trade for China, Dr Singh has advocated liberalizing India's economy.

China's leader, Hu Jintao is also considered a champion of economic liberalization. Within China, the CCP leadership under Hu has been especially accommodating towards the entrepreneurial class and private sector. Hu has also continued to emphasize the development of China's western regions, including a greater opening up of Tibet. In China, there has also been a recent shift of focus from the manufacturing to the service sector (which will prove profitable in the long run when a skilled workforce is assembled). The primary strength of the current Chinese leadership lies in its stability. This is because very few people doubt that Hu Jintao should be at the helm of China's continued modernization (Swaran Singh, 2005b).

The rate at which Sino-Indian economic ties have been expanding is impressive—for instance, from 1999 to 2004 bilateral trade rose from $1.9 billion to $13 billion. In aggregate terms, however, Sino-Indian trade remains low as a percentage of total Chinese and Indian trade (1 percent and 5 percent respectively). Nonetheless, Sino-Indian trade has grown rapidly in the past few years. With both India and China, pledging to eventually bring trade to $100 billion, there is no reason to expect that this goal cannot be reached given the current trends in Sino-Indian trade growth. As both India and China continue to modernize their ports and build basic infrastructure, the possibility for increasing trade remain substantial.

The trade projections of $30 billion by 2010 might indeed have been overly conservative. By the end of 2005, Sino-Indian bilateral trade stood at $18.7 billion, up 37.4 percent from the previous year, representing an import and export increase of 50.5 percent and 27.2 percent respectively (Xu, 2006).

More recent projections see Sino-Indian trade reaching the $100 billion mark by 2010, with some estimates as high as $450 billion (Dawar, 2005). Correspondingly, as this chapter will try to demonstrate, it is not unreasonable to suggest that there is an emerging economic interdependence between China and India and that the Sino-Indian economic relationship has the potential to transform relations from a framework of rivalry and conflict to cooperation.

It is this prospect for Sino-Indian economic engagement that will be examined next. However, before the points of synergy (and their consequences) between the Chinese and Indian economies are discussed, it will be necessary to analyze the precise nature of the current Sino-Indian economic relationship. First the institutional dynamics of Sino-Indian bilateral trade and economic ties will be examined. Thereafter Sino-Indian trade in goods, Sino-Indian trade in services and Sino-Indian bilateral investments will be analyzed.

The institutional dynamics of Sino-Indian trade and economic ties

There has been an evolving institutional framework that has continued to structure Sino-Indian trade and investment relations. The major pillars of the institutional framework are the Ministerial level India-China Joint Group on Economic Relations and Trade, Science and Technology; at the Secretary level, the Joint Study Group (JSG, which was set up during Vajpayee's 2003 visit to China) and at the Joint Secretary level, the Joint Working Group (JWG). The JSG was established in 1988 during PM Rajiv Gandhi's visit to China and has met a total of six times. However, it is the Joint Working Group (JWG) for promoting mutual trade and commerce (established in 1984) that does much of the "hands on work". Since a mechanism for the group was created at the Joint Secretary level in February 2003, it has been mandated to discuss wide-ranging trade-related issues. The JWG, which meets annually, has been the general forum where trade is coordinated between India and China. The JWG on trade and commerce is also supported by a Joint Business Council that represents the business interests of the non-state sector in both India and China.

Since Vajpayee's June 2003 visit to China, the JSG was set up by both sides

> to examine the potential complementarities between the two countries in expanded trade and economic cooperation. The JSG would also draw up a programme for the development of India-China trade and economic cooperation for the next five years, aimed at encouraging greater cooperation between the business communities of both sides.
>
> (Kwatra, 2005: 239)

Another major institutional arrangement that India and China have come to terms with includes a trade agreement on the avoidance of double taxation between the two countries. Finalized in 1996, these arrangements put in place: (1) double taxation avoidance mechanisms; (2) provision of Most-Favored Nation (MFN) status to one another's sea-borne trade commodities; and (3) combating the smuggling of narcotics and arms.

More recently, India and China have commenced a dialogue on the possibility of establishing a bilateral free trade agreement (FTA). This was first discussed during bilateral meetings on 21–22 March 2004, in Beijing. The meeting was co-chaired by the Reserve Bank of India's Deputy Governor, Rakesh Mohan and China's Vice-Minister of Commerce, An Min. It sought to produce a clear schedule/timetable and guideline for the feasible areas of economic cooperation between India and China. Although there remains considerable skepticism in some circles about the viability of a Sino-India FTA in the short term, there are some positive indicators pointing in the opposite direction ("Likely Sino-Indian FTA . . .," 2004: 1).

First, the rapidly expanding Sino-Indian trade relationship has actually prompted experts on both sides to consider the practicality of an FTA and expanding mutual trade and investments. This is especially significant in light of the unresolved border issue and great power suspicions. Second, India's declining resistance to low-cost Chinese goods has been received well in Beijing and has caused many to push ahead with the free trade line of reasoning. Finally, China appears to conceive of FTAs as the next logical step in the evolution of its trading relationships. For instance, China already signed an agreement with ASEAN in November 2002 towards creating a free-trade zone by 2010, which would represent the world's largest FTA (with over 1.7 billion residents and over 2 trillion in trade per year). India too has signed a similar agreement with ASEAN in 2004 that aims to create a FTA of this nature by 2012 (Suraynarayana, 2003: 11).

Thus, as Sino-Indian trade has grown in the past few years, the necessity of institutional coordination has become more apparent. This has led to creation of the JSG and an increase in the role played by the JWG. The institutional engagement between China and India provides a focal point for the coordination of economic policy and will help towards building mutual trust. For functionalists, there is an expectation that as institutional mechanisms appear in coordinating trade, there will be more structural pressure to continue coordinating policy. In the case of European integration the origins of the European Economic Community were traced to the European Coal and Steel Community. As Sino-Indian trade continues to expand and reaches the projected $30 billion, the functional pressure to coordinate economic policy can also be expected to grow.

Sino-Indian trade in goods

Trade between India and China has favored China from 1998–1999 to 2003–2004. In 2003–2004 for instance, India had a trade deficit of over one billion dollars with China. In terms of both volume and percentage growth,

Sino-Indian trade continues to expand. In 2003–2004 for instance, Sino-Indian bilateral trade increased over 45 percent.

The changing nature of Sino-Indian trade relations

India's export basket to China has been traditionally dominated by primary and resource based products. This includes iron ore and primary and semi-finished iron and steel products as well as plastics and chemicals. Chinese exports to India, though more diversified, including resource-based manu-factured items and low-medium level technology products also have remained very basic in nature. Thus, many have characterized the nature of the Sino-Indian trade relationship as "superficial" (Bhalla, 2005; Nairayan, 2005). However, the trade relationship is now showing signs of diversification. Exports of auto components, pharmaceuticals and machinery items, for instance, have been increasing in the past few years. In fact, this product group as a whole has registered growth of over 100 percent between 2002–2003 and 2003–2004.

Major exports from India to China

As noted above, iron ore and primary and semi-finished iron and steel in addition to machinery and instruments, plastic and linoleum products, pro-cessed minerals and cotton yarn constitute the major export items to China from India. These products have registered significant growth between 2002–2003 and 2003–2004. Iron ore, machinery and instruments, petroleum prod-ucts, non-ferrous metals and iron and steel bar/ore have registered a growth of over 100 percent from 2002–2003 to 2003–2004. The share of primary and semi-finished iron and steel, processed minerals and cotton yarn, however, has declined in total exports from India to China. Iron ore and iron and steel accounted for the predominant share (about 47 percent) of the total exports. Exports of other ores and minerals, marine products, inorganic/organic/agro chemicals registered a decline, both in terms of percentage growth and as share of total exports from India to China in this period. According to the Chinese statistics, mineral ores always have had a predominant status in India's exports to China. The percentage of ores, however, has declined from 38.4 percent in 1995 to 31.5 percent in 2003. The percentage of two primary products of cotton, pelts and leather has also declined by a large margin. In the same period, the percentage of manufacturing products has consider-ably increased. The percentage of iron and steel rose by large margin from 4.4 percent to 25.5 percent, plastics and plastic products from 4.7 percent to 7.7 percent, and machinery equipments begin to rank among the top ten products in terms of total export volume recently. The percentage of organic and inorganic chemical products has remained around 10 percent in total.

Major exports from China to India

Electronic goods and organic chemicals comprise a major proportion (nearly 46 percent) of China's exports to India. India's top ten imports from China in 2003–2004 have experienced growth. Items such as silk yarn and fabrics, machinery and electronic goods, inorganic chemicals have registered an increase in growth by over 50 percent with silk yarn and fabrics having registered the maximum growth in this period. According to Chinese data, compared with the commodity structure of China's exports to India in 1995, electric machinery, electronic and audiovideo equipment has registered a sharp increase from 6 percent to 20 percent and, this has become the largest export category from China to India. The percentages of textiles, chemical fibers, optical photographing and medical equipment as well as iron and steel products have also increased significantly, ranking among the top ten products in terms of export volume recently. The percentages of mineral fuels and silk have fallen markedly from 14.1 percent and 12.8 percent to 7.1 percent and 6.8 percent respectively.

Sino-Indian trade in services

The services sector accounts for a considerable share of the GDP in both India (more than 50 percent) and China (more than 30 percent). However, the importance of the service sector in India's economy has increased more rapidly than that in China's economy. Between 1995 and 2002, the contribution of services in India's GDP increased from 43.6 to 50.7 percent and that for China from 30.7 to 33.5 percent (World Bank, 2004). During the same period, India's trade in services as a percentage of its total trade increased from 19.8 to 27 percent and that for China declined marginally from 15.7 to 12.4 percent. In absolute terms, China's export and import of services exceeded that of India's and is increasing. Therefore, the decreasing proportion reflects a much faster growth of China's trade in goods. India and China's ranking among WTO member countries in export and import of commercial services has improved significantly between 1995 and 2003. In 1995, India ranked thirty-fourth and twenty-eighth in services exports and imports, which improved to twenty-first for both exports and imports in 2003. Similarly, in 1995, China ranked sixteenth and twelfth among WTO member countries in exports and imports of services, but had the ninth and eighth positions respectively in 2003. The Revealed Comparative Indices (RCAs) in three broad service sectors—transport, travel and other services, based on IMF Balance of Payment Statistics—indicate that China has a comparative advantage in travel services while India has comparative advantage in other services, including the export of software and other IT-enabled services. Thus, there is potential for enhancing trade in services between the two countries (*Report of the India-China . . .*, 2004).

The current state of Sino-Indian bilateral trade in services

The scale of India-China bilateral investments in the services sector is not very large. Currently, India's investment projects in China exceed China's in India. The list of Indian companies that have a presence, or have plans for establishing a presence, in China, shows the service sectors where India has a bilateral trade interest. Similarly, the Chinese companies working in India, or planning to set up operations show the specific areas of trade interest to China. India's investment in the services sector is focused on IT training, software solutions and higher education, pharmacy, banking and trade, etc. For example, APTECH and NIIT, two IT training and education enterprises of India, have set up over 250 franchises in China; State Bank of India, Bank of India, Punjab National Bank, Bank of Baroda and ICICI Bank have set up representative offices in China; the top software producers and exporters of India including Infosys Technologies, Tata Consultancy Services, have set up their offices and R&D centers in China (Hua, 2005; Kwatra, 2005).

China's investments in India's services sector are mainly in trade and IT-related Research and Development (R&D). For instance, China National Machinery and Equipment Import and Export Corporation, and China Metallurgical Import and Export Corporation have set up their representative offices in India; Huawei Technologies has established its software R&D center in India (Mitra and Roy, 2005).

Sino-Indian bilateral investment

Indian investments in China

The presence of Indian companies in China has also increased substantially, especially in sectors such as iron and steel, textiles, chemicals, automobile components, and pharmaceuticals. Indian companies in China are active in services, like restaurants, entertainment, culture and banking (Mitra and Roy, 2005; Nagesh Kumar, 2005).

According to the Indian Ministry of Finance, total Indian investments approved by the Government over 1996–2004 (June) in China amount to US $96.5 million. According to the Chinese Ministry of Commerce, India had invested in 101 projects in China by the end of 2003 and the actual investment was US $79.1 million. In 2003, 30 new projects involving about US $15.9 million were undertaken (Mitra and Roy, 2005). Among the Indian companies that have set up joint ventures or subsidiaries include pharmaceuticals companies like Ranbaxy, Aurobindo Pharmaceuticals, Dr. Reddy's Laboratories, and IT software companies like Aptech, NIIT, Tata Consultancy Services, Infosys. In the manufacturing sector, Sundram Fasteners Ltd. (for high tensile fasteners), and Aditya Birla Group (for carbon black production) have also set up operations in China (Hua, 2005; Mitra and Roy, 2005).

Many others have opened trade/representative offices in China and might deepen their presence in future.

Chinese investments in India

China is also burgeoning as an important source of FDI in Asia as both state-owned and private Chinese companies are starting to invest abroad. According to statistics released by the Ministry of Commerce, China, Chinese companies invested $2.7 billion abroad in 2002. According to the Ministry of Commerce and Industry, Government of India, during the period January 1991 to March 2004, India approved Chinese FDI of US$ 231.6 million. The approved investments, however, have been slow in materializing as actual inflow has been only to the order of US$ 0.63 million (*Report of the India-China . . .*, 2004: 20). According to the statistics of the Chinese Ministry of Commerce, the total of Chinese investments in India up until 2003 was only about US$ 20.6 million and covered 97 Chinese proposals for foreign collaborations mainly in the telecom, metallurgical, transportation, electrical equipment and financial sectors. Chinese sources suggest that the official figures might underestimate the actual investment, as some Chinese companies tend to invest before they declare their investment to the government. Although there may be discrepancies between Chinese and Indian sources on the inflow of FDI it is nonetheless clear that the existing bilateral investment flows between the two countries hardly represent the potential and synergies that exist between the two large and dynamic economies.[2]

Trade and investment-related linkages

In addition to investment, the exchange of business delegations has increased rapidly between the two states. For instance, in the first half of 2004, more than 60 business delegations were exchanged (Kwatra, 2005: 253; Siddharthan, 2005). These include sector-specific delegations, governmental and semi-governmental delegations, high-level business exchanges and from the Chinese side, tours by provincial representatives of India's IT sector.

Another mode of business exchange between India and China includes the growing number of exhibitions by businesses in both countries. These have included exhibitions in fields such as cotton yarn, processing machinery, chemicals, agricultural products and plastic polymers. Close to 4,000 Indians also participated in the bi-annual Canton fair in Gaungzhou (in South China). China too has increased its participation in Indian exhibitions. For instance, in 2003, China was a partner country in the India Engineering Trade Fair and over 70 Chinese companies participated in the India International Trade Fair (IITF). In 2004, over 200 Chinese companies participated in the IITF and in August 2004, a 100-member Chinese business delegation toured Indian industries in Delhi, Calcutta and Bangalore (Kwatra, 2005: 254). India and China have also organized country-specific shows, for instance, the Confederation of Indian Industries "Made in India" show in Beijing in October 2003 (with over 100 companies participating) and the Guangdong CCPIT's "Made in Guangdong" show in Mumbai in March 2004.

The points of synergy and potential for expansion

As noted earlier, both India and China have to make efforts at diversifying their existing bilateral trade basket which is only currently limited to 20–25 categories. The fact that bilateral trade, particularly Indian exports, is dominated by iron ore exports raises overall doubts about the sustainability of the current high rate of and volume of bilateral trade and growth. In short, there needs to be a move away from dependence on exports of raw materials towards an increase in the share of manufacturing and low, medium and high technology items.

On the reverse side of the coin, though, the potential for the expansion of Sino-Indian trade remains quite significant. The share of bilateral trade in the total trade between India and China remains rather insignificant. For instance, trade between India and China accounted for 5 percent of India's total trade in 2003–2004 and in the same year India's exports to China were three billion dollars while imports were four billion dollars. Overall, exports to China account for only 5 percent of India's total exports and less than 1 percent of China's total imports while Chinese exports account for 5 percent of India's total imports and less than 1 percent of China's total export volume (*Report of the India-China* . . ., 2004). The fact that bilateral trade between India and China is increasing and that trade shares remain relatively small does indicate the potential for significant expansion between the two states. This is further buttressed by trends in total external trade for both states. China's total trade aggregated to $851.21 billion by the end of 2003 (in 2005, closing at $1.4 trillion; "China 2005 Total Trade . . .," 2006), an increase of 37.1 percent over the previous year and between the same period, India registered a growth of 22.3 percent in total trade (*Report of the India-China* . . ., 2004). Coupled with continued high economic growth in both states, the geographical proximity of both India and China, it is clear that there is definite room to intensify economic interaction.

Utilizing the index of revealed comparative advantage, the commodities where India has a comparative advantage in the world market can be identified. Coupled with a list of commodities that are already imported by China from other developing countries, it is possible to project commodity categories of potential export (Kwatra, 2005: Annex-I, 269–270). The areas where efforts could be made to bolster trade include: (1) Pharmaceuticals; (2) Auto-components (this would be intra-industry trade as China is also strong in this sector); (3) Dairy Industry (skimmed milk powder, whey protein concentrate, processed cheese, dairy equipment and dairy husbandry practices); (4) Agricultural products; (5) Machinery and machine tools; (6) Organic and inorganic chemicals.

To discuss a few of these sectors, India, in agricultural terms, is a net exporter of food grains (namely, rice and wheat). India has been fairly successful in developing an elaborate network of grain reserves as well as a system of procurement and distribution. India's farming practices are becoming increasingly mechanized as well. China has also developed a system of "grain security" that, in addition to food grains, also produces sugar and many oilseeds (though the emphasis is again shifting to grain production). In the agricultural field there are many opportunities for cooperation. There are complementarities for many of the oilseeds (such as sesame seeds and groundnut oil) and solvent extracts (soybean and rapeseed). Furthermore, the Chinese have certain strengths in the field of productivity of agricultural crops, including rice and processing of fruits and vegetables, where cooperation is viable (Kwatra, 2005: 263). Both countries could also benefit from sharing experiences about farming practices, rural development and agricultural modernization in general.

In the dairy industry, India is the world's largest producer of milk. India has moved successfully towards cost reduction and technological upgrade in the dairy industry. On the other hand, China has traditionally been a non-milk-drinking society. However, dairy consumption is significantly rising in China, especially in more urban areas. Domestic milk consumption is rising by more than 20 percent annually and although China has over 1600 dairy companies, most do not have their own herds and lack technical expertise. India could play a major role in the development of the Chinese dairy industry and in the supply of dairy products (ibid.: 264).

Following the 2003 Bangkok Agreement, both India and China have made improvements, first, on extending tariff concessions and, second, on reducing the level of non-tariff barriers in place. In the agreement, both countries agreed to provide each other with more preferential customs tariff rate treatments than even for the Most Favored Nations. In accordance with the agreement, China would offer India a List of Tariff Reductions for 217 items with an average preferential margin of 13.5 percent. India also reciprocated with a list of 188 items covering a wide range of categories (*Report of the India-China . . .*, 2004; Hua, 2005).

There are also additional opportunities in the IT sector. There are complementarities in hardware (China) and software (India). Even in the software industries of both countries, China's predominant focus is on products, whereas India has focused on software solutions and contract services. There is great potential in the Chinese market, whose scale is estimated to increase from $2 billion to $6 billion by 2007. China could easily become one of the major importers of India's software and software processing technologies (Dutta, 2005). India could export software installation technologies to China's hardware manufacturers while China could provide hardware to India for its software development. In terms of IT training and education, India is also advanced and both the 2008 Beijing Olympics and the 2010 Shanghai World Expo afford excellent opportunities of coordination in the information technology sector (Swaran Singh, 2005b).

In turn, as India continues to improve its infrastructure, many contractual opportunities are opening up for Chinese construction and engineering firms, especially in the areas of Chinese expertise (electric power and highways).

Additional improvements in facilitating trade are also desirable. Customs valuation, increased efficiency of handling at ports could be improved greatly between the two states (as more than 90 percent of trade between the two states is done through ports). Although both states are currently in the process of port modernization (ports such as Shanghai and Shenzhen have already attained "hub" status), continued improvements in transportation services are necessary to bolster growth in bilateral trade (Bhalla, 2005). The current Customs Cooperation Agreement under consideration would be an important step in the right direction. Second, the harmonization of technical standards in identified areas (such as agriculture) would greatly enhance the flow of trade and cut back disputes emerging from a lack of understanding of each other's technical standards. Finally growing visibility in terms of increased shipping and air links will also help expand trade. In 1996, India and China signed an agreement on cooperation in maritime transport services that aimed at developing and sustaining an effective working relationship between the concerned authorities of the two countries. The agreement provided that each country would assist the other's vessels. More recently the India-Far East Express (INDFEX) Consortium, consisting of the Shipping Corporation of India Ltd, Mumbai, the Dongnama Shipping Company Ltd., Seoul, the Kawasaki Kisen Kaisha Ltd., Tokyo, and the Pacific International Line Ltd., Singapore, have already commissioned INDFEX1 and INDFEX2 direct mainline (large vessels plying long distances) container services linking China and India (Kwatra, 2005: 261).

In terms of air linkages, the current scheduled frequency of flights between India and China is four flights a week, two by China Eastern Airlines and two by Air India. Currently proposals are being discussed to expand the number of flights to seven per week on each side and to put in place direct flights (as Beijing to Delhi is via Shanghai and Delhi to Beijing via Bangkok).

There is also significant room for expansion in tourism. In 2001, China was the largest exporter and importer of travel services among the developing countries and India ranked twelfth. The level of bilateral tourism between the two states, however, remains quite limited. Only 15,422 Chinese traveled to India in 2002 and 159,361 Indians to China in the same year (GOI, 2003). Both of these figures constitute less than 1 percent of each country's total inflow of tourists. Recently, India has been granted "Approved Destination Status" in China for self-paid tourists. Correspondingly, the Ministry of Tourism of India has adopted many measures to facilitate Chinese tourists. As economic relations continue to grow between China and India, this could be one of the areas of the greatest growth in the years to come.

Finally, there is also significant room for cooperation and expansion in the health services sector. In September 1994, an agreement was reached between India and China on cooperation in health and medicine. The agreement involved the set-up of a working group to support collaboration in traditional medicine including yoga and acupuncture, pharmacology and pharmaceuticals, infectious disease, maternal and child healthcare and tropical medicine. Training programs for doctors and the exchange of scientific information and research were also covered in the agreement. More recently, in November 2003, the Indian government officially recognized acupuncture and its various branches (such as acupressure and reflexology) as legitimate medical practice. The demand for these services has been growing in India in the past few years and offers possibilities for cooperation with Chinese specialists. Conversely, yoga and ayurveda are in great demand in China. India is increasingly emerging as a healthcare hub in Asia and many Indian hospitals have gained worldwide credibility and recognition. The cost of medical treatment in India remains only one-fifth of that in other developed countries. In short, India could provide essential medical training to Chinese students to cope with China's growing medical needs (*Report of the India-China . . .*, 2004: 40).

Intra-industry trade possibilities

India and China both benefit from a surplus of low-cost labor. Exports of labor-intensive products are growing rapidly in both countries and undoubtedly, India and China are bound to compete in some areas. However, while it is clear that China has clear comparative advantages in labor-intensive mass-produced goods, India has an ability to competitively produce differentiated niche products like handicrafts, handmade carpets, and so forth. In this sense, there is room for intra-industry trade between India and China.

Second, the nature of economic globalization and patterns of international trade and investment (which have extended production chains beyond national boundaries) afford opportunities for intra-industry trade. So although India and China have comparative advantages in similar sectors such as chemicals, processed metals and alloys, machinery and equipment and textiles, there is room for developing comparative advantages within different sub-sectors and products (and thus intra-industry trade). A prime example, for instance, is how competition between India and China in textile exports has forced Chinese enterprises into the manufacturing and export of garments after importing textile materials from India. Competition can thus be converted into opportunities for mutual benefit. If the economic experiences of the European Union (EU) and the United States are analyzed, it is also clear that states with similar economic structures and factor endowments can have large-scale trade with one another (Gros and Thygesen, 1998: 270; Welfens, 1997: 197–198). Similar countries in terms of per capita income have intensive horizontal intra-industry bilateral trade. In the United States and the EU, for instance, almost 60 percent of trade is intra-industry. The increasing level of per capita incomes between India and China (which is bound to increase the demand for variety and the production of differentiated goods) therefore leads to the expectation that the extent of intra-industry trade between India and China will likely grow (*Report of the India-China . . .*, 2004: 40).

Conclusion

Sino-Indian trade has grown rapidly in the past few years and is being increasingly structured institutionally by the JWG and JSG. Though bilateral investment between India and China remains quite low, there appears to be growing interest among Indian and Chinese enterprises to do business with each other. Although Sino-Indian trade remains low as a percentage of total Chinese and Indian trade, rather than indicating that China and India are poised for competition and conflict, for economists these small percentages indicate the huge potential for expanding trade. As the next two chapters will demonstrate, there is a growing understanding between China and India that seeks to realize the full potential of the Sino-Indian relationship. In short, although there is no overwhelming relationship of complex ("vulnerability") interdependence between India and China (in the Keohane and Nye, 1977, sense), the analysis in this chapter has tried to show that India and China show signs that they have embarked on this path. The Sino-Indian trade relationship is only in its infancy and has only gained a footing in the past five years. There are indications, however, that a relationship of economic interdependence is emerging and can serve as a mitigating factor in the Sino-Indian relationship. Sino-Indian trade has taken on important institutional dynamics, and total trade, including intra-industry, trade continues to grow impressively every year and every quarter. Both India and China, through the JEG, JWG and JSG dialogue, realize where trade can be expanded and what needs to be done to get there (*Report of the India-China . . .*, 2004).

Premier Wen Jiabao's recent visit to the Indian Silicon Valley exemplified the emerging interest shared by both sides to continue constructive economic engagement. As Wen remarked, "the two countries of China and India are not rivals in competition, but friends" (*Renmin Ribao* 2005). As Subramanian Ramadorai, the chief executive of Tata Consultancy Services, one of the largest software consultancy services in Asia noted, "The promise for bilateral relations made by the Chinese premier, will serve as a bridge for bilateral trade between the two countries" (ibid.).

4 China's and India's energy policies

India's energy security policy

According to Daniel Yergin (1988: 11), energy security "is to assure adequate, reliable supplies of energy at reasonable prices and in ways that do not jeopardize major national values and objectives" (quoted in Downs, 2004: 22–23). The national values and objectives emphasized in the traditional study of energy security are state sovereignty and the proper functioning of the economy. As Erica Downs has noted, "Traditional thinking on energy security is state-centric, supply-side biased, overwhelmingly focused on oil and tends to equate security with self-sufficiency" (Downs: 2004: 23; also Fried and Trezise, 1993). As it will be seen, mainstream thinking in India and also China is characteristic of such a calculation.

India's rapid economic rise in the 1990s coincided with a parallel rise in energy consumption. In an effort to reassess India's energy consumption patterns and its future course, the government issued its report, *Hydro Carbon Vision 2025* in 1999 (GOI, 1999b). The document highlights the importance of increasing domestic production of energy and prescribes a regime of deregulation, with the active participation of the private sector (both national and foreign). As Muni and Pant (2005: 13–14) note, currently in India, "there is an acute realization that the Indian economy will increasingly rely on oil and gas imports and will be susceptible to fluctuations in the international energy situation" (see also Chowdhury, 1998; MacDonald and Wimbush, 2000). The recently released *Vision 2025* document thus buttresses the need for a coherent and enduring foreign energy security policy that secures energy imports at sustainable prices and at regular flows. Since price fluctuations or disruptions in the flow of energy resources naturally threaten economic growth, energy policy is inherently linked to both politics and the security domain.

For India, hydrocarbons comprise roughly 42 percent of India's commercial energy consumption (Muni and Pant, 2005: 14). The transportation and manufacturing industries are especially reliant on oil and gas and it is estimated that their share in the total energy supply of India will be 45 percent by 2025 (oil 25 percent and gas 20 percent). Overall, the demand for crude oil and petroleum products is expected to reach 190 million tons by 2012 and 364 million tons by 2025.[1] As India's demands for primary fuel are expected to continue to soar in the coming years, its own domestic production of oil will continue to decline. Production has been stagnating at around 33 million tons per year of late. As Muni and Pant (ibid.: 14–15) note, "It is estimated that demand will grow at the rate of six-to-seven per cent per annum with a corresponding rate of zero per cent growth in the production of oil and gas." Thus, as noted, above, it is expected that by 2015, India will import 75–80 percent of its oil from abroad in 1991–1992, India imported only 50 percent of its oil. "Indian Oil Production . . .," 2002). According to recent estimates, the quantitative volume of crude oil will triple from 2.13 to 7.3 million b/d from 2002 to 2025 ("Tackling Import . . .," 2002: 18). The Indian economy is therefore projected to become increasingly sensitive and vulnerable to the international oil market.

Indian hydrocarbon resources have been estimated at 29 billion tons but only 6.8 million tons of this have been upgraded to in-place reserves. Overall the hydrocarbon recovery rate in India is quite low at 28 percent compared to the world average of 40 percent. India has thus far derived its hydrocarbon production from 6 out of 26 sedimentary basins, covering a 3.14 million sq km area. What this means is that less than 35 percent of the sedimentary basin area in India has actually been explored (Muni and Pant, 2005: 16). The Indian government, realizing both the significance of enhancing the recovery rate and in encouraging further hydrocarbon exploration, has initiated a new exploration and licensing policy that seeks the support of the Indian private sector and foreign multinationals.

Overall, 30 different countries supply India with petroleum crude products. However, the proportions supplied to India between these various countries are highly skewed. Five countries, namely, Nigeria, Saudi Arabia, United Arab Emirates (UAE), Kuwait and Iran account for nearly 80 percent of India's total oil imports. Many analysts agree that such a high concentration for a country that is importing 70 percent of its oil needs is not desirable (ibid.: 18). Consequently India has attempted to address the risks associated with the supply of oil. It is important to note that the supply-side risks have more to do with unfortunate geography (such as narrow passages and choke points), political turmoil and inadequate pipeline infrastructure than with global hydrocarbon reserves (which are fairly large). The disintegration of the former Soviet Union and the emergence of the Central Asian republics seriously affected oil supplies all over the world. In addition, Central Asian hydrocarbon supplies are often hostage to "pipeline politics" (Forsythe, 1996; Ruseckas, 1998; Gidadhubli, 1999). The 1980–1988 Iran-Iraq War, the 1990 Gulf War and the more recent US-British led invasion of Iraq in 2003 also had a major impact on world oil prices. In fact, crude oil and natural prices have hit record highs in the past few years. The proximity of the Persian Gulf to India continues to play a large role in explaining why that region is the main supplier of oil to India.

The Indian government hopes that successful domestic exploration will alter the estimated energy consumption projections. For instance, in October 2002, the Reliance Group made a large gas find off the Vishakhapatnam coast:

> The . . . volume of natural gas is in excess of 7 trillion cubic feet, equivalent to about 1.2 billion barrels or 165 million tons of crude oil. Based on the recoverable reserves of over 5 trillion cubic feet, the gas availability to consumers in the country would increase by almost 60 per cent . . . It has been widely acknowledged by all media and analyst reports that this large gas find would completely change the Basic Energy Equation in India in the coming years.
>
> (Reliance Energy Research Group, 2002: 266)

By and large, India is emerging as a major player in the global oil and gas market (perhaps ranking only behind China). Underscored by the Indian government's New Exploration Licensing Policy (NELP), many international oil companies have taken note and are starting to invest in oil and gas exploration in India. NELP I and II, as Muni and Pant note, "received extremely good responses and both domestic as well as international players are aggressively in the fray for the exploration of potential oil and gas fields (2005: 22). Under NELP II alone, the Indian government awarded 100 contracts in 74 separate exploration blocks. The recently launched NELP IV in May 2003 opened by placing 24 oil blocks for bidding and has also proved to be a major success (ibid.: 22). The Indian government is encouraged by some of the preliminary findings such as the large deepwater gas discoveries made in the Krishna-Godavari basin (*Hindustan Times*, 2003). Domestic oil giants such as the state-owned Oil and Natural Gas Corporation (ONGC), are also actively involved in domestic exploration projects to greatly enhance oil and gas reserves. ONGC expects to double its reserves from the current 6 billion tons oil equivalent to 12 billion tons oil equivalent.

India's new energy policy also seeks to push Indian companies to become more active in its overseas interactions and to reach agreements with other companies in both exploration and sourcing. Correspondingly, the major Indian oil companies, ONGC, Indian Oil Corporation (IOC) and the Gas Authority of India Ltd (GAIL) have reached an agreement to work as a consortium for all international oil and gas exploration and production, transportation and marketing projects overseas. In a deal currently in the works with Daewoo of South Korea to source gas from Myanmar, ONGC will concentrate on oil and gas exploration, IOC on marketing the petroleum and GAIL on transporting and marketing the gas. The agreement has already led to the production of an estimated 112–168 million cubic meters of gas in Myanmar (Ranjan, 2004).

India's ONGC has also been expanding its overseas involvement and negotiating partnerships in Russia, Yemen, Tunisia, Sudan and Iran (*Alexander's*

Gas . . ., 2002). India's burgeoning energy relationship with Iran is perceived to be especially promising given the close geographical proximity between the two states and Iran's vast hydrocarbon resources. Recently, India and Iran agreed to a controversial $22 billion pipeline deal much to the displeasure of the United States, that would supply 5 million tons of gas to India per year for 25 years. The pipeline would be 2775 km long and 760 km of it would have to be routed through Pakistan. However, President Prevez Musharraf has publicly commented on being on board with the plan, as Pakistan will gain lucrative transit fees ("Indo-Iran . . .," 2005).[2] ONGC's other high pro-file operations are located in Vietnam, Russia (Sakhalin Island), Malaysia and Kazakhstan. In Vietnam, ONGC has already produced reserves of 58 billion cubic meters and has discovered 485 billion cubic meters of gas in Russia (and 307 million tons of oil): (Ranjan, 2004). India has also signed a natural gas deal with Qatar in 2002 for 25 years involving IOC, GAIL and Bharat Petroleum. India also continues to participate in gas projects such as "Dolphin" in the UAE and continues to explore the possibility of importing gas from Myanmar and Bangladesh (which would be ideal for supplying Calcutta and India's burgeoning eastern coastal regions) (*Alexander's Gas . . .*, 2002).

India's foreign policy objectives in terms of energy policy thus appear to involve: (1) the mobilization of investment to augment domestic production as well as the expansion and diversification of foreign sources of oil and gas supplies; (2) ensuring the future presence of existing oil supplies by consoli-dating energy ties; (3) hedging against the risks of concentration in the external market; (4) evolving strategies to meet the challenges posed by unfolding conflicts in areas where energy is supplied; and (5) ensuring the safe transit of energy resources to India.

Following the terrorist attacks on 11 September 2001 and the subsequent invasion of Afghanistan and Iraq, security objectives have taken on increas-ing importance. The need for a Middle-East/Asian security dialogue on energy security has long been recognized. As the former executive director of the International Energy Association, Robert Priddle (2000) commented, "Asian countries depend on certain shipping routes to import oil from the Middle East, the traffic volume can be expected to increase substantially. Countries in the region certainly need to cooperate to keep these shipping routes safely open." India's key location between the Persian Gulf and East Asia and its growing naval prowess make it a key strategic player in ensuring energy security in the IOR. Many Gulf countries have become increasingly wary of the US presence in the region and many would likely welcome a larger role for India in the IOR, which has the second largest Muslim popula-tion in world. Japan has also expressed a strong desire to engage in a strategic partnership with India. This was one of the key themes of Prime Minister Junichiro Koizumi's official visit to India in 2005. Recently ships from the Japanese and Indian Navy conducted joint naval exercises near Mumbai (Bhatt, 2005).

China's energy security policy

Since 1993, China has been a net importer of oil and is quickly becoming the second largest oil consumer, trailing only the US (Downs, 2004: 21). By 2010, it is estimated that China will be importing about 150 million tons of oil (40–50 percent of its oil requirements) and by 2020 analysts argue that oil imports could surpass 250 million tons, which would place China on par with Japan. Gas consumption is also expected to significantly rise in China, with imports projected to hit 20–30 billion cubic meters by 2010 and 40–60 billion cubic meters by 2020 (see Dannreuther, 2003; Downs, 2000; Gao, 2000).

This is a major problem for China because, much like India, there is a growing oil deficit. For instance, between 1993 and 2002, China's oil consumption increased from 2.9 million b/d to 5.4 million b/d while oil production only increased from 2.9 million b/d to 3.4 million b/d over the same period (British Petroleum, 2003: 6–9). However, despite the growing oil deficit, it is important to realize that China still does and in the future will continue to rely on domestic resources for most of its energy needs. China has vast coal resources and continues to rely on coal as a primary fuel resource. According to the International Energy Agency, coal constituted 69 percent of China's total primary energy demand in 2000 and is expected to decline to only 60 percent by 2030. Oil will most likely remain China's second most important fuel in the near future as its share of the energy mix is projected to increase only slightly from 25 percent to 27 percent from 2000 to 2030. In the same period natural gas is expected to increase from 3 percent to 7 percent and nuclear and hydropower from 2 percent to 6 percent (International Energy Agency, 2002: 258). However, there is increasing international pressure for China to accelerate its shift to oil and gas, which are cleaner burning and less polluting in comparison to coal. Notwithstanding, even at approximately 25 percent of China's overall energy needs, oil and also gas (which China became a net importer of in 2005) and its secure transit to China are of increasing importance.

Overall, China's proven recoverable reserves of oil and gas are fairly modest, totaling just 2 percent and 1 percent of globally proven recoverable reserves (Dannreuther, 2003: 201). The majority of China's oil-bearing sediment basins have been well explored and the largest oil fields have been producing oil for more than 30 years. Although offshore exploration has led to a series of discoveries over the past 20 years, these fields only account for about 10 percent of China's overall oil production. Furthermore, oil produced domestically is more expensive by international standards. "Lifting costs" in China amount to $12 per barrel whereas they are only $2–$3 per barrel in the Middle East (Soligo and Jaffe, 1999, cited in Dannreuther, 2003: 202). However, since natural gas exploration in China only began in the 1990s, there is optimism that domestic production could be greatly enhanced. Forecasts have Chinese natural gas production jumping from 27 billion cubic meters in 2000 to 60–75 billion cubic meters by 2010 and possibly up to

100 billion cubic meters in 2020. Despite the high costs involved in the production and transportation of natural gas from China's remotest regions (Andrews-Speed, 2001), China has forged ahead with plans for domestic production. In March 2000, construction of a west-to-east pipeline from the Tarim basin in Xinjiang to Shanghai began. Now completed, the project demonstrated major strategic commitments on the part of the Chinese to bolster domestic gas production, despite the costs involved.

Nevertheless, the Chinese government has realized that domestic production will not be enough to deal with the rising demand for energy supplies in the years to come. With increasing reliance on outside sources of energy, China recognizes that a sudden rise in energy prices or a disruption in the supply of energy could have detrimental consequences on economic development and thus national security. Such effects may include lower levels of industrial output, decline in investment and balance of payment problems (Geller *et al.*, 1994). Countries such as India and China, which are pursuing policies of rapid economic development, therefore, have to be extremely cautious of energy security and devise policies accordingly. China's energy policies have been primarily state-led (despite recent market-oriented liberalization and accession to the WTO). The Chinese government has been actively involved in pushing for enhanced domestic energy production and in encouraging more overseas energy investments.[3] Though there are many players and lively debate domestically in China influencing energy security policy,[4] the most important agency involved in making energy policy is the State Development Planning Commission (SDPC), renamed the National Development and Reform Commission in March 2003.

The main objectives of China's energy policy include: (1) increasing China's control over its energy supplies and maximizing the domestic output of oil and gas; (2) increasing investment in overseas oil fields and diversifying the sources of oil and gas supply; (3) the construction of a strategic petroleum reserve system and other infrastructure to bring oil and gas more easily to the Chinese market; (4) closing off oil fields in western China for emergency use; and (5) the continued development of Chinese naval forces to protect China's energy supplies (Yan and Yang, 1999; Zhou, 1999). As Dannreuther (2003: 201) notes, "The principal underlying philosophy of . . . [China's] . . . policy is the perceived danger of dependence on international energy markets and the need for the government to direct the flow of investment into projects that reduce this dependence." An equally pressing consideration for the Chinese is the potential danger of a blockade in the Malacca Strait and in the South and East China Seas or disruptions to oil production in the Middle East. The Chinese government, therefore in addition to building naval forces to protect SLOCs, has also expressed great interest in pipeline projects from adjacent Asian countries and continues to push for the diversification of hydrocarbon resources.

In this regard, the major Chinese oil companies, the China National Petrochemical Corporation (Sinopec), the China National Petroleum Corporation

(CNPC) and the China National Offshore Oil Corporation (CNOOC) have been key players in setting the Chinese energy security agenda. As Downs (2004: 25) notes:

> The influence of these companies is a result of both their oil expertise and their political clout, derived from the Chinese government's increasing fiscal dependence on them and from the fact that their top positions are appointed by the Central Committee of the Chinese Communist Party (CCP), which gives them direct access to the Chinese leadership.

The oil companies are unsurprisingly strong advocates of investment in overseas oilfields as such a strategy helps enhance Chinese energy security.

Chinese oil companies became serious about overseas investments in the late 1990s, first marked by CNPC's pledge of $8 billion for oil concessions in Kazakhstan, Venezuela, Iraq and Sudan. China also has ongoing projects in Algeria, Azerbaijan, Indonesia and Peru (Downs, 2004: 34). As Dannreuther (2003: 203) notes, "at the heart of this strategy lies the recognition that China is surrounded by a 'belt' of untapped oil and gas reserves in Russia, Central Asia and the Middle East." In Africa, another major area of concentration for Chinese energy policy, imports have risen from the continent to account for nearly one-fourth of total oil imports to China (Kondapalli, 2005a: 2). As China moves to decrease its dependence on the Persian Gulf states, this figure is expected to rise to one-third by the end of the next decade. China has signed agreements or is negotiating with several African countries including Nigeria, Gabon, the Central African Republic, Congo, Angola, Niger and Chad. Sudan already provides nearly 8 percent of China's total oil imports (Kondapalli, 2005a: 2).[5]

Russian far-east energy resources are perceived to be especially promising in supplying the growing energy demands of the Chinese eastern coast. Several proposals are in the works for the construction of gas pipelines from Irkutsk and Yakutia (in eastern Siberia), from Sakhalin and other regions in Western Siberia. China is also very keen on plans to build a $2.5 billion pipeline from Russian Lake Baikal to its own Daqing oil field (Russia is also contemplating Japanese proposals, Kondapalli, 2005a). A deal for a crude oil pipeline from the Angarsk region of Siberia has already been reached. A long-discussed $3.5 billion pipeline from Kazakhstan thought to be dead because of economic problems was finalized in 2004 (Ottaway and Morgan, 1997: 1; Sisci, 1997; Rashid and Saywell, 1998: 48).

In 2001, Chinese oil companies produced 180,000 b/d of "equity oil" (*fen'e you*) overseas, which comprised approximately 15 percent of oil imports that year (Xu, 2002). Chinese overseas investments, as Downs (2004: 35) has noted, have focused on the purchase of equity positions in previously discovered oil fields. Rather than undergoing risky and costly exploration, the foreign company in these instances comes to an agreement with the domestic company on production sharing where the output is split. Recently, China has adopted this strategy into Western markets as well. CNOOC's aggressive unsolicited $18.5 billion bid for Union Oil Company of California (Unocal) in June 2005, caused a stir in the United States.[6] Though the bid collapsed as Congressional pressure against China mounted, China has been successful in penetrating the large Canadian oil market. CNOOC has made a $2 billion investment in Albertan oil sands projects and in August 2005, bought a controlling stake in PetroKazakhstan for $3.75 billion. In 2005, there were also continuing rumors that China would make a bid for the large Calgary-based Husky Oil (Reynolds, 2005). The North American equity oil markets in comparison to Africa, the Middle East and Latin America, are looking increasingly attractive for China as it searches for politically and economically stable regions to do business.

China has especially taken advantage of the shift in Sino-Soviet relations, from one of confrontation in the mid-1980s and through much of the Cold War to one of accommodation. China has also been strategically proceeding with its "oil diplomacy" in the Middle East. The establishment of foreign relations with many Gulf States and also Israel has been the first step in this process. In its foreign policy push in this region, China has managed to secure long-term oil supply arrangements from Saudi Arabia, Iran, Oman and Yemen (Calabrese, 1998). In 1999, Jiang Zemin made the first official Chinese state visit to Saudi Arabia and declared that the two states had reached a strategic "oil partnership" where Arab companies were encouraged to counter-invest in Chinese refining and marketing sectors (Xu, 2000; Dannreuther, 2003: 203). In October 2004, China signed a mega-deal with Iran for nearly $100 billion with another $50–100 billion option for cooperation in exploring oil and pipeline infrastructure (Kondapalli, 2005b). The deal is similar to one signed with Australia in 2003 for $40 billion. There are also reports that China is increasingly interested in the hydrocarbon reserves of Myanmar as well as Bangladesh.

Converging Sino-Indian energy interests

The possibility of converging energy interests in the IOR in addition to emerging economic interdependence could also bolster Sino-Indian cooperation in the future. Both India and China have already entered into cooperative agreements with Iran's national oil company and some analysts suggest that a cooperative Asian energy framework would be an attractive option for both India and China (Kumar, 2005; Nairayan, 2005; Zhang and Saika, 2005). Central Asia's abundant hydrocarbon resources, second only to the Middle East, could serve as an essential coordinating point between India and China.

Recent energy deals signed by India and China indicate that a cooperative energy framework may indeed be the most attractive option. On 12 January 2006, during the visit by India's Petroleum and Natural Gas Minister Mani Shankar Aiyar to Beijing, an agreement was reached whereby ONGC Videsh Ltd and the China National Petroleum Corp (CNPC) would place joint bids for promising energy projects in other countries. The importance of this deal cannot be understated. As Siddharth Varadarajan (2006) has noted, "India and China have managed to confound analysts around the world by turning their much-vaunted rivalry for the acquisition of oil and gas assets in third countries into a nascent partnership that could alter the basic dynamics of the global energy market." Emerging Sino-Indian energy cooperation could be the beginning of the creation of a broader Asian energy market, with major geopolitical consequences for the United States.

Since the 1973 Arab oil crisis, the international market for hydrocarbons has become tightly regulated. The Organization of Petroleum Exporting Countries (OPEC) represents the major suppliers' cartel and the demand for oil is primarily driven by the Organization for Economic Cooperation and Development (OECD) member-states. As the oil trade is conducted in American dollars, it ensures that most states around the world have large foreign reserves in greenbacks. Control over the oil market by the US and Western Europe is so extensive that Asian countries pay up to $2–3 more per barrel of oil (the so-called "Asian oil premium").[7] As China and India continue to grow and become more dependent on hydrocarbons, the reliance on institutions, trading frameworks and armed forces from outside Asia will become less and less attractive. Iran is close to both India and China and Central Asia has emerged as a major producer of hydrocarbon resources. Traditional oil suppliers in the Middle East also have a lot to gain if an Asian energy market means greater stability and predictability in prices. As one analyst notes:

> Saudi Arabia may like high prices but not prices that are "unreasonably high." It is not a coincidence that the first overseas tour of King Abdullah [in 2006] is to China, India, Pakistan, and Malaysia and that his agenda, at least in Beijing and New Delhi, involves important energy-related initiatives like the proposed oil reserve facility on Hainan island.
>
> (Varadarajan, 2006)

The nucleus of the recent Sino-Indian energy deal is the proposal for ONGC and CNPC to place joint bids for energy projects and oil facilities in third countries. In December 2005, ONGC and CNPC made a joint $537 million bid to buy the al-Furat oilfields in Syria from PetroCanada ("PRC FM Spokesman . . .," 2006). The two oil giants are also currently working on an acquisition in Russia's Udmurtia Republic. Recent cooperation comes following a period of intense competition and bidding wars. For instance, in August 2005, CNPC agreed to pay $4.18 billion for PetroKazakhstan, outbidding ONGC. Both India and China now appear to realize that more can be gained from cooperation than competition in the field of energy. As the Indian Petroleum and Natural Gas Minister Mani Shankar Aiyar commented to Ma Kai, chairman of China's powerful National Development and Reforms Commission, "When companies from the two sides submit a joint bid, no project would be beyond our reach." As Kai continued, "We should go forward together and bid . . . otherwise it is the third party which wins" (Varadarajan, 2006). The joint acquisition of equity oil and gas thus appears to be one fruitful area where China and India will continue to cooperate.

In addition to placing joint bids, there is room for cooperating on techno-logical grounds in the field of energy. The Chinese have pioneered oil recovery technology that helps sustain production at ageing oil fields (such as Dagang and Daqing) for longer periods of time. As Indian oil fields continue to mature and "peak out," such technology would clearly be beneficial. Chinese companies could also lend their expertise in basin evaluation and drilling. In return, Indian companies could offer state-of-the art IT-enabled exploration and production services. There is also room to further integrate energy trans-port mechanisms (including regional pipelines) and the use of backhaul car-goes (in very large crude carriers) to jointly source crude oil from distant destinations such as Venezuela and West Africa (ibid.).

In his address to Chinese energy specialists in Beijing, India's Petroleum and Natural Gas Minister pointed out that the European economic and politi-cal community had its origins in the European Coal and Steel Union and suggested that Asia could follow this path. As Siddharth Varadarajan notes, "With India and China committed to building strategic petroleum reserves, South Korea offering to work on an 'Inter-Asia Oil and Gas Transportation System,' and Iran planning its own hydrocarbon bourse, such an idea is no longer far-fetched" (ibid.). Correspondingly, both China and India have indi-cated that foreign currency reserves need to be diversified. Yen or euro-based trading in energy would be one way to end the US monopoly of the oil market and to undercut the "Asian Oil Premium" ("Playing it Safe . . .," 2006). According to China's Foreign Ministry spokesman Kong Quan, "China hopes to work with its large neighbor India in energy and other fields in a mutually beneficial way and on the basis of equality so as to achieve our common development" ("PRC FM Spokesman . . .," 2006).

Conclusion

Recent Sino-Indian energy cooperation demonstrates that China and India are developing a mutual understanding. Both states recognize that competing for energy resources in the IOR and abroad may not be the Pareto optimal strategy to pursue. Rather, there is much to be gained from a coordinated Sino-Indian and Asian energy policy. As China's and India's economies continue to expand so will their energy demands. Instead of competing for securing energy resources and bidding up acquisitions, both China and India could effectively coordinate policy to lower costs. Moreover, as energy demand continues to rise, the "Asian Oil Premium" will become more and more unacceptable. This could provide further incentives for coordinating Sino-Indian and Asian energy policy. In short, the coordination of energy policy marks a shift from a Pareto suboptimal to Pareto optimal strategy. China's and India's recent energy agreements indicate that they are both willing to cooperate on this issue and that their strategic perceptions cannot be totally characterized in relative gains or neorealist terms. Correspondingly, the next chapter details the positive trends in the Sino-Indian elite dialogue while acknowledging the continuing irritants in the relationship.

5 The positive trends in the Sino-Indian bilateral dialogue

Introduction

There has been a discernible shift in Sino-Indian elite dialogue.[1] Overall, diplomatic exchanges between India and China have taken a friendlier tone and indicate that a mutual understanding is developing between the world's most populous states. The recent success in the Sino-Indian economic relationship has been a key catalyst in stimulating this emerging understanding. For instance, Premier Wen Jiabao made encouraging comments about the burgeoning Sino-Indian relationship at the ASEAN conference in Vientiane (November, 2004). According to Wen, "We are happy about the rapid growth of India's economy and its continuously enhanced influence in the world." Commenting on the border issue, Wen noted that, "We believe that if abiding by the principle of equal consultation, mutual understanding and mutual accommodation, the two sides can find solutions to this issue through sincere negotiations" ("Wen Jiabao . . .," 2004; Li, 2005).

Wen's comments were followed up during his landmark April 2005 visit to India. During the Sino-Indian bilateral talks there was a discernible push to ensure that Asia's future is cooperative in nature. Apart from agreeing to set a target of increasing Sino-Indian bilateral trade, China officially recognized Indian sovereignty over Sikkim. The establishment of a Sino-Indian strategic partnership, including a five-year plan of economic development and the signing of an agreement on guiding principles to solve the Sino-Indian border dispute, marks an important shift in the relationship, according to the PRC (Fang, 2005). The economic focus of the Sino-Indian relationship was made clear by Wen's choice of Bangalore rather than New Delhi for the historic talks. Regarding India's attempt to gain a UN Security Council seat, India and China issued a joint statement noting that China understands and supports India's aspirations to play an active role in the UN and international affairs. According to some reports, India has already received written commitments from Beijing that it will support New Delhi's bid for a permanent seat on the Security Council (and not support Japan).[2]

Growing military and political consensus

In the years leading up to the 2005 Sino-Indian summit, there have also been a series of high-level military exchanges between China and India. In November 2003, General Wu Quanxu, deputy chief of general staff of the PLA met with Lieutenant General Mohinder Singh, commander of the 4th Corps of the Eastern Military Region of the Indian Armed Froces. Wu and Lt. Gen. Singh stressed the importance of improving relations between the two countries and how cooperation was the only way to ensure common prosperity and the fundamental interests of the people of India and China. During the meeting Gen. Wu also gave Lt. Gen. Singh and his delegation a briefing on the modernization of the PLA and emphasized the desirability of increasing military-to-military exchanges (Yuan, 2003). In his diplomatic tour, Lt. General Mohinder Singh also visited Chinese bases in Tibet, the first such visit since the Sino-Indian border war in 1962 ("Indian Army Delegation . . .," 2003). China's Defense Minister Gen Cao Ganchuan reciprocated and visited India in March 2004.

In the same month (November 2003) a three-vessel Indian warship fleet visited Shanghai for five days to conduct joint naval exercises with PLAN. The Indian fleet, commanded by Rear Admiral R.P. Suthan, flag officer commanding the Eastern Fleet of India, led the guided missile destroyer INS *Ranjit*, the guided missile corvette INS *Kulish* and the replenishment tanker INS *Jyoti* in the search and rescue operation with China's East Sea Fleet, commanded by Zhao Guojun ("Indian Warship . . .," 2003).

Thereafter, India's Army Chief General N.C. Vij made a landmark visit to Beijing from 22–29 December 2004. In his meetings with his Chinese counterpart, PLA Chief of Staff General Liang Guanglie, a "consensus" was reached to continue expanding military-to-military ties and in enhancing cooperation in combating non-conventional security threats ("'Consensus' Between . . .," 2004). In a press release issued by the Indian Embassy on General Vij's visit, it was noted that:

> There was consensus on enhancing military exchanges and cooperation at different levels. Both sides also discussed cooperation in facing non-traditional threats, particularly against international terrorism. The visit of the Chief of Army Staff is an important element of the expanding military contacts between our two countries as part of the overall development of bilateral relations. Both sides attached importance to improving relations and more cooperative exchanges between the two militaries. They noted with satisfaction that peace and tranquility continues to be maintained in the border areas.
>
> ("'Consensus' Between . . .," 2004)

While touring PLA facilities in Shanghai, Qingdao (Shangdong province) and Xi'an, General Vij noted that, "trust between the two militaries has deepened in recent years as bilateral cooperation enhanced in all fields." The Chinese Vice President Zeng Qinghong reciprocated such feelings, noting, "China would like to further expand the friendly relations with India and other neighboring countries to achieve common prosperity" ("Sino-Indian Trust . . .," 2004). As Zeng continued, "China supports an even bigger role for India in international and regional cooperation issues" ("'Consensus' Between . . .," 2004).

During Premier Wen Jiabao's visit to India in April 2005, Yashwant Prasad, Deputy Chief of General Staff of the Indian Navy, held productive talks with the Commander of PLAN Zhang Dingfa in Beijing. Zhang noted that the Chinese and Indian Navies continue to strengthen cooperation in the future and hailed the growing exchanges and deepening understanding between India and China ("PRC Navy Commander . . .," 2005). This was followed up with joint Sino-Indian naval exercises in the Indian Ocean on 1 December 2005. The Chinese missile destroyer *Shenzhen* and the supply ship *Weischanhu* joined the Indian frigate *Gomati* and the patrol ship *Sarda* in the northern waters of the Indian Ocean to conduct joint search-and-rescue exercises codenamed "Sino-Indian Friendship 2005" ("China–India Joint Naval . . ." 2005). During the joint exercises the naval ships of both states drilled on signal communication, joining forces in maneuver, maritime air and search operations, formation supply and rescuing damaged ships.

In May 2005, PLA Chief of Staff General Liang Guanglie, Chief of Staff of the Air Force Lieutenant General He Weirong and the Deputy Commander of the Beijing Military Region Lieutenant General Liu Fengjun visited New Delhi to meet with India's Chief of Army Staff, General J.J. Singh, Chief of Naval Staff Admiral Arun Prakash and Chief of Air Staff General S.P. Tyagi (An, 2005). The two sides had in-depth exchanges on regional and international security, national defense and the armed forces and general relations between India and China, including the border dispute. A wide-ranging consensus was reached where both sides expressed the desire and commitment to enhance mutual understanding and trust and to develop friendship.

In an effort to implement the enhanced CBMs agreed upon by Premier Wen Jiabao and PM Manmohan Singh in April 2005, the two sides discussed modalities. Both Indian and Chinese military officials signed a protocol on additional CBMs regarding military matters. Apart from working out simpler details such as expanding the border meeting points and increasing exchanges between military personnel and training institutions, the two militaries reached an agreement to implement the protocol in areas where previously undefined modalities have led to tensions. These include situations where troops come face-to-face in areas of disputed control and military aircraft flying in disputed airzones ("Indian, Chinese Army . . .," 2005).

The Sino-Indian military and political dialogue has continued in 2006 as well. On 20 February 2006, General Zhang Li, deputy chief of general staff of the PLA met with Lieutenant General Arvind Sharma, Commander of the Eastern Command of India in Beijing. According to Zhang Li, the Chinese armed forces are ready to continue deepening Sino-Indian military cooperation and maintain peace and tranquility in the border regions. Lieutenant General Sharma commented on how the Indian armed forces will strengthen exchanges with their Chinese counterparts in the military field and continue to promote the all-round development of ties between the two countries ("Zhang Li Meets . . .," 2006).

The year 2006 may indeed prove to be a milestone year for Sino-Indian relations. On 1 January 2006, Chinese and Indian heads of government met to officially launch the "China–India Friendship Year" ("RMRB Interviews . . .," 2006 and "Chinese, Indian Leaders . . .," 2006"). Chinese President Hu Jintao claimed that China was willing to work with India to further develop friendship and to enhance dialogue, exchange and cooperation at all levels. The Indian President Abdul Kalam reciprocated the good will and said that both sides have decided to establish "a strategic and cooperative partnership oriented towards peace and prosperity, which not only demonstrates the two sides' determination to cooperate but also creates conditions for raising the bilateral relations to new highs" ("RMRB Interviews . . .," 2006). The Sino-Indian Friendship Year has been unveiled as a series of official exchange activities (over 50) that will be spread out through 2006 (one per week). These activities range from political, economic and military exchanges to cultural, scientific and educational exchanges. Both Chinese President Hu Jintao and Indian PM Manmohan Singh have already agreed to invitations to national visits. In this year the seventh meeting of special representatives on the China–India border question will be held and the Nathu La Pass on the China–India border will be reopened. In his meeting with India's Foreign Secretary, Shyam Saran, Chinese State Councilor Tang Jiaxuan said:

> It is in the fundamental interests of both countries to solve the border issue at an early date . . . the announcement of building a strategic and cooperative partnership by both governments indicates that Sino-Indian relations have entered a new phase of development.
>
> ("China, India Hope . . .," 2006)

As China's Ambassador to India noted of the declaration of 2006 as the Sino-Indian Friendship Year, "Last year I was very busy since bilateral exchanges between the two countries were quite frequent. In the new year I will be even busier . . . I hope from now on every year will be China–India Friendship Year" ("RMRB Interviews . . .," 2006).

China and India are also scheduled to continue discussing a Sino-Indian free trade agreement and exchange cultural delegations. Furthermore, Indian and Chinese Defense Ministers are scheduled to meet in 2006. Cultural exchange between frontier defense troops, joint exercises in anti-terrorism and anti-piracy on the sea have also been scheduled (ibid.).

Overall, both India and China are beginning to acknowledge that the prosperity of Indian and Chinese people will be facilitated by Sino-Indian cooperation. The hawkish element long present in military circles in both India and China appears to be giving way to pragmatism and a general desire at the highest levels to develop a strategic Sino-Indian consensus. As India's Defence Minister Pranab Mukherjee recently noted:

> Our [Sino-Indian] security ties have undergone a change, with the resumption of military ties signified by joint exercises, bilateral visits and sharing of information on military matter of joint interest. By institutionalizing the Sino-Indian dialogue at a political level, with regular exchanges between designated interlocutors, the territorial and boundary differences between our two countries are being addressed purposefully.
>
> ("Indian Defense Minister . . .," 2005)

Commenting on the shifting economic dynamics in Asia, India's Foreign Secretary, Shyam Saran, has also noted how the Sino-Indian relationship has shifted away from traditional preconceptions:

> There is a strong consensus in India on improving and developing our relations with China. Together with China, we have taken a number of positive measures to improve the quality of our relations across a wide range of areas, without allowing the existing differences to affect the overall developing or our ties . . . *the theories of "balance of power" or "conflict of interests," in the context of India-China relations [have become] outdated . . . the key to ensuring long-term security and stable equilibrium in Asia lies in the collective ability of Asian countries to build mutual economic stakes in one another.*
>
> ("Cooperation is Key . . .," 2006: emphasis added)

It is therefore hard to deny that positive changes in the Sino-Indian relationship at the elite level are taking place. The diplomatic encounters that top Chinese and Indian political and military officials are having are creating a consensus—namely, that peace and prosperity are the way of the future. The initiation and intensification of high-level political discourse have moved China and India towards having, as Adler and Barnett note, "dependable expectations of peaceful change." As discussed in the previous chapter, the burgeoning economic relationship has been an important catalyst in this process. As the Sino-Indian relationship deepens over the Sino-Indian Friendship Year of 2006, the positive feedback loop will continue to strengthen. As China and India are in the process of reinterpreting their "social realities," they are showing signs indicative of peaceful change.

The SCO and maritime terrorism

The SCO

There may also be incentives for bolstering Sino-Indian cooperation in Central Asia. One of China's main concerns in Central Asia is security. The collapse of the Soviet Union and the emergence of the Central Asian republics created a level of uneasiness in Beijing concerning the security of China's borders. However, the collapse of the USSR also afforded China new strategic opportunities. As Cornell (2004: 170) notes, "The two most significant developments [with the collapse of the Soviet Union] were the removal of control over the region exercised by a hostile power, the USSR: and increasing Chinese access to the natural resources of Central Asia." China has also been sensitive to how other international players, namely the United States, have sought to increase their presence in the region as well. As Cornell (ibid.: 170) continues:

> The increasing activities of the United States and the NATO in Central Asia, including the Partnership for Peace exercises in Kazakhstan in 1997 . . . as well as an increasing realization of a common interest with Moscow to minimize Western influence in Central Asia, led China to take the lead in turning to the Shanghai 5 group.

The Shanghai 5, comprising Russia, Kazakhstan, Kyrgystan, Tajikistan and China was formed in 1996 as the heads of state of these nations met in Shanghai. The Chinese led meetings witnessed the signing of the "Treaty on Deepening Military Trust in Border Regions" and the "Treaty on Reduction of Military Forces in Border Regions." The annual meetings slowly shifted the emphasis from building trust in border regions to expanding mutually beneficial cooperation in trade and economics. On the fifth anniversary of the Shanghai 5 on 15 June 2001, the heads of state of the members agreed to the accession of Uzbekistan as the sixth member of the Shanghai 5 apparatus (Zhang and Saika, 2005: 43). Correspondingly, the Shanghai 5 was modified with the "Declaration on the Establishment of the Shanghai Cooperation Organization (SCO)." The SCO Charter, which adhered to the purposes and principles of the UN Charter, sought to promote mutual trust among the member states, develop effective cooperation in political affairs, economy and trade, science and technology, culture, education, energy, transportation, environmental protection and maintain regional peace and stability.

In its dealings with Central Asian states, China is primarily concerned with protecting its territorial integrity and national unity, combating terrorism and stabilizing the north-western region, Xinjiang (Zhang and Saika, 2005: 46). China's main threat, as noted in Chapter 3, comes from the ETIM in the northwest. China has been active in trying to solve this problem multilaterally, rather than unilaterally and has used the SCO for exactly such a purpose.

Non-traditional threats such as trans-border terrorism, weapons smuggling, drug trafficking and illegal immigration have been combated under the SCO framework and this has contributed to stabilizing China's north-west frontier (ibid.: 47).

The SCO also highlights China's strategic economic and energy interests in Central Asia. China's growing energy demands, coupled with its desire to diversify sources of energy and dependence on the Strait of Malacca, point to Central Asia and its vast natural resources as a realistic option. China is actively engaged in transforming the SCO from an organization with roots in security issues to one that promotes economic exchange. As one analyst astutely points out:

> China's cooperation with the Central Asian States in the framework of the SCO promotes the integration of the economies in the region, and resolves the common problems of defence and development. It offers broad perspectives for close collaboration between China and the Central Asian States.
>
> (Sun, 2004: 149)

Traditionally, India's Central Asian policy has been largely determined by the Pakistan factor. Many Indian elites continue to believe that the Pakistani government has aided Islamic terrorist organizations that have in turn compromised Indian security interests in the north-west and north-east. With the links between the former Taliban government in Afghanistan and al-Qaeda, the dangers of militant Islam gaining a foothold elsewhere in Central Asia were all too clear for India. As one analyst has noted, for India:

> [T]he basic underlying aim was to ensure that the heart of Asia does not turn hostile to India. Indian policy makers knew it was in their interest to see that these countries also do not end up helping hostile forces or falling prey to the ravages of militant Islam ... The thought that the violence in Kashmir was becoming part of a much wider Pan-Asian pattern was extremely disturbing because it suggested that secular India was facing a much larger and widespread threat.
>
> (Banerjie, 2004: 3–4, in Zhang and Saika, 2005: 49)

The SCO was one of the first international organizations to specifically institutionalize combat against separatism, extremism and terrorism and focus on counter-terrorist measures. The "Shanghai Convention Against Terrorism, Separatism and Extremism" of 15 June 2001, outlined specific directions and procedures for tackling the aforementioned threats. This was followed by the June 2002 "Agreement of the SCO Member States on Counter-Terrorism Regional Structure" at St Petersburg and multilateral joint anti-terrorist military exercises in August 2003 (Zhang and Saika, 2005: 54). Recognizing India's experience in combating terrorism and the converging interests between the SCO member states and India in checking Pan-Asian insurgency, Kazakhstan has been backing New Delhi's entry into the SCO (India currently has observer status. "India Asked to Join . . .," 2002). The SCO could therefore be an attractive venue to expand the Sino-Indian security dialogue and build on bilateral exchanges between the two states that have expressed the need to continue battling terrorism in Asia.[3] As India continues to deal with Kashmiri militants (with the latest Delhi bombings on 29 October 2005), Russia battles with radical Chechnyan groups and China battles nationalist Uighur extremists, there is a clear convergence of interest between the three major Asian powers on the point of preserving territorial integrity and combating Islamic extremism. For India and China, Pakistan's inability to deal with terrorist organizations operating inside Pakistani borders is a large mutual concern, especially since 11 September 2001. In this sense, although Pakistan is a valuable Islamic ally for China, it is also a liability in some ways. According to China's National Defense White Paper, "The threat posed by terrorism, separatism and extremism is still grave" and that "international terrorist forces remain rampant. It seems rather difficult to eliminate completely the root causes of terrorism, making the fight against terrorism a long and demanding task before the international community" (PRC, 2004). The realization that international terrorism is a major threat to peace and stability and that the fight against it is long term will serve to mitigate Sino-Indian rivalry and create pressure for coordination.

Maritime terrorism

In recent years terrorists have increasingly taken to the maritime realm to carry out their attacks. The lawless domain of the sea, home to over 50,000 ships, carrying 80 percent of the world's traded cargo, is vulnerable both as an avenue for land attacks and as a target in itself. Many security experts have commented on how future terrorist attacks will likely emanate from the sea, in unmarked containers and aboard stateless hulls. As Graham Allison notes, "The nuclear weapon that terrorists would use . . . is far more likely to arrive in a cargo container than on the tip of a missile" (Newman, 2006). As Peter C. Newman (2006) notes, Osama bin Laden controls over 20 merchant ships, some of which were implicated in delivering explosives in Tanzania and Kenya in 1998. Although China and India have not been mentioned as specific target states by al-Qaeda, as Britain and the US have, they do continue to combat Islamic terrorism in Xinjiang and Kashmir. India has often raised concerns about the links between Kashmiri extremists and Islamic terrorist groups in Pakistan and abroad. As discussed earlier, Islamic extremists in support of the ETIM have also targeted the Chinese. Bin Laden's taped warnings that "the youths of God are preparing . . . [to] . . . fill your hearts with terror, and target your economic lifeline until you stop your oppression" serves as a warning for all countries deemed to be engaged in "anti-Islamic" activity (quoted in Newman, 2006).

Global hydrocarbon shipments are particularly vulnerable to terrorism as they transit through the IOR. Oil tankers are slow moving and are open targets for pirates and terrorists (Khurana, 2005a, 2005b). The strategic choke points in the IOR—especially the Straits of Hormuz and Malacca, are visibly vulnerable targets for terrorism. The Strait of Hormuz is especially exposed because at its narrowest points it is only 1.5 miles wide and there are no alternative routes. As Khurana (2005a) notes, "Its vulnerability was palpable during the 1984–87 Iran-Iraq *Tanker Wars*, when even neutral vessels were often attacked in the Persian Gulf, leading to a drop in the strait's shipping by 25 percent." The corresponding increase in US naval presence has helped to protect this strategic point but West Asia has always been a region where maritime terrorism has struck. In 1985, the *Achille Lauro*, an Italian cruise ship, was hijacked by Palestinian militants; in 2000, the US warship, *USS Cole* was bombed at Aden and in 2002 al-Qaeda terrorist attacks were carried out against the French supertanker *Limburg* (Khurana, 2005a). 11 September 2001 indicated that terrorist organizations like al-Qaeda are increasingly resorting to unorthodox or unconventional methods of attack. Trade and energy lifelines could be especially attractive targets in this regard. The recent April 2004 attacks on two Iraqi oil terminals at Al Faw is one such example. As Khurana (2005a) notes, "The energy infrastructure and transportation in the Gulf are potential targets despite the overwhelming presence of coalition naval forces."

The Malacca Strait, in addition to its dense shipping traffic, poses many navigational constraints. It is only 1.2 miles wide at its narrowest and 22 m deep at its shallowest (Khurana, 2005a). Recent reports (Luft and Korin, 2004) indeed indicate that:

> There have been cases of terrorist pirates hijacking tankers in order to practise steering them through straits and crowded sea lanes—the maritime equivalent of the Sept.11 hijackers' training in Florida flight schools. These apparent kamikazes-in-training have questioned crews on how to operate ships but have shown little interest in how to dock them.

In one such incident on March 2003, an Indonesian chemical tanker, the *Dewi Madrim*, was boarded by ten armed men who proceeded to steer it through the Strait of Malacca and then left the ship with navigational equipment and technical documents (ibid.)

The major threat to shipping/sea-lines in the South-east Asian straits is piracy. The statistics of International Maritime Bureau indicate piracy attacks have now become bolder—involving the use of automatic weapons and sophisticated equipment for hijackings. London's *Sunday Telegraph* recently reported that there were 1,224 piracy related boardings in 2005, targeting cargo ships (in Newman, 2006).

With the ongoing separatist movements supported by Jammah Islamiyah, the sub-regional Islamic fundamentalist movement linked to al-Qaeda, the waters of Southeast Asia have all the ingredients for maritime terrorism (Watkins, 2004). In South Asia, separatist groups such as the Liberation Tigers of Tamil Elam and its naval wing, the Sea Tigers continue to threaten shipping in the waters surrounding Sri Lanka. Separatist insurgents have frequently hijacked ships and specifically targeted energy resources. For instance, in October 2001, five Sea Tiger boats carried out a suicide attack on the oil tanker *MT Silk Pride* off the coast of northern Sri Lanka. Indonesian separatist groups in Aceh have also often targeted ships carrying oil and other natural resources because they perceive that they have been unfairly denied access to the natural resource wealth of their province. These commodities are easily sold on the black market and the revenue generated is used to fund their movement (Luft and Korin, 2004).

Both India and China are therefore vulnerable to terrorism and piracy on the high seas. China has the world's largest merchant marine and scenarios such as the deliberate scuttling of an oil tanker in the Strait of Malacca or Hormuz are especially alarming. The Indian Navy, with its growing blue-water capabilities could play a major role in the Indian Ocean in ensuring the safe transit of Chinese ships. In turn, pipelines from Russia or Kazakhstan could be routed through Xinjiang to India. China could also reciprocate by ensuring the safe transit of Indian ships bringing hydrocarbons from the Russian Far East to the sub-continent. For China and for other IOR littorals, an increasing role for the Indian Navy in the Indian Ocean is preferable to a strong US presence in the region. China has been particularly wary of the growing US presence in the Middle East and Central Asia. Both China and India were also officially opposed to the US invasion of Iraq in 2003.

As energy demand grows in both China and India, the importance of SLOCs and the safety of strategic choke points such as the Straits of Hormuz and Malacca will also grow. Maritime terrorism is a growing problem and terrorist organizations such as al-Qaeda have been implicated in targeting merchant vessels, using ships to carry out attacks on the ground and plotting possibly catastrophic blockades of strategic choke points. In this sense, maritime terrorism is a problem for all Indian Ocean littoral states and for other states such as South Korea and Japan highly dependent on energy shipments from the Persian Gulf. Piracy is also a major problem in the Indian Ocean and the waters of South-East Asia. These problems require a multilateral approach as they affect many states and should push Asian states towards maritime policy convergence. Recent joint Sino-Indian naval exercises demonstrate that there is a willingness on both sides to collectively tackle issues of maritime terrorism and piracy in the Indian Ocean. Future exercises are already planned for 2006 and will likely be a key theme of Sino-Indian naval cooperation in the years to come. For China, the US growing military and naval presence in the IOR and in Central Asia has not been viewed favorably. In this regard, the Indian Navy's increasing power can be interpreted favorably. This is because a growing role for the Indian Navy in the Indian Ocean is preferable to US and Japanese presence not only for China but also to other littoral states in the IOR. As the geographically central state in the Indian Ocean, a larger role for India and the Indian Navy is far easier to justify.

Continuing irritants in the Sino-Indian relationship

The main irritants in Sino-Indian relations will continue to be the contentious Tibet issue and Pakistan. Although officially New Delhi has recognized Chinese authority over Tibet, there still remain some ambiguities. For instance, India's long-standing policy, as noted in the 2003 India-China declaration has been that it "recognizes that the Tibet Autonomous Region is part of the territory of the People's Republic of China" and "does not allow Tibetans to engage in anti-China political activities in India" ("Declaration on Principles . . .," in Zhang, 2005: 63–64). For India, the new wording of the status of Tibet was "an attempt at a more appropriate 'verbalization' of the Indian position" (Acharya and Deshpande 2003: 21). However, India's use of the word "recognize" instead of "acknowledge" compares to the US stance on Taiwan in 1972 and 1979. Moreover, India has not added the word "inalienable" in front of the phrase "part of the territory of the PRC" (Zhang, 2005: 64). This raises obvious questions as to whether India only recognizes the current status of Tibet and fails to recognize its status as a part of the PRC in history or in the future.

In addition, there are questions over what constitute "anti-China activities." Some have questioned whether allowing the Dalai Lama and his representatives to make international visits to promote the Tibetan independence cause, with documents issued by the Indian Ministry of Home Affairs represents anti-China activities. According to John Garver (2001b: 74), India is effectively host to a Tibetan government-in-exile, headed by the Dalai Lama and based in Dharmshala that is both political and anti-China. For Garver, the 110,000 Tibetan exiles living in India give New Delhi an important way of pressuring Beijing and is the only effective mechanism of leverage that India has over China (Garver, 2001b: 75). As Acharya and Deshpande note (2003: 20), "the concerns on the Indian side regarding the question of Tibet have unquestionably been at the heart of the Sino-Indian boundary dispute." The mainstream position in India, however, is that Tibet is not a crucial issue in Sino-Indian relations because the Indian government is neither an abettor nor an instigator of the political cause of the Tibetans (Ramachandran, 2004: 287).

China's policy on Tibet has been fairly consistent. It advocates that the Dalai Lama admit publicly that Tibet and Taiwan are an inalienable part of China and, secondly, that he stop promoting the Tibetan independence cause. In the meantime China has actively supported Tibet's economic development, encouraged ethnic diversity and developed Tibetan culture (Zhang, 2005: 65). China's main request to India regarding the Tibet issue is for New Delhi to stop implicitly supporting the Tibetan independence movement by allowing the Dalai Lama to travel abroad and then return to India. Thus far, the Tibet issue has not interfered in the progression of Sino-Indian relations as New Delhi continues to balance Beijing's requests with domestic pressure to ensure the rights of Tibetan refugees. The fine balance will likely continue while Sino-Indian economic and political relations continue to improve.

The Pakistan issue in Sino-Indian relations is more sensitive, given China's history of helping Pakistan's nuclear and missile programs. As India's late National Security Advisor J.N. Dixit noted, "The strategic and security cooperation between Pakistan and China can have a negative impact on the regional security environment from India's point of view" (Dixit 2003: 439). China's post-Cold War relationship with Pakistan, however, has tended to focus more on China's domestic concerns and less on India. As noted earlier with Gwadar, most of China's external concerns likely relate more to the United States. The main incentives for China to continue its relationship with Pakistan is: (1) because of China's ongoing problems in Xinjiang and its rebellious Muslim groups; (2) to find an outlet to the Arabian Sea; and (3) to monitor the growing US presence in Central Asia. Pakistan's northern borders lie south of Xinjiang and as an allied state give China support in combating terrorist groups. Furthermore, Pakistan is a key Muslim ally of China and China's gateway to the Islamic world. As discussed earlier, China's involvement in the Gwadar Project may have more to do with decreasing dependence on the Malacca route and in finding more direct access to the Arabian Sea and the Persian Gulf, where China has major energy interests. China's consistent concerns about US military activities overseas remain a fundamental reason why the Sino-Pakistani alliance continues to prosper. China has already pressured the Pakistani government into removing US electronic gadgets in its northern region and appears to have an interest in using Gwadar to monitor US (and growing Japanese) naval activities in the Indian Ocean (Sakhuja, 2005a). As some in China have concluded, "Our relations with Pakistan will not be more important than those with India . . . India has acquired from Russia whatever Pakistan has acquired from us" ("China's Ambassador to India . . .," 2000, in Zhang, 2005: 66).

Overall the Pakistan factor has played a minimal role in interfering with the development of Sino-Indian relations since Pokharan II. As political and economic ties continue to be forged between China and India, Pakistan will likely shift to more and more of a bilateral issue between China and India rather than a triangular one as during the Cold War. Although China has not gone as far as India would like, as Garver (2001b: 231–32 in Shirk, 2004: 91, also Garver, 2005: 222) notes, "China distanced itself from Pakistan during the process of Sino-Indian rapprochement." China no longer sides with Pakistan nor threatens to intervene on the Pakistani side in the Kashmir conflict and furthermore in 1997 pledged to cut off all assistance to nonsafe-guarded nuclear facilities in an agreement with the US (Shirk, 2004: 91). China also solidified its earlier 1998 pledge to stop the transfer of missile technology to Pakistan in November 2000 in another agreement with the US (ibid.: 91). China's decision to reduce military assistance to Pakistan is not only motivated by a desire to improve relations with India and the United States but also because of Chinese concerns that Pakistan may internally collapse. The fear is that Islamic extremists supporting the insurgency in Xinjiang may get their hands on dangerous weaponary.

In general, there is a productive dialogue between India and China at the highest political levels and concerns on both sides are continuously under discussion. According to several high-ranking government officials, both India and China understand the central problems in their relationship and are working actively to ensure that these problems are addressed in due course (Anonymous, 2005). Both sides recognize the prosperous potential of Sino-Indian cooperation and political leaders are trying their utmost to ensure that this potential can be realized (ibid.).

As demonstrated by the April 2005 Sino-Indian summit, there is increasing hope that the current political and economic good will enjoyed by the two states will spill over into a resolution to the border dispute. Leading up to the April 2005 meeting, there were several rounds of boundary talks between India's national Security Advisor Brajesh Mishra and Chinese Deputy Foreign Minister Dai Bingguo in Beijing in October 2003. Another round of talks were held in June 2004 and again in July 2004 between the now deceased J.N. Dixit, Mishra's replacement as India's Special Representative and Dai Bingguo. It now appears that both sides are preparing themselves for the much discussed "east–west swap." As early as 2001, John Garver (2001b: 100) commented that:

> Chinese control of Aksai Chin was important to China's control of Tibet. Indian control of the southern slope is important to its defense of the northeast. This was the geopolitical logic underlying the proposal of an east-west trade-off between Chinese and Indian claims.

India's former ambassador to China, C.V. Raganathan (2001: 132) also commented that a boundary settlement between India and China would have to be on the basis of "political give-and-take and not based on legal arguments." According to one analyst, the most recent discussions between India and China have revealed that:

> Both sides now tend to be preparing for compromise, though what kind of compromise has remained indefinite. It may be "east-west swap." Which means that China gives up its demand for sovereignty in the East sector, while India admits Chinese sovereignty over Aksai Chin in the West.
>
> (Anonymous interview, quoted in Zhang, 2005: 63)

If China were to accept an east–west trade-off, many analysts have noted that China would persist on maintaining sovereignty over the Tawang tract, "a sensitive geopolitical region where evidence of a history of actual administration by the Tibetan government is strongest" (Zhang, 2005: 63).

The Sino-Indian border issue remains one of the major stumbling blocks in the bilateral relationship. To date, progress in this arena has been glacial. However, in recent years there is indication that the tide may be turning. For instance, during Wen Jiabao's visit to India in April 2005, the two states signed an agreement on the *Political Parameters and Guiding Principles for the Settlement of the India-China Boundary Question* consisting of the following provisions (where China, for the first time also recognized Indian sovereignty over Sikkim):

> Article III: The boundary settlement must be final, covering all sectors of the India–China boundary.

> Article IV: The two sides will give consideration to each other's strategic and reasonable interests, and the principle of mutual and equal security.

> Article V: The two sides will take into account, inter alia, historical evidence, national sentiments, practical difficulties and reasonable concerns and sensitivities of both sides, and the actual state of border areas.

> Article VI: The boundary should be along well–defined and easily identifiable natural geographical features.

> Article VII: In reaching a boundary settlement, the two sides shall safeguard due interests of their settled populations in the border areas.

It appears that the two countries are serious about resolving the border issue, with the agreement on Political Parameters and Guiding Principles on the boundary issue as the important first stage of a three-stage process. Currently the two countries are in the second phase that involves developing a framework for final settlement. This is the stage where the hardest negotiation is taking place and where development of the border dispute has been slow.

The third phase involves delineation of the boundary. The India-China Joint Working Group and the India-China Diplomatic and Military Expert Group continue their work under the Agreements of 7 September 1993 and 29 November 1996, including the clarification of the line of actual control (LAC) and the implementation of CBMs. It must be realized that the Sino-Indian border is the largest undemarcated border in the world, involving vast distances and high altitudes. So naturally this will be a long process. The recent opening of the Nathu La Pass and the proposed opening of the Stillwell road, however, are good signs for the future.

Further indication that the border issue may be resolved at some point in the future is that China has in recent years resolved most of its territorial disputes with its other neighbors. For instance, negotiations with Soviet

Union and Vietnam on border issues began in 1964 and 1977 and were not resolved until 2004 and 1999 respectively. The slowness of the boundary negotiations between India and China should be placed in this broader context. China has also signed border agreements recently with Kazakhstan in 2002, Kyrgyzstan in 2004, and Mongolia in 2005 (Sharma, 2006).

Conclusion

Whether the factors discussed in this chapter will eventually lead to the development of true Sino-Indian friendship remain to be seen. What these sections have tried to demonstrate is that we are seeing the early signs of a relationship transforming from one of rivalry, competition and conflict to one of cooperation. As economic ties are bolstered between India and China in the years to come and the political/military dialogue continues, it is reasonable to expect that tensions will continue to subside and mutual understanding will grow.

Conclusion

The Sino-Indian case represents what may be characterized as an ideal case for the debate between neorealists and neoliberals. The former would expect considerations of survival and power to trump economics, whereas the latter would see economic issues transforming the nature of the "game" (i.e. shifting it from a PD game to a more cooperative model). Some analysts have suggested that because of India and China's history of conflict and the unresolved border issue, there is a ceiling to how far relations can progress (Chellaney, 2005; Karnad, 2005). However, an emerging position in Indian academic and government circles is that there is not necessarily any ceiling to how far Sino-Indian relations can go (Dutta, 2005; Anonymous, 2005).

Both sides are becoming more and more convinced that absolute gains can be pursued to the mutual benefit of the people of China and India. Although the rapid development of Chinese and Indian Navies, costing billion of dollars, as well as the acquisitions of other Asian states such as Malaysia, Singapore and Indonesia may raise alarm bells in some circles about the possibility of a naval arms race, these projections remain far-fetched in the absence of clear and targeted threats. It must be realized that many of the recent naval acquisitions in India and China have been quite necessary as both states have relied on outdated ships and submarines from the early post-WWII period for much of their security needs. Both India and China, large countries with diverse interests and increasingly reliant on energy imports from abroad, are developing their navies along with their economies to safeguard their security interests. In India, the current nature of Chinese activities in the IOR does not pose any serious threats to Indian security, thus, most analysts are not alarmed by suggestions that China has plans to encircle India (Anonymous, 2005). Correspondingly, India's engagement with ASEAN does not specifically target China and is part of a broader strategy of enhancing global economic ties (as both ASEAN states and India have relied to heavily on the US and the EU markets in the past). In addition, as discussed earlier, China's threat perceptions of India are quite low and China will remain preoccupied with the Taiwan issue first and foremost.

The real wild cards in the Sino-Indian relationship may prove to be Japan and the United States. China continues to have a "love–hate" relationship with Japan while Japan is starting to carve out a larger foreign policy agenda. Japan has been increasingly wary of Chinese naval development and maritime activities in Eastern Asian waters. There exist serious Sino-Japanese historical disputes, such as Japanese war crimes committed in World War II and visits to war memorial sites by high-ranking Japanese officials—not to mention disputes over maritime gas fields in contentious island groups. Recently, in 2004 a Chinese survey ship ventured into the exclusive economic zone of Okinotori Island and was followed by the intrusion of a Chinese submarine into Japanese waters ("Indian Author Sees . . .," 2005). There is also the North Korea issue that continues to loom as a security threat in East Asia. The future of Sino-Japanese relations may have an important consequence for Sino-Indian relations as Indo-Japanese relations have continuously improved following Pokharan II. If China becomes increasingly aggressive in the international arena, the Indo-Japanese relationship would take on a new context.

The United States will remain the most important external power that will shape the future of Sino-Indian relations (Frankel and Harding, 2004). If the United States decides to balance against rising Chinese power in the future, many would see India as a key partner in the balancing equation. However, many Indian elites clearly do not wish to play the role of a "US pawn" in the American game of great power balancing (Dutta, 2005). There is a strong desire in India to maintain an autonomous foreign policy and to follow what is best for India (Hoffmann, 2004: 34). In this sense, India is trying to balance between gaining the most it can gain from its partnership with the US while allaying Chinese fears and continuing to advocate a deepening of Sino-Indian ties. Leftist political pressure in India will continue to check the Indo-US partnership if it heads down the path of targeting China. As China has been apprehensive about being "ganged up on" by a Indo-US strategic partnership (and thus has been nervous about growing US-India ties), India has conversely been uneasy about the prospect of intensifying Sino-US relations. Sino-US collaboration in the early 1970s was in many ways targeted against India (Malik, 2001). Furthermore many Indian elites remain convinced that plans to launch a western attack during the 1971 Indo-Pakistani War were halted because of US support for Pakistan. In this sense, US involvement in Asian affairs may play on the fears of decision-makers in China and India and have the effect of destabilizing Sino-Indian relations.

The world, however, has changed significantly from the days of the Cold War. US involvement in the sub-continent had everything to do with balancing against the Soviet Union and its aligned partners (such as India). Since 11 September 2001 the United States has been working closely with China, Pakistan and India to combat terrorism (Pant, 2004). In this way Chinese, US and Indian interests converge. In some important ways the United States will serve to moderate Sino-Indian tensions. This is because 20 percent of China's trade is with the United States, not to mention the substantial amount of FDI coming in from the United States. Conversely, only 4 percent of US trade is conducted with China (CIA World Fact Book 2004). Although the United States runs a large trade deficit with China, the asymmetries in total trade are an important source of leverage for the United States (Keohane and Nye, 1977). With India also conducting a fifth of its trade with the US, the US enjoys "soft-power" leverage in Indo-US relations as well. The US has cultivated a strong economic and political relationship with both China and India and has much to offer both states (Pant, 2004: 326). In this way there is a greater pressure for both India and China to "bandwagon" with the United States (Wohlforth, 1999). The US will use and has used this leverage in addition to its military strength to pressure China on checking its aggressiveness on issues such as Taiwan. As the Indo-US and Indo-Japanese relationship continue to strengthen following Pokharan II, India has less to fear in terms of a Chinese threat. It is reasonable to expect that the United States and Japan would get involved in the event of a Sino-Indian crisis.

This was demonstrated by President's Clinton's involvement in the Indo-Pakistani nuclear standoff in 1998. The last thing the United States wants is a conflict between two nuclear states such as India and China. In this sense, the United States will play a key role in moderating Sino-Indian tension if outstanding issues arise in the years to come. As Paul Kennedy, once a leading proponent of the US decline theory has conceded, never before in history has such a disparity in power existed between the major power in the international system and the other powers (Kennedy, 2002, in Pant, 2004). The US is so far ahead of other states in the international system that it doesn't need to worry about "balancing" against China. Rather the US has pursued a policy of engagement with both India and China in an effort to make the rise of China and India a peaceful one. As of now, the US does not need India to do its bidding in Asia. The Japanese would be far more capable in this regard. Conversely, both China and India have much more to lose than gain in challenging the United States and its position in the international system. The same is true of the Sino-Indian relationship—China and India have a lot more to lose from competing with one another than from cooperating to pursue mutual gains. In this way the world is no longer the same one that existed when China and India fought their border war in 1962. Both China and India are facing pressures to integrate into the US-led international economy and in their bilateral relations are realizing that there is much to gain from cooperation within this international environment.

Despite these two wildcards in the future of Sino-Indian relations, the most important factor in assessing the changing nature of the relationship is the current state of Sino-Indian bilateral relations. Although there remain some difficulties over the undemarcated boundary, Tibet and Pakistan, overall, the commitment at the very top levels of government in both China and India, including the military, indicate that relations will continue to improve. Both India and China recognize that there is much to be gained from continued engagement as represented by efforts to bring trade figures eventually to $100 billion ("ASEAN's 'Change of Heart' . . .," 2004). There is no reason to expect that Sino-Indian relations will once again spiral downward given the positive momentum generated in recent years. Both India and China have set out on the path of creating dependable expectations of peaceful change and as long as the political will remains, Sino-Indian relations will continue to progress. The Indian nuclear genie is out of the bottle and has come to be accepted by the international community—there is nowhere to go but to forge ahead.

Summary

This book has tried to demonstrate that there are emerging empirical discrepancies in the Sino-Indian relationship that cannot easily be explained within a neorealist framework. These two discrepancies primarily include the shifting nature of the Sino-Indian economic relationship and the development of a cooperative Sino-Indian bilateral dialogue.

In the economic realm, an attempt was made to show that the Sino-Indian economic relationship is growing rapidly and that total bilateral trade figures have risen markedly in the past few years. Projections that Sino-Indian trade can hit $100 billion in the next five to ten years do not seem far-fetched if trade continues to grow at its current rate and if a free trade agreement is reached between China and India. The points of synergy in Sino-Indian trade and the areas where there can be future growth were explored in an attempt to demonstrate that the future of the Sino-Indian economic relationship may be promising. There are indeed many fruitful areas where interchange could be deepened.

The Sino-Indian economic relationship is also increasingly taking on an institutional dynamic, as it is being framed and guided by the JSG and the JWG. As trade between China and India intensifies and grows ever more complex in the years to come, the pressure for further institutional coordination will also grow. In the economic realm, as the neoliberal functionalist argument holds, China and India could very well have set down the path of complex interdependence. The economic sphere demonstrates the potential that low political engagement has in transforming the Sino-Indian relationship.

Importantly, this book has also tried to demonstrate that the mitigating factors in the Sino-Indian relationship are not entirely structural-functional. In both China and India, the political will to alter the nature of the Sino-Indian relationship from a lens of conflict and rivalry to cooperation has grown. At the military-to-military and at the political levels, China and India have demonstrated a willingness to resolve outstanding disputes, to continue building the burgeoning Sino-Indian economic relationship and to frame the Sino-Indian bilateral relationship in increasingly cooperative terms. According to the literature on sociological transformation, China and India could be considered to be building dependable expectations of peaceful change and reinterpreting their social realities.

The structural-functional pressure to continue economic cooperation to realize mutual gains, coupled with an emerging elite consensus that aims to create dependable expectations of peaceful change, bodes well for the future of Sino-Indian relations. Viewed together, the economic and political spheres indicate that there are factors mitigating Sino-Indian rivalry and competition. These emerging developments cannot easily be explained in strictly neorealist terms. In the absence of a clear (and mutual) external military threat, China and India have seemingly set forth on the path of interdependence and cooperation. This book, by utilizing insights from neoliberal theories of interdependence and constructivism, has pushed for a richer realist explanation of the Sino-Indian relationship. One of the central themes of this book has been that an entirely neorealist approach to Sino-Indian relations is bankrupt and ignores how the relationship is currently changing. Therefore, a synthetic theoretical approach was developed here that linked theories of interdependence and sociological transformation to more qualified realist arguments. The continuing irritants in the Sino-Indian relationship (the Pakistan and border issues), as well as China and India's attempts to position themselves in the global balance of power, may best reflect the realist aspects of Sino-Indian relations. For China, the United States is the main strategic competitor and the only superpower in international relations. The Gwadar Project and China's growing presence in the IOR may have more to do with the United States than India. There is a strong desire in New Delhi to bring India on par with the other major powers in international relations. However, both China and India's great power aspirations do not necessarily point towards conflict. Rather, China and India have begun to realize that there is more to gain from cooperation and coordination than rivalry and conflict. Correspondingly mutual threat perceptions have declined and currently remain limited in nature.

Soaring energy demands, on which economic and national growth depend, have increased the importance of the IOR and the Indian Ocean's SLOCs. Sino-Indian naval modernization and presence in the IOR reflect this growing importance. India's pre-eminent position in the Indian Ocean and PLAN's logistical limitations, coupled with the threat of maritime terrorism also create pressure for coordinating maritime policy. Furthermore, India's growing trade with ASEAN and China's preeminent position in the South China Seas indicate that naval coordination and reciprocation may be preferable to rivalry. Protecting strategic choke points in the Indian Ocean such as the Straits of Hormuz and Malacca is in the mutual interest not only of China and India but also other Indian Ocean littoral states.

In 2006, the Sino-Indian friendship year, both China and India also established a basis for future energy cooperation. This was best exemplified by the ONGC and CNPC joint energy exploration deal. In the energy sector, there may be much more for both China and India to gain from cooperation than from rivalry. Rather than competing with one another for foreign equity oil and driving up the costs of acquisition, China and India are learning that it may be more beneficial to coordinate policy to meet domestic energy needs.

In short, neorealist arguments that depict the Sino-Indian relationship in terms of a regional struggle for power overlook many important dimensions of the Sino-Indian relationship. The security dilemma argument is too simplistic, as it ignores how low political engagement may be transforming the nature of the "game." Moreover, there is a growing elite consensus in China and India that is committed to sustaining peaceful relations, expanding trade and resolving outstanding issues. Liberal theories of economic interdependence and sociological theories of communication provide great insight into how the current state of Sino-Indian relations are changing. Only by relaxing the rigid assumptions of neorealism and employing a richer realist framework that does not ignore issues related to economic interdependence and shifting social conditions can the full picture of Sino-Indian relations be appreciated. That relationship is in the process of profound transformation. As Wen Jiabao noted at the ASEAN conference in December 2004, Sino-Indian cooperation is eventually going to "catch the attention of the whole world."

Notes

Introduction

1 There are two main strains of realism, offensive and defensive. Offensive realists like John Mearsheimer (2001) note that states seek to maximize their power whereas defensive realists like Kenneth Waltz (1979) have argued that states seek to balance power and to preserve the status quo.

2 In his "steps-to-war" model, Vasquez (1993, 1995) has argued that the absence of a boundary dispute between two rivals all but ensures that the conflict will not escalate to war. Conversely, however, evidence also suggests that the presence of territorial disputes significantly affect hostility levels and the prospects for escalation to war (Diehl 1999: xv).

3 See also Alexander Wendt (1995) and Friedrich Kratochwil (1993) for similar arguments on neorealism's inability to account for structural change.

4 See also Krasner (1983), March and Olsen (1998) and Powell (1994).

5 For instance, North and Weingast's (1989) example of the British monarch ceding financial authority to Parliament in efforts to increase revenue-generating capacity—reducing prospects for unilateral reneging on accumulated debts.

6 Dunn's specific concern, in the interwar context was with the problem of dealing with revisionist powers—those that sought to upset the status quo. According to Dunn, "the problem of peaceful change calls for procedures adapted to persuasion, investigation, the discovery of compromises [and] the revealing of real interests" (1937: 84). Overall, Dunn stresses the importance of negotiation and the role of international organizations and concludes that "the most promising way to meet these difficulties [of peaceful change] seems to be to turn . . . toward the idea of a freer international trade with all countries" (ibid.: 130).

7 There exists a significant "Cold War" literature on the security dynamics within the Indian Ocean Region (Kohli, 1978; Booth, 1984; Dowdy and Trood, 1985; Majeed 1986; Misra, 1986; Kaushik, 1987; Singh, 1993; Roy-Chaudhury, 1995). On the nuclear security balance (Thomas, 1993; Thomas and Gupta, 2000; Dittmer, 2001; Yuan, 2001; Perkovich, 2004)

8 On Sino-Indian border issues and the prospects of settlement (Hoffman, 1994; Sidhu and Yuan 2001; Swamy, 2001; Ganguly, 2004). The boundary issue has been one of the few areas within Sino-Indian scholarship that has been well covered elsewhere. There have been many book-length studies on this issue and progress on the border question in Sino-Indian relations has been glacial—this makes an original contribution in this area extremely difficult to make. The approach taken here was to acknowledge that the border question remains an important one (for instance, see the final section of Chapter 5) and to simply document the major developments (see Chapter 1). The book instead focuses on issues that have not

been covered as well by scholars (maritime, economic, energy and elite dialogue) and where major developments have occurred in recent years.

1 The history of Sino-Indian relations

1 For detailed information, see Chaturvedi (1991), Lamb (1964, 1968), Lall (1989), Van Eekelen (1964), Hoffmann (1990), Maxwell (1970), Mehra (1989), Ram (1973), Vohra (1993), Sandhu (1988) Saigal (1979), Sharan (1996) and Woodman (1969).
2 Sino-Soviet relations had already deteriorated far enough by 1960–1961 to consti-tute a split, even though most scholars define the split as finalizing in 1963–1964. For a detailed discussion of the events leading to the Sino-Soviet split of the early 1960s, see Jones and Kevill (1985: 17–59), Medvedev (1986: 30–43), Griffith (1964: 33–207) and Zagoria (1962: Chapters 8–17).

2 The Indian Ocean and China and India's naval strategy and modernization

1 One can draw a comparison with how the US threatened to cut off Japanese oil supplies in South-East Asia prior to the 1941 Japanese attack on Pearl Harbor.
2 This refers to the influential naval doctrine of the Russian Naval Commander Admiral Sergei Gorshkov (1910–1988).
3 If one compares the capabilities of the American blue-water navy with the current Chinese Navy it then becomes clear how China will be capable of projecting power at a distance if it acquires a blue-water navy. The American Navy is easily able to monitor the world's strategic waterways with its carrier groups and logistical infrastructure. It is such a blue-water capability that China seeks to gain.
4 These reports indicate China's acquisition of a new type of nuclear-powered submarine, high speed airship, and missile destroyers from Russia and the modern-ization of China's anti-ship missile launchers, primary guns, secondary guns, rocket-type anti-submarine deep-sea bombs, ship-to-air missile systems, helicopter embarkation systems and so forth.
5 The 052B-class will be additionally equipped with Russian SHTIL–1 ship-to-air missiles.
6 For an extended treatment of this war, see Lall (1989), Sharan (1996), Maxwell (1970), Saigal (1979).
7 India also makes it possible for the Dalai Lama and his officials to travel abroad by issuing the necessary documents and in this way enables the Tibetan issue to remain before the world community.
8 If the border problem is not resolved and the influx of Bangladeshi Muslims continues, Assam will become the second Indian state with a majority Muslim population (the other being Jammu and Kashmir).
9 Sri Lanka has often accused India of sympathizing with the Tamil rebel groups and has argued that Tamil Nadu continues to supply terrorist groups with financing.
10 For more information on the possible overland trade effects of these new networks, see Garver (2005: 205–228).
11 See note 10.
12 Blue-water is a term from maritime strategy used in conjunction with brown and green water. Brown water refers to littoral ocean areas within 100 nautical miles of the coastline. Green water refers to ocean areas from about 100 nautical miles to the next major land formation. Blue water, as noted, refers to the ability to project force at a distance of 1500 nautical miles and beyond the coast. For more information, see Till (2004) and also Sondhaus (2004).
13 This will be discussed in the sections and chapters to follow.

14 The navy's original carrier, the *Vikrant* was decommissioned in 1997.
15 The nuclear submarine INS *Chakra* (Charlie class) was leased from Russia in 1988 and returned in 1991. The lease of the submarine provided the Indian Navy with valuable information about the maintenance and operation of nuclear submarines. It is not surprising then that the ATV program has been modeled on the Charlie-class design.
16 The two submarines are currently under completion at Komsomolsk-on-Amur Shipbuilding Plant in Russia. See Majumdar (2005).
17 Some reports indicate that the *Akula* Class SSN K–154 Tigre, under the command of Aleksey Burilichev was successful in shadowing the US Navy's Ohio-class ballistic missile armed nuclear submarines (SSBNs). See Majumdar (2005).
18 The BrahMos was a joint-venture between Indian DRDO and Russian NPO Mashinostroyeniya.
19 The submarines will be built at the Mazgaon Docks in Mumbai and will be introduced in a timely fashion as several of India's older submarines are slated to be decommissioned by the time the Scorpene is ready.
20 The pipeline would be 2775 km long, 760 km of which is through Pakistan. Pakistan, however, would gain substantial transit fees and President Prevez Musharraf has been on board with the plans ("Indo-Iran . . .," 2005). India currently imports 70 percent of its current crude oil and gas needs and its use of gas and oil is expected to double by 2020 (Anbarasan, 2005).
21 As one analyst notes, the US has refused to even share Theatre Missile Defense (TMD) fully with the Japanese (Bidwai, 2004; Subramanian, 2005).
22 Recently declassified archival evidence detailing Sino-US talks in the early 1970s supports this school of thought. For more information, see Malik (2002).
23 This issue is taken up in more depth in the final section of Chapter 5, "The continuing irritants in Sino-Indian relations and the global balance of power."
24 Also see PRC (2004).
25 Ibid.
26 ASEAN commenced free-trade negotiations with Japan and South Korea in April 2005. Singh also noted that the telecom sector would require $25 billion in investment over the next five years and that the power sector would require $75 billion over the same period (Jiang, 2004).

3 Chinese and Indian economic liberalization and the nature of the Sino-Indian economic relationship

1 This will be discussed later in this chapter. Briefly though, it had to do with the Congress Party's belief that the key to eradicating poverty in India lay in introducing capitalism into the countryside.
2 Part of the reason for discrepancy is the fact that some Chinese investments in India are routed through Hong Kong.

4 China's and India's energy policies

1 By comparison, the US currently imports around 500 million tons of oil per year (Dannreuther, 2003: 205).
2 India currently imports 70 percent of its current crude oil and gas needs and its use of gas and oil is expected to double by 2020 (Anbarasan, 2005).
3 For more information on the differences between the market and state-led strategies for energy security, see Toichi and Naitoh (2001) for the latter, and Morse and Jaffe (2001) for the former.
4 For a full assessment on the internal dynamics of Chinese policy formulation, see

Downs (2004), Tanner (2002), Lieberthal and Oksenberg (1988), Gilboy (2002) and Andrew-Speeds *et al.* (2002).
5 Kondapalli also notes the importance of energy security for Chinese officials was demonstrated in 2005 when China used its veto on the UN Security Council over the Sudan issue. This was the first time that China had used its veto other than on the Taiwan issue (Kondapalli, 2005b).
6 Unocal controls more than 500 million barrels of oil in North America and also has large natural gas reserves in South-east Asia as well as a stake in a big Azerbaijan oil field (Johnson, 2005).
7 The role of speculators who trade in oil futures on the New York Mercantile Exchange and the International Petroleum Exchange is also important and has driven the price of oil to record highs in the past few years.

5 The positive trends in the Sino-Indian bilateral dialogue

1 China and India have complex domestic political structures and a full analysis of the relationship between elites, institutions and domestic government structures were beyond the scope of this book.
2 This reference is to a report issued by Agence France-Presse noted in Fang (2005). Also see, "Looking Forward to . . . 2005."
3 China thus far has been reluctant in allowing India's entry without also allowing Pakistan in. In response, India has been reluctant to back China's entry into SAARC.

Bibliography

Abraham, Itty (1999) *The Making of the Indian Atomic Bomb*. London: Zed Books.

Acharya, Alka and Deshpande, G.P. (2003) "'Talking of and with China,' in Prime Minister Vajpayee's China Visit, June 2003: Reflections and Comments," *Occasional Studies* 1, New Delhi: Institute of Chinese Studies.

Adler, Emmanuel and Barnett, Michael (eds) (1998) *Security Communities*. Cambridge: Cambridge University Press.

AFP (1994) 6 October, FBIS-NES–94–194.

Ahrari, Ehsan (1998) "China's Naval Forces Look to Extend their Blue-water Reach," *Jane's Intelligence Review*, April, 31–36.

Alam, Muzaffar and Subrahmanyam, Sanjay (eds) (1998) *The Mughal State, 1526–1750*. Delhi: Oxford University Press.

Alexander's Gas and Oil Connection (2002) 7:3, 6 February.

Alker, Hayward R. and Biersteker, Thomas (1984) "The Dialectics of World Order," *International Studies Quarterly*, 28: 121–142.

An, Zhiping (2005) "PLA Chief of General Staff Liang Guanglie Meets Leaders of Indian Armed Forces," *Xinhua*, Beijing, 24 May, from World News Connection.

Anbarasan, Ethirajan (2005) "Wither India-Iran Ties?" *BBC News*, World Edition, South Asia, 29 September.

Andrews-Speed, Philip (2001) "The Challenges Facing China's Gas Industry," *LNG Journal*, May/June: 26–29.

Andrews-Speed, Philip, Liao, Xuanli and Dannreuther, Roland (2002) *The Strategic Implications of China's Energy Needs*. New York: Oxford University Press.

Anonymous interviews (2005) New Delhi, July.

Anzera, Giuseppe (2005) "The Modernization of the Chinese Navy," *The Power and Interest News Report*, 12 September.

Arun, T.G. and Nixon, F.I. (2000) "Privatization in India: Miles to Go . . .?" in Nicholas Perdikis (ed.) *The Indian Economy: Contemporary Issues*. Singapore: Ashgate, pp. 69–93.

"ASEAN's 'Change of Heart' Prompted by India's Fast Growth Rate" (2004) *The Asian Age*, New Delhi, 4 December.

Ashley, Richard (1986) "The Poverty of Neorealism," in Robert O. Keohane (ed.) *Neorealism and Its Critics*. New York: Columbia University Press, pp. 255–301.

Ashraf, Tariq (2004) "Doctrinal Reawakening of the Indian Armed Forces," *Military Review*, 84(6): 53–62.

Athwal, Amardeep (2004) "The Sino-Soviet Split: The Key Role of U.S. Nuclear Superiority," *Journal of Slavic Military Studies*, 27: 271–297.

Axelrod, Robert (1984) *The Evolution of Cooperation*. New York: Basic Books.

Axelrod, Robert and Keohane, Robert (1993) "Achieving Cooperation under Anarchy Strategies and Institutions," in D. Baldwin (ed.) *Neorealism and Neoliberalism*. New York: Columbia University Press, pp. 85–115.

Baer, George W. (1994) *One Hundred Years of Sea Power: The United States Navy, 1890–1990*. Stanford, CA: Stanford University Press.

Banerjie, Indranil (ed.) (2004) *India and Central Asia*. London: Brunel Academic Publishers.

Bansal, Alok (2005a) "Resurgence of Violence in Balochistan: Causes and Implications," paper presented for the Institute for Defense Studies and Analyses, New Delhi.

—— (2005b) Personal interview, IDSA, New Delhi, June.

Basham, A.L. (1954) *The Wonder That Was India*. New York: Grove Press.

Baum, Richard (1994) *Burying Mao: Chinese Politics in the Age of Deng Xiaoping*. Princeton, NJ: Princeton University Press.

Beaton, Leonard and Maddox, John (1962) *The Spread of Nuclear Weapons*. London: Chatto and Windus.

Bedi, Rahul (2004) "Russian Help Bolsters N-submarine Program," *The Deccan Herald*, 6 June.

—— (2005) "India the Developing World's Top Arms Buyer," *Irish Times*, 21 September.

"Beijing to Buy 30 Russian Jets." (1999) *Asian Defense Journal*, November 1999.

Bennett, Andrew and George, Alexander L. (1997) "Process Tracing in Case Study Research," paper presented at the MacArthur Foundation Workshop on Case Study Methods, Belfer Center for Science and International Affairs (BCSIA), Harvard University, 17–19 October.

Berlin, Donald (2004) "The 'Great Base Race' in the Indian Ocean Littoral: Conflict Prevention or Stimulation?" *Contemporary South Asia*, 13(3): 239–255.

Bernstein, R. and Munro, R.H. (1997) "China I: The Coming Conflict with China," *Foreign Affairs*, 76(2): 12–22.

Beukel, Erick (1994) "Reconstructing Integration Theory: The Case of Educational Policy in the EC," *Cooperation and Conflict*, 29(1): 33–54.

Bhaduri, Amit and Nayyar, D. (1996) *The Intelligent Person's Guide to Liberalization*. New Delhi: Penguin Books.

Bhalla, A.S. (2002) "Sino-Indian Growth and Liberalization," *Asian Survey*, 42: 419–439.

Bhalla, Madhu (2003) "Extricating Sino-Indian Economic Relations from Security Agendas," *Defense and Technology*, August: 62–67.

—— (2005) Personal interview, JNU, New Delhi, July.

Bhatt, Arunkumar (2005) "Japanese Warships on Goodwill Visit," *The Hindu*, Chennai, 23 August.

Bidwai, Praful (2004) "India-U.S. Tech: A Fool's Bargain," *Rediff*, 18 October.

Bindra, A.P.S. (1980) "Indian Navy." *Raison d'être, Navy International*, 85: 726–735.

Booth, Kenneth (1984) *The Indian Ocean: Perspectives on a Strategic Arena*. Centre for Foreign Policy Studies, Dalhoise University, Halifax, Nova Scotia.

British Petroleum (2003) *BP Statistical Review of World Energy 2003*. London: British Petroleum.

Brown, M.E., Coté, O.R. and Lynn-Jones, S.M. (2000) *The Rise of China: An International Security Reader*. Cambridge, MA: MIT Press.

Buiter, William and Patel, Urjit (1992) "Debt, Deficits and Inflation: An Application to the Public Finance in India," *Journal of Public Economics*, 47: 171–205.

Burley, Anne-Marie and Mattli, Walter (1993) "Europe Before the Court: A Political Theory of Legal Integration," *International Organization*, 47(1) 41–76.

"Burma to Promote Implementation of Sino-Burmese Border Agreements," (2004) *Xinhua* [in English], Beijing, 24 July.

"Burma Strongman Vows to Bring Democracy, Crush Anti-Indian Rebels," (2004) *AFP*, Hong Kong, 29 October.

Bussert, James C. (2004) "China Builds Destroyers Around Imported Technology," *Signal*, August.

Buzan, Barry, Jones, Charles and Little, Richard (1993) *The Logic of Anarchy: Neorealism to Structural Realism*. New York: Columbia University Press.

Cable, Vincent (1995) "China and India: Economic Reform and Global Integration," *World Development*, 23: 1475–1494.

Calabrese, J. (1998) "China and the Persian Gulf: Energy and Security," *Middle East Journal*, 52(3): 351–361.

—— (1999) "China's Policy Towards Central Asia: Renewal and Accomodation," *Eurasian Studies*, 16: 75–99.

Calder, Kent (1996) "Asia's Empty Gas Tank," *Foreign Affairs*, 75(2): 55–69.

Carr, E. H. (1939) *The Twenty Years Crisis, 1919–1939*. New York: Harper Torchbooks.

Castex, Adm. R. (ed.) (1994) *Strategic Theories*. Annapolis, MD: Naval Institute Press.

Chai, Joseph C.H. (ed.) (2000) *The Economic Development of Modern China:* Vol.III: *Reforms and Opening up Since 1979*. Cheltenham: Elgar Reference Collection.

Chandra, Bipin (1994) *Ideology and Politics in Modern India*. New Delhi: Har-Anand Publications.

Chang, Felix (2001) "Chinese Energy and Asian Security," *Orbis* 45(2): 1–25.

Chaturvedi, Gyaneshwar (1991) *India-China Relations: 1947 to Present*. Agra: M.G. Publishers.

Chellaney, Brahma (2005) Phone interview, New Delhi, July.

Chen, Kuan-I. and Uppal, J.S. (1971) *Comparatiave Development of India and China*. New York: The Free Press.

Cheng, Allen T. (2004) "Labour Unrest Is Growing in China," *International Herald Tribune*, Hong Kong, 27 October.

Chi, Mo (2004) "Perspective of China's Formidable Weapons for Attacking Taiwan," *Sing Tao Jih Pao*, 6 May, FBIS-CPP20040506000084.

Chibber, Pradeep (1995) "Political Parties, Electoral Competition, Government Expenditures and Economic Reforms in India," *Journal of Development Studies*, 32(1): 74–96.

"China 2005 Total Trade Hits 1.42 Trillion", (2005) *Daily Times*. Available at: http://www.dailytimes.com.pk/default.asp?page=2006%5C01%5C11%5Cstory_11-1-2006_pgs_34

"China Builds New Type Frigate," (2003) *Kanwa News*, 20 July.

"China Emerges as a Maritime Power" (2004) *Jane's Intelligence Review*, October.

"China's Foreign Trade Rises Some 30 Times in 24 Years" (2002) *People's Daily*, Beijing, 30 December.

"China, India Hope for Early Solution to Border Issue" (2006) *Xinhua*, Beijing, 10 January.

"China-India Joint Naval Exercise Staged in Indian Ocean" (2005) *Jiefangjun Bao*, Beijing, 12 December.

"China Installs Russian Air-defense Missile on Domestic Destroyers" (2003) *Kanwa News*, 30 April.

"China Launches a Powerful New Super-warship" (1999) *Jane's Defence Weekly*, 3 February.

"China Outlines 21st Century Oil Strategy" (2002) *Zhongxinshe*, 11 November, from World News Connection.

China Today: Defense Science and Technology (1993) Beijing: National Defense Industry Press, 2 vols.

"Chinese, Indian Leaders Exchange Congratulations on Launching of Friendship Year" (2006) *Xinhua*, Beijing, 1 January.

"Chinese Navy Chief Meets Chief of Army Staff of Bangladesh" (2004) *Xinhua* [in English] Beijing, 22 September.

"China's Ambassador to India: Sino-Pakistani Relations Will Not Threaten India" (2000) *Lianhe Zaobao*, Singapore, 18 March.

"China's Statement on India's Nuclear Tests" (1998) *Beijing Review*, 1–7 June.

Chiu, Yu-Tzu (2004) "Taiwan Science Council to Launch New Division in India," *Taipei Times*, 17 November.

Choudhury, Uttra (2004) "ASEAN, India, China, Japan, Korea Can Create Asian Powerhouse: Indian PM," *AFP*, Hong Kong, 19 October.

Chowdhury, Rahul Roy (1998) "An Energy Security Policy for India: The Case of Oil and Natural Gas," *Strategic Analysis* 21(11): 1671–1683.

Chu, Yun-kai (2003) "China, Pakistan Joint Military Exercise Aims at Breaking Potential Circle of Containment," *Hong Kong Hsin Pao*, Hong Kong, 30 October, FBIS-CHI–2003–1030.

CIA (2004) *The World Fact Book 2004*. Dulles, VA: Potomac Books.

Cohen, Stephen P. (2001) *India: Emerging Power*. Washington, DC: Brookings Institution Press.

Cohen, Stephen S. and Zysman, John (1987) *Manufacturing Matters: The Myth of the Post-Industrial Economy*. New York: Basic Books.

Cole, Bernard D. (2001) *The Great Wall at Sea: China's Navy Enters the Twenty-First Century*. Annapolis, MD: Naval Institute Press.

"'Consensus' Between India, China to Expand Military-to-Military Ties" (2004) *Jammu Daily Excelsior*, 30 December, FBIS-NES–2004–1230.

"Cooperation is Key in Sino-Indian Ties: Saran" (2006) *The Asian Age*, New Delhi, 12 January.

Corbett, Sir Julian (ed.) (1905) *Fighting Instructions, 1530–1816*. London: Navy Records Society.

—— (1907) *England in the Seven Years War*, 2 vols. London: Longmans, Green.

Cornell, Svante E. (2004) "Regional Politics in Central Asia: The Changing Roles of Iran, Turkey, Pakistan and China," in Indranil Banerjie ed. *India and Central Asia*. London: Brunel Academic Publishers, pp. 154–182.

Cox, Robert (1986) "Social Forces, States and World Orders: Beyond International Relations Theory," in R. Cox (ed.) *Neorealism and its Critics*. New York: Columbia University Press, pp. 204–255.

Dabhade, Manish and Pant, Harsh V. (2004) "Coping with Challenges to Sovereignty: Sino-Indian Rivalry and Nepal's Foreign Policy," *Contemporary South Asia*, 13(2): 157–169.

Dannreuther, Roland (2003) "Asian Security and China's Energy Needs," *International Relations of the Asia-Pacific*, 3: 197–219.

Das, P.S. (2001) "Indian Ocean Region in India's Security Calculus," *Journal of Indian Ocean Studies*, 9(3): 315–323.

—— (2005) "Maritime Dimensions of Security in the Indian Ocean," *Proceedings— U.S. Naval Institute*, 131(3): 68–70.

Davis, James W., Finel, Bernard, Goddard, Stacie, Van Evera, Stephen, Glaser, Charles and Kaufmann, Chaim (1998–1999) "Taking Offense at Offense-Defense Theory," *International Security*, 23(3): 179–206.

Dawar, Niraj (2005) "Prepare Now for a Sino-Indian Trade Boom." *Financial Times* [online] Richard Ivey School of Business, Hong Kong. Available: <http://www.ivey.com.hk/news_31_Oct_05.html> [accessed 11 February, 2006].

Deaton, A. (2001) "Computing Prices and Poverty Rates in India, 1999–2000," Princeton University Research Program in Developmental Studies.

"Declaration on Principles for Relations and Comprehensive Cooperation Between the People's Republic of China and the Republic of India" (2003) Beijing, 23 June [online]. Available: <http://www.chinaembassy.org.in/eng/ssygd/zygx/xy/>.

Deng, Xiaoping (1993) *Selected Works of Deng Xiaoping: Book Three*. Beijing: People's Press.

Desai, Ashok (1999) "The Economics and Politics of Transition to an Open Market Economy: India," OECD Development Center Technical Papers, no. 155, Paris: OECD.

"Design Concept of China's New Generation Frigate." (2003) *Kanwa News*, 20 July.

Deutsch, Karl (1957) *Political Community and the North Atlantic Area*. Princeton, NJ: Princeton University Press.

—— (1966) *The Nerves of Government*. New York: The Free Press.

Diehl, Paul F. (ed.) (1997) *A Road Map to War: Territorial Dimensions of International Conflict*. Nashville, TN: Vanderbilt University Press.

Dittmer, Lowell (2001) "South Asia's Security Dilemma," *Asian Survey*, 41(6): 897–906.

Dixit, J.N. (1996) *My South Block Years: Memoirs of a Foreign Secretary*. New Delhi: UPSB.

—— (2003) *India's Foreign Policy 1947–2003*. New Delhi: Picus Books.

Documents on the Sino-Indian Boundary Question (1960) Beijing: Foreign Languages Press.

Donhang (1999) 26 May, FBIS-CHI–99–0604.

Doughtery, James and Pfaltzgraff, Robert (1981) *Contending Theories of International Relations*. New York: Harper and Row.

Dowdy, William L. and Trood, Russell B. (1985) *The Indian Ocean: Perspectives on a Strategic Arena*. Durham, NC: Duke University Press.

Downing, John W. (1996a) "China's Evolving Maritime Strategy, Part 1," *Jane's Intelligence Review*, 8(4): 129–133.

—— (1996b) "China's Evolving Maritime Strategy, Part 2," *Jane's Intelligence Review*, 8(4): 186–191.

Downs, Erica S. (2000) *China's Quest for Energy Security*. Santa Monica, CA: RAND Corporation.

—— (2004) "The Chinese Energy Security Debate," *The China Quarterly*, 177: 21–41.

Dray, William (1959) "'Explaining What' in History," in P. Gardiner (ed.) *Theories of History*. Glencore, IL: Free Press, pp. 403–408.

Dreze, Jean and Sen, Amartya (1995) *India: Economic Development and Social Opportunity*. Delhi: Oxford University Press.

Dunn, Frederick Sherwood (1937) *Peaceful Change; A Study of International Procedures*. New York: Council on Foreign Relations.

Durkheim, Emile (1893) *De la Division du travail sociale: Etude sur l'organisation des societes superieres*. Paris: F. Alcan.

Dutta, Saikat (2004) "Navy Charts New Course with First Doctrine," *The Indian Express*, 26 April.

Dutta, Sujan (2004) "Navy Takes Plunge for Nuclear Muscle," *Telegraph India* [online]. Available: <www.telegraphindia.com/1040624/asp/nation/story_3409050. asp> [accessed 11 October, 2005].

Dutta, Sujit (2005) Personal interview, IDSA, New Delhi, July.

Dzever, Sam and Jaussaud Jacques (eds) (1999) *China and India Economic Performance and Business Strategies of Firms in the Mid-1990s*. London: Macmillan Press.

Eckstein, Alexander (1977) *China's Economic Revolution*. Cambridge: Cambridge University Press.

Elleman, Bruce (2002) "Recent Works on the Chinese Navy," *Naval War College Review*, 45(3): 1–10.

Elvin, Mark (1973) *The Pattern of the Chinese Past*. Stanford, CA: Stanford University Press.

"EU3 to Call for Emergency IAEA Talks on Iran in Feb," (2006) *Reuters*, London, 16 January.

Fairbank, John (1992) *China: A New History*. Cambridge, MA: Harvard University Press.

Fang, Tien-sze (2005) "China Focuses on Improving Relations in South Asia," *Taipei Times*, 27 April.

FewSmith, Joseph (2001) *China Since Tiananmen: The Politics of Transition*. Cambridge: Cambridge University Press.

Finnemore, Martha (1996) *National Interests in International Society*. Ithaca, NY: Cornell University Press.

Fisher, Richard (2003) "PLA Air Force Equipment Trends," in Stephen Flanagan and Michael Marti (eds) *The People's Liberation Army and China in Transition*. Washington, DC: National Defense University Press.

"Former Indian Official to Attend Cooperation Conference in Taiwan" (2004) *Taipei Times*, Taipei, 11 November.

Forsythe, Rosemarie (1996) *The Politics of Oil in the Caucasus and Central Asia*. Oxford: Oxford University Press.

Foucault, Michel (1982) "The Subject of Power," *Critical Inquiry*, 8: 777–795.

Frankel, Benjamin (1996) "Restating the Realist Case," in Benjamin Frankel (ed.) *Realism: Restatements and Renewal*, London: Frank Cass and Co.

Frankel, Francine (1978) *India's Political Economy 1947–1977*. Princeton, NJ: Princeton University Press.

Frankel, Francine and Harding, Harry (eds) (2004) *The India-China Relationship*. New York: Columbia University Press.

Fried, Edward R. and Trezise, Philip H. (1993) *Oil Security: Retrospect and Prospect*. Washington, DC: Brookings Institution.

Fu, Xiaoqing (2004) "India's 'Look East' Policy: Geopolitical, Historical and Perceptional Changes," *Contemporary International Relations*, 14(9): 33–48.

Gabriel, Jurg Martin (1995) "The Integration of European Security: A Functional Analysis," *Aussenwirtschaft*, 50(1): 135–160.

Ganguly, Sumit (2002) "India's Alliances 2020," in Michael R. Chambers (ed.) *South Asia in 2020*. Strategic Studies Institute, pp. 363–385.

—— (2004) "India and China: Border Issues, Domestic Integration, and International Security," in Francine Frankel and Harry Harding (eds) *The India-China Relationship*. New York: Columbia University Press, pp. 103–134.

Gao, S. (2000) "China," in P.B. Stares (ed.) *Rethinking Energy Security in Asia*. Tokyo: Japan Center for International Exchange, pp. 43–58.

Garver, John (1996) "Sino-Indian Rapprochement and the Sino-Pakistan Entente," *Political Science Quarterly*, 111(2): 323–347.

—— (2001a) "The Restoration of Sino-Indian Comity Following India's Nuclear Tests," *The China Quarterly*, 168: 865–889.

—— (2001b) *Protracted Contest: Sino-Indian Rivalry in the Twentieth Century*. Seattle: University of Washington Press.

—— (2002) "The Security Dilemma in Sino-Indian Relations," *India Review*, 4: 1–38.

—— (2005) "China's Influence in Central and South Asia: Is it Increasing?" In David Shambaugh (ed.) *Power Shift: China and Asia's New Dynamics*. Berkeley, CA: University of California Press, pp. 205–228.

Geller, H., DeCicco, J., Laitner, S. and Dyson, C. (1994) "Twenty Years After the Embargo: U.S. Oil Import Dependence and How it Can be Reduced," *Energy Policy*, 22: 471–485.

Gernet, Jacques (1982) *A History of Chinese Civilization*. Trans. J.R. Foster and Charles Hartman. Cambridge: Cambridge University Press.

Gidadhubli, R.G. (1999) "Oil Politics in Central Asia," *Economic and Political Weekly*, 34(5): 260–263.

Gilboy, George (2000) "China's Energy Security Policy after September 11: Crossing the River when the Stones are Moving," *CERA Private Report*, February 2002.

Gill, Bates (2005) "China's Evolving Regional Security Strategy," in David Shambaugh (ed.) *Power Shift: China and Asia's New Dynamics*. Berkeley, CA: University of California Press, pp. 247–266.

Gilpin, Robert (1981) *War and Change in World Politics*. Cambridge: Cambridge University Press.

—— . (1996) "No One Loves a Political Realist," *Security Studies*, 5: 3–28.

Global Information System Naval Staff (2004) "PRC Appears Ready to Field New Trimaran Fast Missile Warship," *Defense and Foreign Affairs Daily*, 5 October.

Glosny, Michael A. (2004) "Strangulation from the Sea: A PRC Submarine Blockade of Taiwan," *International Security*, 28(4): 125–160.

Goldman, Jeffrey B. (1996) "China's Mahan," *U.S. Naval Institute Proceedings*, March: 44–47.

Goldstein, Lyle and Murray, William (2004) "Undersea Dragons: China's Maturing Submarine Force," *International Security*, 28(4): 161–196.

Goldstein, Melvyn C. (1989) *A History of Modern Tibet, 1913–1951*. Berkeley, CA: University of California Press.

Goncharov, Sergei N., Lewis, John W. and Litai, Xue (1993) *Uncertain Partners: Stalin, Mao and the Korean War*. Stanford, CA: Stanford University Press.

Gopalan, R. (2001) "A Discussion Paper on China's Competitiveness," Department of Commerce, Government of India, New Delhi.

Government of India (1959) *White Paper No. 1*. New Delhi: Ministry of External Affairs.

—— (1971) *Annual Report, 1970–1971*. New Delhi: Ministry of Defense.

—— (1973) *Annual Report, 1972–1973*. New Delhi: Ministry of Defense.

—— (1999a) *Economic Survey 1998–1999*. New Delhi: Ministry of Finance.

—— (1999b) *Hydrocarbon Vision 2025*. New Delhi: Planning Commission.

—— (2003) *Tourist Statistics, 2002*. New Delhi: Ministry of Tourism and Culture.

Graham, A.C. (1989) *Disputers of the Tao*. La Salle, IL: Open Court Press.

Gray, Colin S. (1999) *Modern Strategy*. Oxford: Oxford University Press.

Grieco, Joseph M. (1990) *Cooperation among Nations: Europe, America and Non-tariff Barriers to Trade*. Ithaca, NY: Cornell University Press.

Griffith, William (1964) *The Sino-Soviet Rift*. Cambridge, MA: The MIT Press.

Gros, Daniel and Thygesen, Niels (1998) *European Monetary Integration*. New York: Longman.

Guozheng (1999) 24 May, FBIS-CHI–99–0602.

Haas, Ernst (1958) *The Uniting Europe: Political, Social, and Economic Forces 1950–1957*. Stanford, CA: Stanford University Press.

—— (1968) "Technology, Pluralism and the New Europe," in Joseph Nye (ed.) *International Regionalism*. Boston: Little Brown, pp. 149–176.

Hagerty, Devin T. (1991) "India's Regional Security Doctrine," *Asian Survey*, 31: 351–363.

Hall, Peter (2003) "Aligning Ontology and Methodology in Comparative Politics," In James Mahoney and Dietrich Rueschemeyer (eds) *Comparative Historical Analysis*. Cambridge: Cambridge University Press.

Han, Fanzhou, Xianjie, Chen and Feng, Xu (2003) "Record of Surveying of China's Marine Territory by Marine Surveying and Mapping Forces," *Liberation Army Daily*, 11 December, 2002 in FBIS-CHI–2002–1211, 8 January, 2003.

Handel, Michael, I. (2001) *Masters of War: Classical Strategic Thought*, 3rd edn. London: Frank Cass.

Hansen, Valerie (2000) *The Open Empire: A History of China to 1600*. New York: W. W. Norton.

Harding, Harry (1987) *China's Second Revolution: Reforms after Mao*. Washington, DC: The Brookings Institution.

Hattendorf, John B. (1991) *Mahan on Naval Strategy*. Annapolis, MD: Naval Institute Press.

Hersh, Seymour M. (1983) *The Price of Power: Kissinger in the White House*. New York: Summit Books.

Herz, John (1950) "Idealist Internationalism and the Security Dilemma," *World Politics*, 2: 157–180.

Heuser, Beatrice (2002) *Reading Clausewitz*. London: Pimilco.

Hindustan Times (2003) New Delhi, 9 May.

Hoffmann, Steven A. (1990) *India and the China Crisis*. Berkeley, CA: University of California Press.

—— (2004) "Perception and China Policy in India," in Francine Frankel and Harry Harding (eds) *The India-China Relationship*. New York: Columbia University Press.

Holls, Martin and Smith, Steve (1990) *Explaining and Understanding International Relations*. Oxford: Oxford University Press.

Holmes, James R. and Yoshihara, Toshi (2005) "The Influence of Mahan upon China's Maritime Strategy," *Comparative Strategy*, 24: 23–51.

"Hong Kong Agency Reports on Speed of China's Navy Modernization" (2000) *Zhongguo Tongxun She*, 12 February, in SWB FE/3766 G/6–7, 17 February.

Hu, Shih (1937) *The Indianization of China: A Case Study in Cultural Borrowing*. Cambridge, MA: Harvard University Press.

Hua Biyun. (2005) "A Bright Future for China-India Economic Cooperation Based on Equality and Mutual Benefit," In C.V. Ranganathan (ed.) *Panchsheel and the Future: Perspectives on India-China Relations*. New Delhi: Institute of Chinese Studies, Centre for the Study of Developing Societies, pp. 271–286.

Hucker, Charles O. (1975) *China to 1850: A Short History*. Stanford, CA: Stanford University Press.

Hunt, Michael H. (1996) *The Genesis of Chinese Communist Foreign Policy*. New York: Columbia University Press.

Ikenberry, John G. (2003) *International Relations Theory and the Asia-Pacific*. New York: Columbia University Press.

"India Asked to Join Central Asian Grouping" (2002) *The Hindu*, Chennai, 13 February.

"India Outlines Vision of Future Nuclear Navy" (2004) *Jane's Defense Weekly*, 29 June.

"India to Build Six French Submarines under Pact" (2005) *The Hindu*, Chennai, 7 October.

"Indian Army Delegation to Visit Chinese Bases in Tibet" (2003) ABC Radio Australia News [online]. Available: http://www.abc.net.au/ra/newstories/RANewsStories_991044.htm [accessed November 8, 2005].

"Indian Author Sees Birth of 'Concert of Asia' as Answer to US 'Strategy' of Blocs" (2004) *The Telegraph*, Calcutta, 18 December.

"Indian, Chinese Army Chiefs to Discuss 'Enhanced Confidence Building Measures.'" (2005) *The Hindu*, Chennai, 28 May.

"Indian Defense Minister on Ties With China, US Role in Asia-Pacific Region" (2005) *The Hindu*, Chennai, 30 January.

"Indian IT Companies Said 'Willing' to set up Industries in Burma" (2004) *Burmanet News*, 3 November.

"Indian Navy Will Become Leaner and Meaner" (2004) *Press Trust of India*, 4 November.

"Indian Oil Production and Consumption." (2002) Centre for Monitoring the Indian Economy, Mumbai.

"Indian Warship Fleet Winds Up Visit." (2003) *China Daily*, Beijing, 14 November.

"Indo-Iran Pipeline Project Gets to Step on the Gas" (2005) *India Daily*, 9 February.

"Indo-U.S. Ties under Bush" (2004) *India News Online*, 8 November.

Inskip, Ian (2002) *Ordeal by Exocet: HMS Glamorgan and the Falklands War, 1982*. London: Chatham.

International Energy Agency (2002) *World Energy Outlook 2002*. Paris: OECD/IEA.

Jaffrelot, Christophe (2003) "India's Look East Policy: An Asianist Strategy in Perspective," *India Review*, 2(2): 35–68.

Jefferson G.H. and Rawski, T.G. (1994) "Enterprise Reform in Chinese Industry," *Journal of Economic Perspectives*, 8(2): 47–70.

Jervis, Robert (1978) "Cooperation Under the Security Dilemma," *World Politics*, 30: 167–214.

Jiang, Yaping (2004) "India's UPA Government Forges Closer Ties with ASEAN in Globalization Era" *Xinhua*, Beijing, 28 December.

Jing, Yan Shi (1998) "India and Foreign Capital," in Surjit Mansingh ed. *Indian and Chinese Foreign Policies in Comparative Perspective*. New Delhi: Radiant Publishers, pp. 200–220.

Johnson, Arik (2005) "China on the Prowl: CNOOC Bid for Unocal Must First Overcome Chevron," *Competitive Intelligence* [online], 24 June. Available: <http://www.aurorawdc.com/ci/000330.html> [accessed 9 November, 2005].

Jones, Peter and Kevill, Sian (1985) *China and the Soviet Union 1949–84*. London: Longman.

Jones, Sean M. Lynn (1995) "Offense-Defense Theory and Its Critics," *Security Studies*, 4(4): 660–691.

Jordan, John (1994) "The People's Liberation Army Navy (PLAN)," *Jane's Intelligence Review*, 6(6): 275–282.

Joshi, Vijay and Little, I.M.D. (1996) *India's Economic Reforms 1991–2001*. Oxford: Clarendon Press.

Kamath, V.A. (1954) "India and the Sea Power," *USI Journal*, 84: 84–100.

Kane, Thomas M. and Serewicz, Lawrence W. (2001) "China's Hunger: The Consequences of a Rising Demand for Food and Energy," *Parameters*, 31: 63–75.

Kanwal, Gurmeet (1999) "India's Security Challenges as a New Century Dawns," *Indian Defence Review*, October–December: 30–45.

Karnad, Bharat (2005) Personal interview, CPR, New Delhi, July.

Kaushik, Devandra (1987) *Perspectives on Security in Indian Ocean Region*. New Delhi: Allied.

Kazi, Reshmi (2004) "India's Naval Aspirations," Institute of Peace and Conflict Studies, 23 August, Article no. 1472.

Kearsley, Harold K. (1997) *Maritime Power and the Twenty-First Century*. Aldershot: Dartmouth Press.

Keat, Russell and Urry, John (1982) *Social Theory as Science*, 2nd edn. London: RKP.

Kennedy, Paul (2002) "The Eagle Has Landed," *Financial Times*, 2 February.

Keohane, Robert O. (1984) *After Hegemony: Cooperation and Discord in the World Political Economy*. Princeton, NJ: Princeton University Press.

—— (1986) "Theory of World Politics: Structural Realism and Beyond," in Robert O. Keohane ed. *Neorealism and its Critics*. New York: Columbia University Press, pp. 158–204.

—— and Nye, Joseph S. (1977) *Power and Interdependence*. New York: Longman.

Khera, S.S. (1968) *India's Defence Problem*. Bombay: Orient Longmans.

Khilnani (1999) *The Idea of India*. New York: Straus and Giroux.

Khurana, Gurpreet (2005a) "Security of Maritime Lifelines: Exploring Sino-Indian 'Confluence,' " paper prepared for the Institute for Defense Studies and Analyses, New Delhi.

—— (2005b) "Maritime Terrorism in Southern Asia," *Indian Defence Review*, 20(1): 54–63.

—— (2005c) Personal interview, IDSA, New Delhi, June.

King, Gary, Keohane, Robert and Verba, Sidney (1994) *Designing Social Inquiry*. Princeton, NJ: Princeton University Press.

Kochhar, Rajesh (2000) *The Vedic People: Their History and Geography*. New Delhi: Orient Longman.

Kohli, S.N. (1978) *Sea Power and the Indian Ocean*. New Delhi: Tata McGraw-Hill.

Kondapalli, Srikanth (2001) *China's Naval Power*. New Delhi: Knowledge World.

—— (2004) "The Dragon at Sea: China's Naval Expansion," New Delhi: Institute for Defense Studies and Analyses.

—— (2005a) "China's 'String of Pearls' Strategy: Creeping Entry into Indian Ocean," New Delhi: Institute for Defense Studies and Analyses.

—— (2005b) Personal interview, IDSA, New Delhi, July.

Krasner, Stephen (1983) *International Regimes*. Ithaca, NY: Cornell University Press.

Kratochwil, Friedrich (1993) "The Embarrassment of Changes: Neorealism as the Science of Realpolitik without Politics," *Review of International Studies*, 19(1): 63–80.

Kraus, Richard (2004) "China in 2003: From SARS to Spaceships," *Asian Survey*, 44: 1.

Kuhn, Thomas (1962) *The Structure of Scientific Revolutions*. Chicago: University of Chicago Press.

Kumar, Nagesh (2005) "Towards an Asian Economic Community: A Longer-term Vision of Sino-Indian Partnership," in C.V. Ranganathan ed. *Panchsheel and the Future: Perspectives on India-China Relations*. New Delhi: Institute of Chinese Studies, Centre for the Study of Developing Societies, pp. 349–369.

Kumar, Nanda (2005) Personal interview, IDSA, New Delhi, July.

Kumar, Siddhartha (2004) "Shwe's Visit to Start 'Constructive Engagement,'" *The Asian Age*, New Delhi, 22 October.

Kuo, Deborah (2004) "Ample Room for Taiwan, India to Improve Political Ties," *Central News Agency*, Taipei, 12 November.

Kwatra, Vinay (2005) "India-China Trade and Economic Relations: Current Status and Prospects," in C.V. Ranganathan (ed.) *Panchsheel and the Future: Perspectives of India-China Relations*. New Delhi: Institute of Chinese Studies, Centre for the Study of Developing Societies, pp. 237–271.

Lakatos, Imre (1970) "Falsification and the Methodology of Scientific Research Programmes," in Imre Lakatos and A. Musgrave (eds) *Criticism and the Growth of Knowledge*. Cambridge: Cambridge University Press.

Lall, A. (1962) *Negotiating Disarmament*. Ithaca, NY: Cornell University Press.

Lall, John (1989) *Aksaichin and Sino-Indian Conflict*. New Delhi: Allied Publishers.

Lamb, Alastair (1964) *The China-India Border*. London: Praeger.

—— (1968) *Asian Frontiers: Studies in a Continuing Problem*. New York: Praeger.

Langlois, John D. (2002) "Pressures on China from the Asian financial Crisis," in A.S. Alexandro H. S. Ostry and R. Gomez (eds) *China and the Long March to Global Trade*. London: Routledge.

Lebow, Richard Ned (1996) "Cold War Lessons for Political Theorists," *The Chronicle of Higher Education*, 42: 20, B2.

Lee, Jae-hyung (2002) "China's Expanding Ambitions in the Western Pacific and the Indian Ocean," *Contemporary Southeast Asia*, 24(3): 549–568.

Legro, Jeffrey and Moravcsik Andrew (1999) "Is Andybody Still a Realist?" *International Security*, 24(2): 5–54.

Leung, Keung and Chin, Steve S.K. (eds) (1983) *China in Readjustment*. Hong Kong: University of Hong Kong Press.

Levy, Jack (1984) "The Offense/Defense Balance of Military Technology: A Theoretical and Historical Analysis," *International Studies Quarterly*, 28(2): 219–238.

Lewis, John Wilson and Litai, Xue (1994) *China's Strategic Sea Power: The Politics of Force Modernization in the Nuclear Age*. Stanford, CA: Stanford University Press.

Li, Jing (2005) "China Willing to Work with India to Develop Bilateral Ties," *Zhongguo Xinwen She*, Beijing, 1 February, from World News Connection.

Liao, Wen-chung (1995) *China's Blue Water Strategy in the 21st Century: From the First Islands Towards the Second Islands Chain*. Occasional Paper Series, Taipei: Chinese Council of Advanced Policy Studies.

Lieberthal, Kenneth and Oksenberg, Michel (1988) *Policy Making in China: Leaders, Structures and Processes*. Princeton, NJ: Princeton University Press.

"Likely Sino-Indian FTA Conducive to Nation" (2004) *China Business Weekly*, Beijing 12 April.

Lindberg, Leon N. (1963) *The Political Dynamics of European Economic Integration*. Stanford, CA: Stanford University Press.

Liu, Xinru (1988) *Ancient India and Ancient China*. New Delhi: Oxford University Press.

Liu, Xuecheng (1994) *The Sino-Indian Border Dispute and Sino-Indian Relations*. Lanham, MD: University Press of America.

"Looking Forward to Fourth Climax of Development in Sino-Indian Relations: Interview with Chinese Ambassador to India Sun Yuxi" (2005) *Xinhua*, Beijing 1 April.

Luft, Gal and Korin, Anne (2004) "Terrorism Goes to Sea," *Foreign Affairs*, Institute for Analysis of Global Security, November/December.

MacDonald, Juli A. and Wimbush, S. Enders (2000) "Thinking About India's Energy Security," a paper presented at the Science Application Information Center, Washington, DC, April 2000.

Maddison, Angus (1998) *Chinese Economic Performance in the Long Run*. Paris: OECD Development Center.

Mahan, Capt. A.T. (1890) *Influence of Seapower upon History 1660–1783*. New York: Scrivener.

—— (1911) *Naval Strategy: Compared and Contrasted with the Principles and Practice of Military Operations on Land*. Boston: Little, Brown.

Maitra, Ramtanu (2005) "India Bids to Rule the Waves," *Asia Times*, 19 Oct.

Majeed, Akhtar (ed.) (1986) *Indian Ocean: Conflict and Regional Cooperation*. New Delhi: ABC Publishing House.

Majumdar, Sayan (2005) "Akula for the Indian Navy," India Defence [online]. Available: <www.indiadefence.com> [accessed 15 October, 2005].

Malik, Mohan (2001) "South Asia in China's Foreign Relations," *Pacifica Review*, 13(1): 73–90.

—— (2002) "Zhou, Mao and Nixon's 1972 Conversations on India," *Issues and Studies*, 38(3): 184–219.

Manning, Robert (2000) *The Asian Energy Factor*. New York: Palgrave.

Mansingh, Surjit. (1994a) "India-China Relations in the Post-Cold War Era," *Asian Survey*, 34(3): 285–300.

—— (1994b) "China-Bhutan Relations," *China Report*, 30(2): 177–194.

Mansingh, Surjit and Levine, Steven I. (1989) "China and India: Moving Beyond Confrontation," *Problems of Communism*, 38(2–3): 30–49.

March, James G. and Olsen, Johan P. (1998) "The Institutional Dynamics of International Political Orders," *International Organization*, 52(4): 943–969.

Margolis, Eric S. (2005) "India Rules the Waves," *Proceedings of the United States Naval Institute*, 131(3): 66–70.

Mathur, Anand (2002) "Growing Importance of the Indian Ocean: Post-Cold War Era and its Implications for India," *Strategic Analysis*, 26: 4.

Maxwell, Neville (1970) *India's China War*. London: Jonathan Cape.

Mearsheimer, John (1995) "Back to the Future: Instability in Europe after the Cold War," in Michael E. Brown, Sean M. Lynn-Jones, and Steven E. Miller (ed.) *The Perils of Anarchy: Contemporary Realism and International Security*. Cambridge, MA: MIT Press, pp. 3–54.

—— (2001) *The Tragedy of Great Power Politics*. New York: W.W. Norton and Company.

Medvedev, Roy (1986) *China and the Superpowers*. New York: Basil Blackwell.

Mehra, Parshotam (1989) *Negotiating with the Chinese, 1846–1987*. New Delhi: Reliance Publishing House.

Mehrotra, L.L. (1997) *India's Tibet Policy: An Appraisal and Options*. New Delhi: Tibetan Parliamentary and Policy Research Centre.

Mirchandani, G.G. (1966) *India's Nuclear Dilemma*. New Delhi: Popular Books.

Misra, R.N. (1986) *Indian Ocean and India's Security*. New Delhi: Mittal.

Mitra, Amit and Anjan Roy (2005) "An Overview of India-China Trade and Investments," in C.V. Ranganathan ed. *Panchsheel and the Future: Perspectives on India-China Relations*. New Delhi: Institute of Chinese Studies, Centre for the Study of Developing Societies, pp. 286–303.

Mitrany, David (1948) "The Functional Approach to World Organization," *International Affairs*, 24(3): 350–363.

Mohan, C. Raja (2003) *Crossing the Rubicon: The Shaping of India's New Foreign Policy*. New Delhi: Penguin Books India.

—— (2005a) "While Delhi Lets Chennai Write its Lanka Policy, China Scripts New Chapter," *The Indian Express*, 2 June.

—— (2005b) Phone interview, New Delhi, July.

Mohanty, Deba R. (2004) "Coming of Age: The Indian Navy in the 21st Century," *Military Technology*, 28(7): 93–101.

Morgenthau, Hans (1948) *Politics Among Nations*. New York: Knopf.

Morse, E.L. and Jaffe, A.M. (2001) *Strategic Energy Policy Challenges for the 21st Century*. James Baker III Institute for Public Policy, Rice University.

Mukherji, Biman (2004) "India Rolls out Red Carpet for Burma's Military Strongman," *AFP*, Hong Kong, 25 October.

Muni, S.D. and Pant, Girijesh (2005) *India's Search for Energy Security: Prospects for Cooperation with Extended Neighborhood*. New Delhi: Rupa Company.

Munro, Ross H. (1999) "Chinese Energy Strategy," in *Energy Strategies and Military Strategies in Asia*, report prepared for the Office of Net Assessment, Department of Defense, United States of America, Washington, DC.

Nairayan, Raviprasad (2005) Personal interview, IDSA, New Delhi, July.

Namoodiri, Udayan (2004) "New Intensity," *The Pioneer*, 18 December.

Nanda, Harbaksh Singh (2004) "India-U.S. Furthers Strategic Ties," *United Press International, The Washington Times*, 22 October.

Naughton, Barry (1994) "Chinese Institutional Innovation and Privatization from Below," *American Economic Review: Papers and Proceedings* 84(2).

Nehru, Jawaharlal (1946) *The Discovery of India*. New York: John Day Company.

"New Generation Warships for the PLA Navy" (2004) *Military Technology*, February.

New York Times (1998) 13 May.

Newman, Peter C. (2006) "Terror Already Has its Sea Legs," *The Globe and Mail*, 11 March.

Niazi, Tarique (2005a) "China's March on South Asia," The Jamestown Foundation, *China Brief*, 3 June.

—— (2005b) "Gwadar: China's Naval Outpost on the Indian Ocean," The Jamestown Foundation, *China Brief*, 28 February.

Niebuhr, Reinhold (1950) *The World Crisis and American Responsibility*. New York: Association Press.

"No Drift in Policy on Pakistan: Natwar Singh" (2004) *The Hindu*, Chennai, 23 December.

North, Douglass C. and Weingast, Barry R. (1989) "Constitutions and Commitments: The Evolution of Institutions Governing Public Choice in Seventeenth-Century England," *Journal of Economic History*, 4: 803–32.

Nurske, Ragner (1953) *Problems of Capital Formation in Underdeveloped Countries*. New York: Oxford University Press.

Oi, Jean (1999) *Rural China Takes Off: Institutional Foundations of Economic Reform*. Berkeley, CA: University of California Press.

Ottaway David B. and Morgan, Dan (1997) "China Pursues Ambitious Role in Oil Market," *Washington Post*, 26 December.

Paik, K.W. (1995) *Gas and Oil in Northeast Asia*. London: Royal Institute of International Affairs.

Paine, S.C.M. (1996) *Imperial Rivals: China, Russia, and Their Disputed Frontier*. New York: M.E. Sharpe.

Palit, D.K. and Namboodri, P.K.S. (1982) *Pakistan's Islamic Bomb*. New Delhi: Vikas.

Panikkar, K.M. (1946) *India and the Indian Ocean: An Essay on the Influence of Sea Power on Indian History*. London: G. Allen and Unwin.

—— (1957) *India and China: A Study of Cultural Relations*. Bombay: Asia Publishing House.

Pant, Harsh V. (2004) "The Moscow-Beijing-Delhi 'Strategic Triangle': An Idea Whose Time May Never Come," *Security Dialogue*, 35: 311–328.

Park, A. and Wang, S. (2001) "China's Poverty Statistics," *China Economic Review*, 12: 384–395.

Paul, T.V. (ed.) (2004) *Balance of Power: Theory and Practice in the 21st Century*. Stanford, CA: Stanford University Press.

"Pentagon Briefs India on Anti-missile System" (2005) *Organization of Asia-Pacific News Agencies*, 9 September.

People's Republic of China, General Office of the State Council (1999) *Circular Concerning Encouraging Enterprises to Conduct Overseas Processing and Assembly Business*. Beijing: Ministry of Foreign Economic and Trade Cooperation, State Economic and Trade Commission and the Ministry of Finance.

—— (2003) *Circular of the State Administration of Foreign Exchange on Relevant Issues Concerning Deepening the Reform of Foreign Exchange Administration on Overseas Investment*. Beijing: Ministry of Foreign Economic and Trade Cooperation, 15 October.

—— (2004) *China's National Defense in 2004*. Beijing: Information Council of the State Office of the People's Republic of China, December.

Perkins, D. (2000) "Industrial and Financial Sector Policies in China and Vietnam." Mimeo, Department of Economics, Harvard University, Cambridge, MA.

Perkovich, George (1999) *India's Nuclear Bomb*. Berkeley, CA: University of California Press.

—— (2004) "The Nuclear and Security Balance," in Francine Frankel and Harry Harding (eds) *The India-China Relationship*. New York: Columbia University Press, pp. 178–219.

"Playing it Safe: Lessons from China's Reserves Management" (2006) *The Hindu Business Line*, 23 January.

Powell, Robert (1994) "Anarchy in International Relations Theory: The Neorealist-neoliberal Debate," *International Organization*, 48: 313–344.

Praval, K.C. (1990) *Indian Army After Independence*. New Delhi: Lancer International.

"PRC Navy Commander Zhang Dingfa Hails China-India Navy Relations" (2005) *Xinhua*, Beijing, 12 April.

"PRC FM Spokesman Sets Positive Tone for Indian Oil Minister's Visit" (2006) *AFP*, Hong Kong, 12 January.

"Presidents of Pakistan, China Expected to Open Gwadar Port Before Year-end" (2004) *Islamabad The News* [in English], Islamabad, 27 November.

Price, Richard and Reus-Smit, Christian (1998) "Dangerous Liaisons? Critical International Theory and Constructivism," *European Journal of International Relations*, 4: 259–294.

Priddle, Robert (2000) "The IEA's Role in Asian Energy Security Cooperation," Seminar on Energy Security in Asia, Tokyo, March.

Rachman, G. (1996) "Containing China," *Washington Quarterly*, 19(1): 129–140.

Radtke, Kurt (2003) "Sino-Indian Relations," *Perspectives on Global Development and Technology*, 2(3–4): 499–520.

Raganathan, C.V. (2001) "Sino-Indian Relations in the New Millenium: Challenges and Prospects," *China Report*, 37(2): 129–140.

Ram, Mohan (1973) *Politics of Sino-Indian Confrontation*. New Delhi: Vikas.

Ramchandran, K.N. (2004) "India-China Interactions," in K. Santhanam and Srikanth Kondapalli (eds) *Asian Security and China 2000–2010*. New Delhi: Shipra Publications.

Ranjan, Amitav (2004) "A Corner of Foreign Oil Field," *Indian Express*, 25 January.

Rasgotra, M.K. (1991) "India's Security and the Sea," *Strategic Analysis* 14: 1040–1057.

Rashid, Ahmed and Saywell, Trish (1998) "Beijing Gusher," *Far Eastern Economic Review*, 26 February.

Ray, J.K. (1967) *Security in the Missile Age*. New Delhi: Allied Publishers.

Reardon, Lawrence (2002) *The Reluctant Dragon: Crisis Cycles in Chinese Foreign Economic Policy*. Hong Kong: Hong Kong University Press.

Reeve, John (2001) "The Rise of Modern Naval Strategy *c*. 1850–1880," in David Stephens and John Reeve (eds) *Southern Trident*. Crows Nest, Australia: Allen and Unwin, pp. 7–24.

Reliance Energy Research Group (2002) *Reliance Review of Energy Markets*. Mumbai, Reliance Industries Limited, December.

Renmin Ribao (2005) "Construct a Bridge Leading to the Future," 13 April, FBIS-CHI-2005-0412, from World News Connection.

Report of the India-China Joint Study Group on Comprehensive Trade and Economic Cooperation (2004)

Reynolds, Richard "China Invests in Canadian Energy Sector," *Day to Day*, 27 September, 2005. Available: <http://www.npr.org/templates/story/story.php?storyId=4865764> [accessed 4 December, 2005].

"RMRB Interviews PRC Ambassador to India on Sino-Indian Relations, Friendship," (2006) *Renmin Ribao*, Beijing, 26 January.

Rose, Leo (2000) "India and China: Forging a New Relationship," in Shalendra D.

Sharma (ed.) *The Asia-Pacific in the New Millenium*. Berkeley, CA: University of California Press, pp. 224–238.

Rosencrance, Richard (1986) *The Rise of the Trading State: Commerce and Conquest in the Modern World*. New York: Basic Books.

Roy, D. (1996) "The 'China Threat' Issue: Major Arguments," *Asian Survey*, 37(8): 758–781.

Roy-Chaudhury, Rahul (1995) *Sea Power and Indian Security*. London: Brassey's.

Rudolph, Lloyd I. and Hoeber Rudolph, Susanne (1987) *In Pursuit of Lakshmi: The Political Economy of the Indian State*. Chicago: University of Chicago Press.

Ruggie, John Gerard (1986) "Continuity and Transformation in the World Polity: Toward a Neorealist Synthesis," in Robert O. Keohane (ed.) *Neorealism and Its Critics*. New York: Columbia University Press, pp. 131–158.

—— (1998) "What Makes the World Hang Together? Neo-Utilitarianism and the Social Constructivist Challenge," in *Constructing the World Polity: Essays on International Institutionalization*. New York: Routledge.

Ruseckas, Laurent (1998) State of the Field Report: Energy and Politics in Central Asia. *Access Asia Review*, 2(1): 46–50.

Sae-Liu, Robert (1999) "Beijing Will Wait and See Before Building New Super Warship," *Jane's Defence Weekly*, 18 August.

Sagan, Scott D. (1986) "1914 Revisited: Allies, Offense and Instability," *International Security*, 11(2): 151–175.

Saghal, Arun (2005) Personal interview, USI, New Delhi, July.

Saich, Tony (2001) *Governance and Politics of China*. New York: Palgrave.

Saigal, J.R. (1979) *The Unfought War of 1962*. New Delhi: Allied Publishers.

Sakhuja, Vijay (2005a) Personal interview, IDSA, New Delhi, July.

—— (2005b) "Project Seabird: An Example of India's Maritime Prowess," New Delhi: Observer Research Foundation.

Salameh, Mamdouh G. (1995–96) "China, Oil and the Risk of Regional Conflict," *Survival*, 37(4): 133–146.

Sandhu, Bhim (1988) *Unresolved Conflict: China and India*. New Delhi: Radiant Publishers.

Schelling, Thomas (1960) *The Strategy of Conflict*. Cambridge, MA: Harvard University Press.

Schmitter, Phillip C. (1969) "Three Neo-Functionalist Hypotheses about European Integration," *International Organization*, 23(1).

—— (1971) "A Revised Theory of European Integration," in L.N. Lindberg and S.A. Scheingold (eds) *Regional Integration: Theory and Research*. Cambridge, MA: Harvard University Press, pp. 234–264.

Schweller, Randall (1997) "New Realist Research on Alliances: Refining, not Refuting, Waltz's Balancing Proposition," *American Political Science Review*, 91(4): 927–930.

Scobell, Andrew (2002) "'Cult of Defense' and 'Great Power Dreams'," in Michael R. Chambers (ed.) *South Asia in 2020*. Washington, DC: Strategic Studies Institute, pp. 329–361.

Seekington, Ian (2002) "China Reforms: A Mixed Legacy for a New Generation," *Asian Affairs*, 33:3.

Segal, Gerald and Yang, Richard H. (eds) (1996) *Chinese Economic Reform: The Impact on Security*. London: Routledge.

Sen, Bhowani (1962) *Evolution of Agrarian Relations in India*. New Delhi: People Publishing House.

Sen, Tansen (2001) "In Search of Longevity and Good Karma: Chinese Diplomatic Missions to Middle India in the Seventh Century," *Journal of World History*, 12(1): 1–28.

Sengupta, Prasun K. (1999) "Airborne ASW Systems in Asia-Pacific," *Asian Defense Journal*, 10(October): 30–34.

Sharan, Shankar (ed.) (1996) *India, Tibet and China: An Agonising Reappraisal*. New Delhi: India Tibet Friendship Society.

Sharma, Devika (2006) "China May Be 'Ultimately Trusted' to Settle Border Dispute," New Delhi, Institute of Peace and Conflict Studies, 13 April.

Sharma, Harvir (2001) "China's Interests in Indian Ocean Rim Countries and India's Maritime Security," *India Quarterly*, 58(4): 67–88.

Sharma, Shri Ram (2003) *India-China Relations 1972–1991*. New Delhi: Discovery Publishing House.

Shirk, Susan L. (2004) "One-Sided Rivalry: China's Perceptions and Policies toward India," in Francine Frankel and Harry Harding (eds) *The India-China Relationship*. New York: Columbia University Press, pp. 75–103.

Shulman, Mark (1995) *Navalism and the Emergence of American Sea Power, 1882–1893*. Annapolis, MD: Naval Institute Press.

Siddharthan, N.S. (2005) "Global Economic Environment: Common Concerns and Policy Options for India and China," in C.V. Ranganathan (ed.) *Panchsheel and the Future: Perspectives on India-China Relations*. New Delhi: Institute of Chinese Studies, Centre for the Study of Developing Socities, pp. 303–327.

Sidhu, Waheguru Pal Singh and Yuan, Jing-dong (2001) "Resolving the Sino-Indian Border Dispute," *Asian Survey*, 41(2), 351–376.

—— (2003) *China and India: Cooperation or Conflict?* Boulder, CO: Lynne Reinner.

Singh, Jasjit (1986) "Regional Naval Power: Retarded Growth," *World Focus*, 7: 13–22.

—— (ed.) (1993) *Maritime Security*. New Delhi: Institute for Defense Studies and Analyses.

—— (1999) *Asian Security in the 21st Century*. New Delhi: Institute for Defense Studies and Analyses.

Singh, Jaswant (1998) "Against Nuclear Apartheid," *Foreign Affairs*, 77(5): 41–52.

Singh, K.R. (2002) *Navies of South Asia*. New Delhi: Institute for Defence Studies and Analyses, pp. 195–218.

—— (2004) "India, Indian Ocean and Regional Maritime Cooperation," *International Studies*, 41(2).

Singh, Nihal S. (1986) *The Yogi and the Bear: A Study of Indo-Soviet Relations*. New Delhi: Allied Publishers.

Singh, Satyindra (1992) *Blue Print to Blue Waters: The Indian Navy, 1951–1991*. New Delhi: Lancer International.

Singh, Sukhwant (1981) *India's Wars Since Independence: Defence of the Western Border*, Vol. 2. New Delhi: Vikas.

Singh, Swaran (1999) "The Kargil Conflict: The Why and How of China's Neutrality," *Strategic Analysis*, 23(7): 1083–1094.

—— (2005a) *China-India Economic Engagement: Building Mutual Confidence*. New Delhi: Centre de Sciences Humaines.

—— (2005b) Personal interview, JNU, New Delhi, July.

Singh, Udai Bhanu (2005) Personal interview, IDSA, New Delhi, June.

"Sino-Indian Trust Promoted upon Indian Army Chief's China Tour" (2004) *Xinhua*, Beijing, 29 December.

Sisci, Francesco Lao Xi (1997) "Giant Oil Deals Move China onto World Stage," *Asia Times*, 6 June.

Soligo, R. and Jaffe, A.M. (1999) "China's Growing Energy Dependence: The Costs and Policy Implications of Supply Dependence," in *China and Long-Range Asia Energy Security: An Analysis of the Political, Economic and Technological Factors*. James Baker III Institute for Public Policy, Rice University, USA.

Sondhaus, Lawrence (2004) *Navies in Modern World History*. London: Reaktin Books.

"Southwest China Finds Ocean Outlet" (2001) *Far Eastern Economic Review*, 21 February.

Srinivasan, T.N. (2004) "Economic Reforms and Global Integration," in Francine Frankel and Harry Harding (eds) *The India-China Relationship*. New York: Columbia University Press, pp. 219–267.

Stein, Burton (1980) *Peasant, State and Society in Medieval South India*. Oxford: Oxford University Press.

Storey, Ian and Ji, You (2004) "China's Aircraft Carrier Ambitions: Seeking Truth from Rumours," *Naval War College Review*, 57(1): 77–93.

Subramanian, R.R. (2005) Personal interview, IDSA, New Delhi, July.

Sun, Zhuangzhi (2004) "Economic Collaboration in Central Asian Region and the SCO," in K. Santhanam and Ramakant Dwivedi (eds) *India and Central Asia: Advancing the Common Interest*. New Delhi: Anamaya Publishers, pp. 144–151.

Suraynarayana, P.S. (2003) "India for Strong Ties with ASEAN," *The Hindu*, Chennai, 2 July.

Swaine, Michael D. (2005) "China's Regional Military Posture," in David Shambaugh (ed.) *Power Shift: China and Asia's New Dynamics*. Berkeley, CA: University of California Press, pp. 266–289.

Swaine, Michael D. and Tellis, Ashley J. (2000) *Interpreting China's Grand Strategy: Past, Present and Future*. Santa Monica, CA: RAND.

Swamy, Subramanian (2001) *India's China Perspective*. New Delhi: Konrak Publishers.

—— (2003) *Economic Reforms and Performance: China and India in Comparative Perspective*. Delhi: Konrak Publishers PVT Ltd.

Swanson, Bruce (1982) *Eighth Voyage of the Dragon: A History of China's Quest for Sea Power*. Annapolis, MD: Naval Institute Press.

"Tackling Import Dependence" (2002) *Petroleum Economist*, India Section, December.

Tai Yang Pao (1999) 1 November in SWB FE/3691 G/3–4 2, November.

Tanham, George (1992) "Indian Strategic Culture," *Washington Quarterly*, Winter: 129–142.

Tanner, Murray Scot (2002) "Changing Windows on a Changing China: The Evolving 'Think Tank' System and the Case of the Public Security Sector," *The China Quarterly*, 171: 559–574.

—— (2004) "China Rethinks Unrest," *Washington Quarterly*, 27(3).

Tarrow, Sidney (1998) *Power in Movement*. Cambridge: Cambridge University Press.

Tellis, Ashley J. (1985) "The Naval Balance in the Indian Sub-Continent," *Asian Survey* 25: 1186–1213.

—— (2001) *India's Emerging Nuclear Posture*. Santa Monica, CA: RAND.

Thakurdas *et al.* (1944) *A Plan of Economic Development of India*. London: Penguin Books.

Thokchom, Khelen (2004) "Train to Myanmar Gets Nod," *The Telegraph*, Calcutta, 25 November.

Thomas, Raju G. C. (1986) *Indian Security Policy*. Princeton, NJ: Princeton University Press.
—— (1993) *South Asian Security in the 1990s*. London: Brassey's.
—— (2000) *India's Nuclear Security*. London: Lynne Rienner.
Thomas, Raju G. C. and Gupta, Amit (2000) *India's Nuclear Security*. Boulder, CO: Lynne Rienner.
Thomas, Raju G. C. and Ramberg Bennett, (eds) (1990) *Energy and Security in the Industrializing World*. Lexington, KE: University of Kentucky Press.
Till, Geoffrey (2004) *Seapower: A Guide for the Twenty-First Century*. London: Frank Cass.
Toichi, T. and Naitoh, M. (2001) "Japan's Energy Security and Petroleum Policies," *Oxford Energy Forum*, 3–4 May.
Toussaint, Auguste (1967) *History of the Indian Ocean*. Trans. June Guicharnaud. Chicago: University of Chicago Press.
United States of America (2004) *2004 Report to Congress on China's WTO Compliance*. Washington, DC: United States Trade Representative, 11 December.
—— Office of the Secretary of Defense (2005) *Annual Report to Congress: The Military Power of the People's Republic of China* 2005. Washington, DC: United States Department of Defense.
Uppal, J.S. (1984) *Indian Economic Planning: Three Decades of Development*. Delhi: Macmillan India Ltd.
Uttam, Jitendra (2003) "Economic Growth in India and China: A Comparative Study," *International Studies*, 40(4): 319–347.
Van Eekelen W.F. (1964) *Indian Foreign Policy and the Border Dispute with China*. The Hague: Martinus Nijhoff.
Van Evera, Stephen (1994) "Hypotheses on Nationalism and War," *International Security*, 18(4): 5–39.
—— (1998) "Offense, Defense and the Causes of War," *International Security*, 22(4): 5–43.
Varadarajan, Siddharth (2006) "India, China and the Asian Axis of Oil," *The Hindu*, Chennai, 24 January.
Vasquez, John A. (1993) *The War Puzzle*. Cambridge: Cambridge University Press.
—— (1995) "Why Do Neighbors Fight?: Proximity, Interaction, or Territoriality," *Journal of Peace Research*, 32: 277–293.
Veit, Lawrence A. (1976) *India's Second Revolution: The Dimensions of Development*. New York: McGraw-Hill.
Vertzberger, Yaacov (1983) *The Enduring Entente: Sino-Pakistan Relations, 1960–80*. New York: Praeger.
Viswesvaraya, Sir M. (1934) *Planned Economy for India*. Bangalore: Bangalore Press.
Vohra, Sahdev (1993) *The Northern Frontier of India: The Border Dispute with China*. New Delhi: Intellectual Publishing House.
Wales, H.G. Quartich (1967) *The Indianization of China and Southeast Asia*. London: Bernard Quartich Ltd.
Waltz, Kenneth N. (1979) *Theory of International Politics*. New York: McGraw-Hill.
—— (1986) "Reflections on *Theory of International Politics*," in Robert O. Keohane ed. *Neorealism and Its Critics*. New York: Columbia University Press, pp. 322–347.
Wang, Lianhe Xinwen (2002) UDN News [online]. Available: <http://udnnews.com/CB/NEWS/FOCUSNEWS/POLITICS/647735.shtml> [accessed 5 October, 2005].

Wang, Xingwang (2002a) "Views on Theory of Dominant Operations: On Domination of Information and Traffic," *Zhonguo Junshi Kexue*, 20 June, FBIS-CPP20021204000144.

Wang, Yanlai (2003) *China's Economic Development and Democratization*. Burlington, USA: Ashgate Publishing House.

Watkins, Eric (2004) "Facing the Terrorist Threat in the Malacca Strait," *Terrorist Monitor* 2:9, The Jamestown Foundation, 6 May.

Weber, Steve (1990) "Realism, Détente, and Nuclear Weapons," *International Organization*, 44(1): 55–82.

Wegner, Alfred (1966) *The Origin of Continents and Oceans*. Trans. John Biram. New York: Dover Publications.

Welfens, Paul (ed.) (1997) *European Monetary Union*. New York: Springer.

"Wen Jiabao Holds Talks with Visiting Burmese Prime Minister" (2004) *Xinhua*, Beijing, 12 July, 2004 FBIS-EAS-2004-0712.

"Wen Jiabao Says China Willing to Expand Cooperation with India" (2004) *Xinhua*, Beijing, 30 November.

Wendt, Alexander (1987) "The Agent-Structure Problem in International Relations Theory," *International Organization*, 41: 335–370.

—— (1995) "Constructing International Politics," *International Security*, 20: 71–81.

—— (1998) "On Constitution and Causation in International Relations," *Review of International Studies*, 24: 101–117.

—— (1999) *Social Theory of International Politics*. Cambridge: Cambridge University Press.

Wohlforth, William C. (1999) "The Stability of a Unipolar World," *International Security*, 25(1): 5–41.

Wolpert, Stanley (1989) *A New History of India*, 3rd edition. Oxford: Oxford University Press.

Woodman, Dorothy (1969) *Himalayan Frontiers: A Political View of the British, Chinese, Indian and Russian Rivalries*. New York: Praeger.

"Work Division at Central Military Commission Reported" (1999) *Tai Yang Pao*, Hong Kong, 27 September, in SWB FE/3652 G/10, 29 September.

World Bank (1983) *China: Socialist Economic Development*, vol. 1. Washington, DC: World Bank.

—— (1996) *India: Country Economic Memorandum*, Report No. 15882-IN, Washington, DC: World Bank.

—— (2000) *India; Policies to Reduce Poverty and Accelerate Sustainable Development*. Report No. 19471-IN. Washington, DC: World Bank.

—— (2004) *World Bank Development Indicators*, Washington, DC: World Bank.

"World Oil Chokepointsx" (2004) Energy Information Administration, Department of Energy, United States of America [online]. Available: <http://www.eia.doe.gov/emeu/cabs/choke.html> [accessed 3 November, 2005].

Wright, Richard N.J. (2000) *The Chinese Steam Navy, 1862–1945*. London: Chatham.

Wu, Sofia (2004) "Premier Calls for Closer Taiwan-Japan-India Cooperation," *Central News Agency*, Taipei, 12 November.

Xie, Zhijun (2001) "Asian Seas in the 21st Century: With So Many Rival Navies, How Will China Manage?" *Junshi Wenzhai*, 1 February, FBIS-CPP10010305000214.

Xinhua (1999a) Beijing, April 21, FBIS-CHI-99-0421.

—— (1999b) Beijing, 10 June in SWB FE/3559 G/11 12 June.

Xu, Changwen (2006) "New Chapter in Sino-Indian Trade," *Beijing Review* [online]

Available: <http://www.bjreview.com.cn/06–09-e/w–4.htm> [accessed 10 February, 2006].

Xu, X. (2000) "China and the Middle East: Cross Investment in the Energy Sector," *Middle East Policy Council*, 7(3): 122–136.

Xu, Yihe (2002) "China Energy Watch: Look Over Great Wall for Oil," *DJES*, 7 March.

Yan, Xu (1993) *True History of the Sino-Indian Border War*. Hong Kong: Cosmos Books.

Yan, X. and Yang, J. (1999) *Fuelling China in the Twenty-first Century: A Report to Raise the International Competitiveness of China's Oil Industry*. Beijing: Enterprise Management [in Chinese].

Yergin, Daniel, Eklof, Dennis and Edwards Jefferson , "Fuelling Asia's Recovery," *Foreign Affairs*, 77(2): 34–50.

Yijian, Liu (1999) "China's Future Naval Construction and Naval Strategy," *Strategy and Management*, 5: 96–100.

Yuan, Jing-dong (2001) "India's Rise After Pokharan II," *Asian Survey*, 41(6): 978–1001.

Yuan, Tian (2003) "Wu Quanxu meets with Visiting Indian Military Guests," *PLA Daily*, Beijing, 18 November.

Zagoria, Donald (1962) *The Sino-Soviet Conflict 1956–61*. Princeton, NJ: Princeton University Press.

Zhan, Jun (1994) "China Goes to the Blue Waters: The Navy Seapower Mentality and the South China Sea," *Journal of Strategic Studies*, 17(3): 180–208.

Zhang, Guihong (2005) "Sino-Indian Security Relations: Bilateral Issues, External Factors and Regional Implications," *South Asian Survey*, 12(1): 61–73.

—— and Saika, Jaideep (2005) "India-China and the Shanghai Cooperation Organization," *Aakrosh*, 8(26): 42–59.

"Zhang Li Meets Commander of Eastern Command of India" (2006) *Jiefangjun Bao*, Beijing, 21 February.

Zhang, Wei Wei (2000) *Transforming China: Economic Reforms and its Political Implications*. London: Macmillan Press.

Zhang, Wenmu (2001) "The Global Geopolitical System and India's Future Security," *Strategy and Management*, 3: 43–52.

Zhang, Xiao-guang (2000) *China's Trade Patterns and International Comparative Advantage*. London: Macmillan Press.

Zhiyong, Shao (2001) "India's Big Power Dreams," *Beijing Review*, 12 April: 9–10.

Zhou, F. (1999) "Challenges Facing the Energy Industry of China in the Twenty-first Century," *China Energy*, 12(3): 3–6 [in Chinese].

Index

Printed in the United States
by Baker & Taylor Publisher Services